AF522484

School Psychology Ethical Practices

School Psychology Ethical Practices

Gurpreet Kaur

School Psychology Ethical Practices

ISBN 978-93-5111-504-5

Published in 2015 in India by

RANDOM PUBLICATIONS

4376-A/4B, Gali Murari Lal, Ansari Road
New Delhi-110 002
Phone : +9111-43580356, 011-23289044, 011-43142548
e-mail: sales@randompublications.com,
info@randompublications.com, randomexports@gmail.com

Reprinted 2019

Type Setting by : Friends Media, Delhi-110089
Digitally Printed at: Replika Press Pvt. Ltd.

Preface

School psychology is a field that applies principles of clinical psychology and educational psychology to the diagnosis and treatment of children's and adolescents' behavioural and learning problems, to teachers, politicians and other responsible persons in the instituationalized education systems with pedagogic, didactic or systemic-organizational problems, sometimes also integrating parents of school children to find common solutions. School psychologists help children and youth succeed academically, socially, behaviourally, and emotionally. They collaborate with educators, parents, and other professionals to create safe, healthy, and supportive learning environments that strengthen connections between home, school, and the community for all students.

School psychologists assist with trauma and crisis; work with children, teachers, and families to deal with hurdles that are preventing success; educate and expand skills to cope with problems. They utilize prevention and early intervention to limit troubles in children's lives and in the school environment. They help to create an equal and encouraging school, bring attention to mental health issues and develop ways to deal with issues individually and school-wide, they team up with teachers and parents to address effective behaviour plans, and ensure acceptance and value of diversity.

This book focuses on how a school psychologist can operate and create change within the educational system instead of focusing solely on the diagnosis and treatment of an individual. It focuses on the significant issues, new developments, and scientific findings that continue to change the practical landscape. It is a must-read for practitioners, students, and faculty, and an ideal resource for parents seeking a scientific approach to the efficacy of school psychology practices.

Author

Contents

1

Practice of School Psychology

The discipline of psychology is fundamental to teaching, learning and child development. School psychologists have training and experience in the core areas of psychology and education and represent the pursuits of both fields. They occupy a uniquely pivotal position at the intersection of both professions, and therefore can significantly advance the accomplishment of a broad range of school goals in the areas of behavior, learning and mental health. They offer a problem-solving orientation based on research, empirically proven practices, and data-based decision making, which is applied to the design and implementation of effective academic and behavioral interventions. Their traditional role encompasses prevention, assessment, counseling and consultation.

The contemporary paradigm of school psychology practice is driven by two decades of significant advances in assessment and intervention techniques which can substantially improve positive educational outcomes in students. Modern assessment and intervention techniques, and the practice of school psychology in general, are characterized by the following:

a. an emphasis on consultation, functional behavioral assessment, curriculum-based measurement, and ecological assessment of learner/environment systems applied to the design of instructional, social, emotional and behavioral interventions;

b. a focus on service outcomes, accountability and data-based decision making that links assessment directly to intervention;

c. a data-based problem-solving orientation emphasizing empirically supported interventions;

d. a focus on wellness and health, prevention, counseling and building competencies with a concomitant de-emphasis on pathology, deficits and labeling; and

e. a systemic orientation characterized by the provision of a comprehensive, integrated program of school psychological services to all learners, their families and those who serve them.

The emphasis placed by the previous generation of school psychologists on testing for deficits followed by categorization and placement is slowly fading into obsolescence and evolving into a new paradigm whereby school psychologists apply a comprehensive range of assessment and intervention skills at every level of the system. This shift in emphasis is in keeping with the Connecticut State Board of Education's vision of how school psychologists and other student support services specialists (i.e., school counselors, school nurses, school social workers, health educators and speech and language pathologists) make unique contributions to students' attainment of educational achievement and personal-social well-being.

These guidelines describe a model of exemplary school psychology practice. As these guidelines are implemented across the state, the potential to substantially improve the social, emotional, behavioral and academic development of students, families, school personnel and their communities is profound.

The mission of school psychologists is to promote educationally and psychologically healthy environments for all children and youth by implementing research-based, effective programs that prevent problems, enhance independence and promote optimal learning.

All children and youth deserve a free and appropriate public education in a safe and nurturing school environment that promotes cognitive, physical, social and emotional development and encourages family involvement.

The future well-being of a community depends on the commitment of finances and resources to develop and maintain accessible support systems for children and families today.

Children learn best in communities where educators are valued and treated with respect, and are learners themselves.

All children have a right to at least one caring and capable adult in their lives.

Early effective interventions and collaborative services will best prepare children for success in the future.

School psychologists are change agents and facilitators who collaborate with key stakeholders in families, schools and communities to promote the healthy development of *all* children and youth.

School psychologists have unique training that encompasses learning and cognition, as well as social and emotional development, and provides an integrated perspective of service within the context of the school.

School psychologists respect individual differences of students and families, and recognize that diversity contributes to a strong and just society.

School psychologists promote early interventions and data-based decision making to support children and families.

Scope of Practice of School Psychologists

School psychologists serve students of all ages and their families, as well as the systems or agencies that serve them. Most school psychologists work in public schools, but some work in various other settings including private schools, universities, school-based health centers, correctional facilities, research organizations and private practice.Their broad training in the core areas of psychology and education puts them in an ideal position to integrate and coordinate educational, psychological and behavioral health servicesThey are positioned to make meaningful contributions anywhere an integration of educational and psychological knowledge bases can be brought to bear in solving a problem or accomplishing an educational goal.

Domains of School Psychology Leadership and Function

Documents published by the National Association of School Psychologists, the American Psychological Association and the Connecticut State Department of Education outline the scope of practice of school psychologists. The organization of this section borrows significantly from the conceptualization of domains of school psychology practice published in *School Psychology:A Blueprint for Training and Practice II* the NASP *Standards for Training and Field Placement Programs in School Psychology*, and the NASP *Guidelines for the Provision of School*

Psychological Services.This section also draws from and builds on *Developing Quality Programs for Pupil Services:A Self-Evaluative Guide.*

Domain I: Data-Based Decision Making and Accountability

School psychologists are problem solvers. They are experts at collecting data, analyzing and integrating information, and measuring outcomes for educational and psychological interventions.This broadly defined assessment and accountability orientation informs every activity of school psychologists as they work to help accomplish the goals of the school system. Some examples of the contributions school psychologists can make in this domain are as follows:

1. School psychologists assess educational outcomes and their instructional implications for individuals, groups or districts using achievement or mastery tests, student portfolios, performance-based assessment and curriculum-based measurement. They contribute in this way to meeting school district accountability standards.
2. School psychologists evaluate individual students using a variety of assessment methods including testing, observation, interviewing and reviewing of existing data to determine students' educational needs, and design and evaluate interventions to address those needs.
3. School psychologists collect data on individual students, classrooms and programs to design effective interventions to enhance service delivery and to evaluate the effectiveness of those interventions.
4. School psychologists assess aspects of the classroom and school environments that contribute to or detract from the social, emotional and academic development of students using classroom ecological and functional behavioral assessment data.

Domain II: Interpersonal Communication, Collaboration and Consultation

School psychologists possess interpersonal skills to foster communication and collaboration among school personnel, families, students and the community. They have expertise in systems consultation at the individual, classroom, school and district levels. Some examples of the services school psychologists can offer in this domain include the following:

1. School psychologists act as change agents at all levels of the system by facilitating communication and cooperation among all members of the school community.

2. School psychologists facilitate cooperation and collaboration among teachers, administrators and other school professionals, and can facilitate effective operation of various kinds of school-based teams.
3. School psychologists consult with parents or guardians, teachers and administrators to help with problem solving in the home, classroom, school and district.

Domain III: Effective Instruction and Development of Cognitive/ Academic Skills

School psychologists help classroom teachers and other school personnel develop challenging but appropriate academic goals for all students, and apply learning and cognitive theory to the development of instructional strategies. They work with other educators to apply empirically demonstrated instructional processes to facilitate student achievement. Examples of school psychologists' contributions in this domain include the following:

1. School psychologists help teachers develop alternative instructional strategies or programs to meet the needs of all students in the classroom.
2. School psychologists provide other educators with timely research on instruction from the psychological and educational literature.
3. School psychologists help special education staff members develop appropriate goals, strategies and outcome measurement methods for students with special needs.

Domain IV: Socialization and Development of Life Competencies

School psychologists help develop challenging but appropriate affective, behavioral and socialization goals for all students, and promote school environments where all members of the school community treat one another with respect. They use intervention strategies such as behavioral intervention; consultation; individual, group, classroom and family counseling; and schoolwide programs to enhance school climate and reduce alienation. Some examples of the contributions school psychologists can make in this domain are the following:

1. School psychologists design and implement individual, classroom and schoolwide programs in social skills, social problem solving, conflict resolution, decision making and life skills.

2. School psychologists design and implement alternative approaches to classroom management and student discipline, behavior management, ecological intervention and enhancement of classroom climate.
3. School psychologists provide individual, group, classroom and family counseling to help students perform better socially, emotionally and academically.

Domain V: Student Diversity in Development and Learning

School psychologists have expertise in the psychology of individual differences and apply this knowledge to develop and implement interventions based on the individual characteristics of the person, family or system.They possess knowledge of, and sensitivity to, individual abilities and disabilities and diverse racial, cultural, biological, ethnic, socioeconomic, linguistic and gender-related backgrounds, and apply that knowledge across a broad range of strategies to promote student development and learning. Some examples of how school psychologists can help in this domain are the following:

1. School psychologists help identify the specific learning needs of individual students and develop instructional strategies for schools to meet those needs.They assess cognitive abilities, social and emotional functioning, academic performance and sensory-motor skills, and diagnose a full range of psychological and educational strengths and disorders as they pertain to the educational process.
2. School psychologists foster sensitivity to diversity issues within the school community and promote the integration of the diverse talents and strengths of all groups into the educational programs of the school.

Domain VI: School Structure, Organization and Climate

School psychologists provide leadership in organizing schools in ways that promote learning, high expectations for excellence, and a sense of caring, safety and community. Some examples of services school psychologists can offer in this domain include the following:

1. School psychologists help design and participate in student support teams, coordinated school-based health teams, school climate committees, character education committees, and
2. other efforts dedicated to improving school climate and service to students.

3. School psychologists help design school policies on such issues as grading, discipline, referral systems, complaint procedures and transitions.

Domain VII: Prevention, Wellness Promotion and Crisis Intervention

School psychologists develop schoolwide comprehensive programs that make school psychological services available to all students. As health care providers, they emphasize prevention and wellness throughout the school community. In the event of a crisis, they provide leadership in helping students, school personnel, families and the community to respond and to heal. Some examples of the contributions school psychologists can make in this domain are the following:

1. School psychologists help design and implement wellness and health promotion programs in areas such as substance abuse, nutrition and eating disorders,AIDS prevention and stress management.
2. School psychologists provide a variety of health promotion activities to improve morale, reduce stress, reduce absenteeism and improve wellness among school staff members.
3. School psychologists design programs to prevent and intervene in situations involving serious academic, behavioral or emotional difficulties.
4. School psychologists design and implement procedures to support students, school staff members and families during times of crisis.
5. School psychologists collaborate with other school service providers in designing a comprehensive and integrated system of school psychology services within the school community.
6. School psychologists can help teach units in the health curriculum for students in all grades, or secondary-level courses in psychology or social sciences.

Domain VIII: Home-School-Community Collaboration

School psychologists, individually or in collaboration with other professionals (e.g., teachers, student support services specialists, community providers), design and implement programs to encourage home-school collaboration. They provide parent counseling, training and consultation to promote student learning and development. They take a leadership role in promoting collaboration and coordination with community agencies and resources. Some examples of how school psychologists can help in this domain are the following:

1. School psychologists design and conduct a variety of activities for supporting parents and families and enhancing the home-school connection. Such activities may include parent training in effective discipline and behavior management, study skills, understanding school rules and procedures, and how to participate effectively in special education meetings and parent/teacher conferences.
2. School psychologists participate in parent conferences, facilitate positive interactions between parents and school staff members, and help resolve conflicts that may occur.
3. School psychologists work with parent and community organizations to promote parent-school collaboration and act as a resource for educational or psychological knowledge.
4. School psychologists facilitate collaboration among community resources to develop integrated efforts to address the needs of the school community.

Domain IX: Research and Program Evaluation

School psychologists apply their knowledge of statistics, measurement and research design to evaluate school programs. They interpret and explain their analyses in a clear way to school personnel and the public. Some examples of how school psychologists can contribute in this domain are the following:

1. School psychologists make psychometrically sound recommendations regarding a school district's testing policies and procedures.
2. School psychologists help school personnel analyze and interpret data generated from a variety of sources within the school system.
3. School psychologists help design research protocols to answer local school district questions about their programs or practices.They assist in data-based program evaluation and decision making.They also design research to address more fundamental questions in the fields of education or psychology.

Domain X: Legal, Ethical Practice and Professional Development

School psychologists accept their obligation to maintain the highest level of legal, ethical and professional practice. They pursue a plan of continuing professional development for themselves, and contribute to the professional development of colleagues by providing professional presentations, professional writing, clinical supervision or other forms of continuing professional development. Examples of how school psychologists can help in this domain are the following:

1. School psychologists offer staff development activities for school personnel in areas such as instructional strategies, classroom management, psychological development and understanding the needs of all students.
2. School psychologists consult with administrators and other school personnel to develop comprehensive school psychology programs that are consistent with best practices in the field.

Domain XI: Information Technology

School psychologists apply their knowledge of technology in ways that enhance the quality of their services. Some examples of services school psychologists can offer in this domain include the following:

1. School psychologists use information sources and technology to access current research and professional literature to apply to solving problems.
2. School psychologists consult with other professionals regarding the selection and use of instructional and adaptive technology when designing programs and interventions for students.

In countires districts there exists a mixture of the old and new models, with some districts and even some individual school psychologists within the same district further along than others in the adoption of the new model. In those districts adopting a comprehensive service delivery model, the results have been positive.The examples provided in Appendix B are not meant to be an exhaustive survey of school psychological services in Connecticut, but are offered to give some idea of school psychology practices already being implemented in urban, suburban and rural districts that exemplify the range of services proposed in these guidelines.

Making Optimal Use of School Psychological Services

School psychology services, like other school district resources, are typically overtaxed and in short supply. School district personnel need to make thoughtful decisions about how to make optimal use of these resources. School administrators in Connecticut have had to be creative in optimizing and protecting available school psychological services that promote social, emotional, and academic learning, such as those described in Appendix B.

Naturally, the question arises as to the practicality of implementing a service delivery model that shifts the emphasis of service to prevention, systemic intervention, and collaboration. In today's educational environment, the model espoused in these guidelines is not only practical, but necessary in order to meet the needs of all students despite limited resources. Rising student enrollments continue to outpace districts' ability to provide school psychological services within the old model. Schools can no longer afford to wait for children to fail and then assign school psychologists to treat them one by one. Under the new model, school psychologists deliver services that prevent the need for special education and other costly specialized services. While school psychologists will likely continue to provide remedial services, greater emphasis on prevention, consultation, collaboration and indirect services will prevent students from failing and obviate the need for more expensive, more intrusive interventions.

School administrators are encouraged to learn more about the skills school psychologists bring to districts to ensure that they are getting the most out of their existing staff. Administrators and school psychologists can work together to pilot innovative deployment of school psychologists in their districts.To ensure that resources are being used effectively and efficiently, administrators can make use of school psychologists' skills in data-based decision making and program evaluation, and their knowledge of empirically supported interventions.

Administrators might consider the following strategies to optimize use of school psychological services:

1. providing clerical support to minimize certain paperwork and activities that do not require professional skills or oversight;
2. using time-saving technology (e.g., laptop computers, test-scoring software);
3. enabling school psychologists to expand, and make full use of, expertise in specialized areas (e.g., neuropsychology, positive behavioral supports, autism);

4. reviewing district requirements and practices that yield relatively little value per time invested (e.g., unnecessarily extensive re-evaluations); and
5. making staff assignments strategically so as to support and protect high-yield projects and activities.

The cost-benefit equation clearly favors the practices espoused in these guidelines. School psychologists and administrators must be resourceful to ensure that school psychological services deliver on their potential to improve education for Connecticut's students.

Future Trends in the Practice of School Psychology

The practice of school psychology, although rooted in the traditional broad foundations of assessment, prevention, counseling and consultation, evolves over time as new challenges arise and new methodologies are developed to meet those challenges. Now and for the foreseeable future, school psychology will continue to emphasize the following outcomes for students, families and schools:

a. improved academic competence for all children;
b. improved social-emotional functioning for all children;
c. enhanced family-school partnerships and parental involvement in schools;
d. more effective education and instruction for all learners; and
e. increased child and family services in schools that promote health and mental health and are integrated with community services.

School psychologists will increasingly incorporate into everyday practice the following themes:

a. a focus on evidence-based approaches to assessment, intervention and practice;
b. a reduced emphasis on traditional individual assessment and increased emphasis on linking assessment directly to intervention and accountability;
c. increased focus on families and improving academic, social and emotional functioning of students through family-school collaboration;
d. incorporation of public health models into school practice, basing prevention strategies on systemic assessments of risk and protective factors;

e. increased collaboration among professions (counseling, social work) and across specialties of psychology (school, counseling, clinical); and

f. increased incorporation of cross-cultural competency in all aspects of practice.

Much of what is here predicted as future practice in school psychology is occurring to varying degrees in Connecticut already. School districts that promote practice consistent with these outcomes and themes will emerge as leaders in school psychology programming in Connecticut over the next several years.

School Psychologist Credentialing

All school psychologists must be certified by the State Department of Education. Minimal training requirements for certification include completion of a planned program of study in school psychology at an accredited institution with at least sixty graduate credits, and completion of a full year supervised school psychology internship. The initial educator certificate may be issued on a limited basis for an intern who is currently enrolled in a graduate program and has completed all requirements other than the internship.

Beyond the entry-level requirement of certification by the State Department of Education, some school psychologists pursue more advanced credentialing.

The Nationally Certified School Psychologist (NCSP) credential is granted to State Department of Education certified school psychologists who pass the written examination and meet the training and experience standards of the National School Psychology Certification Board.

Some school psychologists have, or pursue, doctoral-level training in school psychology and are granted the Ph.D., Psy.D., D.Ed. or Ed.D. in school psychology.

Some school psychologists who hold a doctorate are also licensed as psychologists by the state's Department of Public Health. Licensure generally requires the doctorate with a yearlong internship and an additional year of supervised postdoctoral work experience, and passage of a written examination.

Some doctoral-level school psychologists are also board certified as school psychologists by the American Board of Professional Psychology

(ABPP) and are fellows of the American Academy of School Psychology.This credential requires State Department of Education certification and Department of Public Health licensure as described above and, in addition, a written evaluation of the school psychologist's practice and an oral examination by ABPP.

Licensed doctoral-level school psychologists with particular training and experience as health care providers may also be listed with the National Register of Health Care Providers in Psychology (NRHCPP).

Many certified school psychologists also hold graduate degrees and certifications or licensure in teaching, counseling, administration and supervision, and other related professional fields.

Practice of School Psychology in the Private Sector

Most school psychologists practice within the public school sector, but some also practice within the private sector. Practice in the private sector is regulated by both the *Principles for Professional Ethics* and Connecticut state statute.

In accordance with ethical principles, a school psychologist in private practice would not accept referrals from families residing in the school district in which the school psychologist is employed.

A school psychologist who is certified by the State Department of Education may provide school psychological services to a school district on a contractual basis for the purpose of procuring specialized services not available within the school district (e.g., bilingual evaluation, neuropsychological evaluation, program planning for a child with autism, clinical supervision) or to provide coverage for a leave of absence.

A school psychologist who also holds a license as a psychologist from the State Department of Public Health may perform additional functions under that license consistent with his or her areas of competence.

Training Standards for School Psychologists

In Connecticut, training to become a school psychologist emphasizes preparation in child development, mental health, evaluation and diagnosis, school organization, learning and behavior. Standards for training programs are such that the following competencies are expected upon completion of the program:

I. School psychologists demonstrate *foundational knowledge* in the following areas:

   A. Child development

   B. Human diversity

   C. Educational and special education law

   D. Ethics

   E. History of and best practices in school psychology

   F. Information technology

   G. Systems psychology

II. School psychologists demonstrate *general skills* in the following areas:

   A. Reading, writing, math

   B. Interpersonal communication and relationship building

   C. Scientific problem solving

III. School psychologists demonstrate *specialized skills* in the following areas:

   A. Direct service

   1. Assessment of students' cognitive, academic, social-emotional and behavioral functioning

   2. Development, implementation and evaluation of individual and group interventions (e.g., counseling, behavior modification, whole-class group, entire-school programs, etc.) that address cognitive, social, emotional and physical problems of students

   3. Crisis intervention

   4. Early intervention screening

B. Indirect service

C. Consultation and collaboration with teachers, support staff, administrators, parents and community agencies

   D. In-service education for teachers, support staff, administrators and parents

   E. Needs assessment

IV. School psychologists demonstrate *prevention strategies* at the individual and system levels.

A. The cognitive, social, emotional and physical growth of *all* students will be nurtured through whole-class lessons and schoolwide programs to promote a safe, positive climate for the entire school community.

B. Programs will be developed, implemented and evaluated according to best practices and current research.

C. Resources will be provided for school and community members.

D. School psychologists will assist in the design of policies, plans and rules that promote a safe, positive climate for the entire school community.

V. School psychologists are committed to *professional growth* through:

A. Personal goal setting and accountability

B. Supervision

C. Seeking to provide best practices

D. Engaging in professional development activities

E. Reflective practice

F. Ethical practice

G. Professional advocacy

H. Professional organization affiliation

School psychologists conduct assessments to provide information that is helpful in maximizing student achievement, educational success, psychological adjustment and behavioral adaptation. They use assessment techniques and instruments that have established validity and reliability for the purposes and populations for which the procedures are intended. When a student's sensory, motor or language skills, or behavior, compromise the validity of a test, the school psychologist describes how the assessment varied from standard conditions and adjusts interpretation of results accordingly. .

School psychologists recognize the strengths and limitations of their training and experience and only engage in practices in which they are competent. Nonbiased assessment procedures and program recommendations are chosen that maximize the student's opportunities to be successful in the general culture while respecting the student's ethnic background. Multifaceted assessment batteries include a focus on the student's strengths.

Evaluation of bilingual students

Evaluation of bilingual students is conducted in the student's dominant spoken language or alternative communication system. All student information is interpreted in the context of the student's sociocultural background and the setting in which he or she is functioning. If interpreters are used, they are trained so that the test administration is conducted in a manner that approximates standardization procedures as closely as possible. An effort is made to identify and minimize any bias on the part of the interpreter so as not to invalidate the evaluation data. Recognition is given to the fact that the difficulty level of a test item often changes when it is translated into a different language. In addition, school psychologists must be aware of potential discrimination when test items are not as familiar to persons from a different cultural background as they are to persons from the norming group.

References

New Brunswick Department of Education (2001). *Guidelines for professional practice for school psychologists.* Fredericton, NB: Author.

Reynolds, C.R. and Gutkin,T.B. (1998). *The Handbook of School Psychology (3rd ed.).* New York: John Wiley & Sons, Inc.

Sheridan, S.M. and Gutkin,T.B. (2000).The ecology of school psychology: Examining and changing our paradigm for the 21st century. *School Psychology Review, 29,* 485-502.

Thomas,A. and Grimes, J. (Eds.) (2002). *Best practices in school psychology IV.* Bethesda, MD:The National Association of School Psychologists.

Ysseldyke, J., Dawson, P., Lehr, C., Reschly, D.J., Reynolds, M., and Telzrow, C. (1997). *School psychology: A blueprint for training and practice II.* Bethesda, MD: National Association of School Psychologists.

2

Science-Based Psychological Practice in Schools

The Darwin's words are as true for school psychological practice as they are for the phyla. As school psychology transitions into an outcome-oriented profession, we continue to evolve new ways to bring science into applied practice in schools. This evolution is critical to the continued importance and viability of school psychology in U.S. schools. In the years since the inception of school psychology, many applications of science in practice have occurred, each with increased effectiveness. We stand at the threshold of the next iteration in that direction.

Science as a Foundation of Psychological Practice

The idea of science driving applied practice in psychology is not a new one. Indeed, when clinical psychology was brought into being in 1949 in a joint meeting between the National Institutes of Health and the American Psychological Association, a unanimous conclusion was reached after an historic 2-week conference in Boulder, CO. In sum, it was agreed that the training of clinical psychologists should include an equal emphasis on both research and practice. It was believed that research was a vital and important part of practice that could yield valuable insights and important implications for practice. It was further argued that involvement in the clinical process would bring researchers into immediate contact with important research issues.

The ideal practitioner, then, was conceived of as a scientist practitioner. This person would have the skills to apply the scientific method to studying problems in the natural universe (one definition of science). This person also would have the experience and savvy to work effectively in applied settings. This model was predicated on the medical model. That is, problems were conceptualized as residing primarily within patients, and the role of the therapist was to treat illness and to maximize human functioning and adjustment. Thus, the model was reactive, waiting for problems to occur and then responding to them. It was also an n 5 1 approach in that individuals most often were the focus of therapy as opposed to groups or systems.

In the decades since this historic conference, applied psychology has grown and matured. School psychology has embraced many of the same concepts as clinical psychology and has clearly promoted the importance of science in both training and practice. This value is illustrated clearly by the inclusion of specific competencies by the National Association of School Psychologists (NASP) in School Psychology: A Blueprint for Training and Practice III and in their Standards for School Psychological Services.

Many approaches to importing science into practices exist, whether explicitly or implicitly referenced as such. These include behavioral consultation, the IDEAL problem-solving model, functional analysis of behavior/functional behavioral assessment, the scientist practitioner model, curriculum-based measurement, applied behavior analysis, action research, and the Heartland Area Education Agency 11 problem-solving model. Each model contains unique features, protocols, and language. In some cases, specific philosophies of science or theoretical orientations predominate, and differential emphasis is placed on alternate parts of the process.

Foundation of Science-Based Practice in Schools

No matter which specific approach or model of sciencebased practice is considered, four thematic questions guide practitioner thinking:

— Is there a problem and what is it?

— Why is the problem happening?

— What can be done about the problem?

— Did the intervention work?

Taken together, these questions are referred to as the problem-solving method. A graphic depiction of this problem-solving logic set is contained in Figure 1.

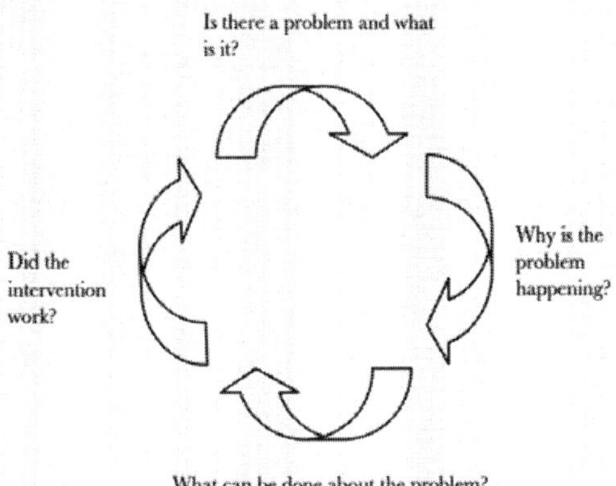

Figure 1. Problem-solving logic set.

Clearly, problem solving is a logical process that most people do every day, which adds to its practical appeal. Problem-solving practices are intuitive, easy to understand, and easy to explain to parents and teachers alike.

Educational Problem Solving

In educational problem solving, it often makes sense to define problems as the difference between environmental expectations and what an individual does. Problems defined this way reflect naturalistically and accurately situations in educational settings. Indeed, most educational problems are brought to light when student performance deviates significantly from teacher expectations in classrooms. No matter where a problem falls on the severity scale, from mild through severe, the same thinking predominates in problem definition. Two things must be operationalized: What is the individual expected to do? What is he or she actually doing? The difference between these two measurements represents the problem, not the behavior that is the subject of the problem solving. This distinction may appear trivial. It is not. For example, physical aggression is not a problem if it occurs at the expected zero rate. The discrepancy between expectancy and performance in this case is zero, so there is no problem. If, however, Nancy is expected to turn in 70% of her homework to pass her American Government class and she is turning in less than 20%, there is a 50 percentage-point discrepancy between expectations and her actual performance, a substantial problem in most high schools. That the problem resides in the discrepancy is a key problem-solving concept that typically is easy to grasp.

There are important implications of defining problems as discrepancies. First, a discrepancy or difference score causes problem solvers to become objective about the nature of a problem. Important problem-related variables are defined in a way that promotes agreement about ''what the problem is'' by all involved parties.

When there is objective agreement regarding a problem, there also can be objective agreement ''that the problem is improving'' as interventions are effective. Second, discrepancy-based problem definitions allow direct scaling of problem magnitude. The larger the discrepancy between observed performance and the standard, the larger the problem. Third, discrepancy-based problem definitions most often are created based on naturally occurring units of behavior, which usually lend themselves directly to analysis and intervention.

For example, if a behavior of concern (response class) is aggression, direct measurement of the problem may include counting all incidents of kicking, hitting, or throwing of projectiles within a time span. The number of acts could then be compared to a peer standard collected during the same observation periods. The same problem could be quantified less directly through rating scales or personality tests that yield a standard score, a diagnosis, or description of personality variables. The former problem definition in this case lends itself directly to clear analysis and intervention using clearly articulated procedures with a high likelihood of successful resolution of the problem. The latter process may not.

The scientific method requires observation to drive hypothesis. When problems are defined in naturalistic behavioral units as discrepancies between what is expected and what occurs, direct observation drives problem analysis (i.e., hypothesis generation). The problem identification phase of problem solving tracks directly to the first stage of scientific investigation; that is, observation of the environment as the basis for further analysis. Precise tools that yield consistent, objective measurement are used to provide a clear, unambiguous index of the situation. Problem definition then sets the stage for the second problem-solving phase: problem analysis.

Why Is the Problem Happening?

After operationalizing the problem, an analysis of problem etiology ensues. The purpose of problem analysis is to identify interventions for student problems that are (a) directly and empirically linked to problem occurrence and(b) have a high likelihood of successful outcome. Low-level inferences predominate. That is, inferences are typically made about student skills rather than abilities; inferences are made about student behaviors, rather than the traits the behaviors may represent; and, most important, inferences are made about the relationships between observed student performance and the highest likelihood variables related to observed performance.

The necessity of low-level inferences in turn drives the types of assessments that are completed to assist in problem analysis. In most cases, school psychologists move away from assessments of student disability. to measures of student ability. Indeed, one school psychologist has captured the concept underlying problem analysis when describing its purpose as ''diagnosing the learning enabled''. Instead of measuring student performance to find disabilities, our purpose is to diagnose the conditions under which students' learning is enabled. Assessment for problem analysis requires quite different skills and procedures from those traditionally used in special education entitlement assessments. The key to effective problem analyses is crafting clear summary statements or hypotheses that plausibly link observed performance to presumed causes (i.e., deduced from direct observation) of the performance problems, which in turn leads to treatment recommendations with a high probability of success. The general form of the logic is:

— For skill problems (can't do issues): X problem is occurring because of Y. Therefore, if we do Z, the problem will be reduced (recall here that the problem is represented by a discrepancy).

— For performance problems (won't do issues): When X problem occurs, the student does Y in order to (description of contingency). Therefore, if we do Z, the problem will be reduced.

The interventions represented by Z are thus logically linked to the analysis of the problems. Variables that served as targets for the problem analysis often, in this case, translate directly into actions that can be taken to enable learning.

As with problem identification, the critical shift in assessment for problem analysis is in thinking. The thinking shift in turn drives practice shifts. Rather than selecting tests for their technical characteristics and marketing, most competent problem-analysis assessments do not rely on published tests at all. In most cases, materials used for these assessments are selected directly from the materials and situations the students are working with in school. While these materials may not have been validated empirically for the purpose of disability identification, they operationalize the performance demands of the present environment and consequently are the most performance-valid assessment materials available.

Operationally, school psychologists need to be able to tease out variables related to observed levels of performance in relation to direct environmental demands. The difference between problem-solving practice and historical practice is illustrated in the following example where two different approaches to analyzing the same student's reading problems are presented.

One school psychologist may describe a student's reading performance as two standard deviations discrepant from the student's verbal ability with possible emotional overlays. These factors may indicate the presence of dysphonemic dyslexia, which may lead to prescribing a multisensory approach to reading instruction. These are impressive sounding words, but not particularly helpful from an instructional perspective. What exactly is dysphonemic dyslexia? What specifically does it mean for this particular student? What skills does the student have and not have? What is the probability that a multisensory approach to instruction will work with this student and not with other students? What functional increment of information does the assessment process add?

A school psychologist from a problem-solving orientation would likely assess the same student's reading skills directly. A sample of the student's oral reading would be collected. Specific-level tests (specific tests of component reading skills) would be given in priority order (skills with the highest probability of contributing to the reading problem are assessed first), yielding a general picture of the student's component reading skills. Resulting analyses might hypothesize that the student's reading comprehension deficits result from (a) a lack of direct phonics instruction, which has caused the student to read disfluently; (b) the student not linking new information to prior knowledge; (c) the student not understanding critical vocabulary words in the passages read; and/or (d) the student not monitoring meaning while reading.

These data-based observations then would be used to develop a need-specific intervention program tailored to the individual student. The difference between the former and latter reading assessments is the ability to directly pinpoint the specific skills that a student does or does not have and the level of inference needed to program instruction. As a general rule, the higher the level of inference used to prescribe instruction, the less certain we can be in the effectiveness of the intervention prescribed.

Professional judgment and experience play as significant a part in the analysis of problems as they did in problem identification. Indeed, it is not possible in problem-solving systems for school psychologists to competently analyze student performance in any performance domain if they do not have significant knowledge in that domain. More than any other component of problem solving, problem analysis requires assessors to have broad and deep knowledge about the subject matter they are assessing. It is not possible to competently analyze the etiology of developmental reading problems if the school psychologist does not understand the process of learning to read. In the same way, it is not possible to discuss the etiology of behavior problems without reference to an accepted professional framework for understanding behavior. The content knowledge and experience requirements placed on school psychologists are perhaps the greatest professional development challenge associated with implementation of a problem-solving system.

The problem analysis phase of problem solving corresponds directly to the second stage of scientific investigation, that of creating hypotheses regarding variables that could plausibly explain the occurrence and nonoccurrence of the problem. To assist in hypothesis development, school psychologists can use whatever diagnostic measurements they choose, but those with most utility are those that measure student behaviors most closely resembling the behaviors that are considered problematic in the natural environment.

What Can Be Done About the Problem?

Once problems are defined and analyzed, the most complex part, if not the most challenging part, of problem solving is completed. When problem analysis is completed accurately, reasonable environmental modifications with plausible connections to problem remediation usually become apparent.

At this point, based on data collected from problem identification and problem analysis, educational interventions can be put in place.

There is a series of components that need to be thought through in setting up interventions. An intervention is defined in this context as a planned modification of the environment made for the purpose of changing behavior in a prespecified way. Specifically, who will do what, when, and in what manner needs to be determined. A specific goal for the intervention may be set in measurable terms, and procedures for monitoring the effectiveness of the intervention must be put in place. Any supports or materials that will be needed to carry out the intervention need to be located or created, and any training for implementers needs to be completed if necessary.

It is important that multicomponent interventions be considered for significant problems to ensure the highest likelihood of success. Not all components will be necessary for every intervention; however, all of the components should be considered thoughtfully in all cases.

The intervention process in education is analogous to the component in the scientific investigation process that tests hypotheses. In this instance, educational programs are put in place based on reasoned hypotheses (derived from problem analysis) in an attempt to confirm the accuracy of the problem analysis (hypothesis). Just as experiments in science are conducted to allow inferences to be made about hypotheses, interventions in education allow us to draw inferences regarding the accuracy of our hypotheses and to improve student performance in the deal.

Did the Intervention Work?

The final question addressed by the problem-solving process regards evaluation of interventions, both formatively and summatively. Because it is not possible to predict with certainty the effectiveness of any educational intervention prior to its implementation, a progress-monitoring process must be put in place to evaluate intervention effectiveness. As with other components of the problem-solving process, procedures used to monitor progress vary in their rigor, precision, and comprehensiveness. The important feature of progress-monitoring systems is the ability to accurately illustrate progress over time. Typically, the behavior that was used to operationalize the existence and magnitude of the educational problem is used as the indicator of progress in progress-monitoring systems. Data are collected multiple times per week, and a pattern of behavior emerges over time, which is often depicted graphically. Using systematic procedures and decision rules to examine the pattern of performance, the effectiveness of an intervention can be determined. Extensive resources are available on monitoring student performance.

At some point during intervention, the magnitude of the problem is revisited. A process very similar to procedures used to identify the initial problem ensues. Student performance is measured and compared with a standard of acceptable performance, and a performance discrepancy is identified. Two standards of comparison are now available to assist in evaluating the magnitude of the discrepancy. As before, current performance can be evaluated against the criterion of acceptable performance, and the size of the problem can be gauged in an absolute sense. Also, the size of the discrepancy can be evaluated in light of the size of the discrepancy at the time of problem identification.

The program evaluation component of problem solving is analogous to evaluation of hypotheses in scientific inquiry. The intervention provides the basis, and the monitoring and measurement provide the evaluation. Generally, if interventions work in improving performance, an inference can be drawn that the analysis of the problem was accurate (our hypotheses are supported). More precisely, the analysis was sufficient to result in significantly improved performance. In applied practice, this level of support for the analysis is sufficient. For problem solvers, the purpose of their efforts is socially meaningful behavior change. When intervention efforts result in this outcome for clients, universality of hypothesis application is secondary.

Using the Problem-Solving Method Alone in Schools

In the early days of problem solving, the problem-solving method just described provided an extremely valuable and important springboard for science-based practices in schools. It provided the thinking structures necessary for framing school-based problems, for analyzing their etiology, for deriving hypotheses about potentially effective solutions, and for testing the effectiveness of these solutions. These thinking structures are foundational to all data-based implementations of the scientific method in practice. And, indeed, the problem-solving method did improve educational practice. It provided an iterative, self-correcting approach to treatment of educational problems. It provided an empirical method to select treatments from the universe of possibilities, and it allowed parents and teachers to evaluate objectively whether the treatments being applied were working.

What the problem-solving method when used alone lacked was a supportive context for implementation and structures within schools that embraced and promoted science-based practices. Most teachers and administrators in schools were not trained in application of the problem-solving method, and most educational structures (e.g., methods for problem identification, referral processes, service delivery structures) and practices were not driven using science or student outcome data as a guide. As such, early application of the problem-solving method relied heavily on experts to bring the practices to schools, to provide the structures for application (e.g., a consultation framework), and for these individuals to provide assessment and intervention services when referrals were received. Most often, the problem-solving method was used for moderate to severe problems after these problems had manifested in the school environment. As such, problem solving was not positioned well to address problems early when the problems are most workable. Moreover, there were no school-based structures in place to address these shortcomings.

Despite these limitations, adoption of the scientific method as a decision-making structure for applied psychology began the process of embedding science in the practice of school psychology. Use of hypothesis testing to drive treatment was a novel idea, but one with great merit. Application of these procedures produced improvements in client outcomes that set the stage for the next evolutionary step.

Bringing Science to Schools

Moving education toward a problem-solving enterprise requires changing both system structures and practices within the system. The historical special education system structures grew out of legal mandates (Education for All Handicapped Children Act of 1975, the Individuals with Disabilities Education Act [IDEA]) that dictate many structures and practices. From the Individualized Educational Program (IEP) development through procedural safeguards and due process provisions, special education structures have remained fixed for more than 30 years. How might a shift to a problem-solving structure occur if so many things are dictated? The answer is that the ''whats'' of special education are fixed. For example, no matter where one lives in America, students with disabilities are guaranteed heightened due process, procedural safeguards, quality assessments, and IEPs. Considerable variability in how these "whats" are carried out is allowed to states by the federal Office of Special Education Programs. For example, states have wide latitude in how special education identification, assessment, and programming are carried out. One state may use a simple discrepancy process for identifying students with learning disabilities, another might use regression-based formulae to identify similar students, and a third state may use functional assessment procedures and noncategorical identification procedures. All can be legal. What is critical is that districts and states ensure that the basic requirements of law are met.

Deploying the Problem-Solving Method as a Decision-Making Structure: Heartland's Problem-Solving Model Shifting structures in special education requires rethinking some of the assumptions underlying how our system was structured originally. Most important is rethinking how services can be delivered in direct relation to need. States and districts in most cases have organized their services typologically. That is, students with similar types of needs are grouped together to make service delivery to these students efficient (consider talented and gifted education, Title I, and special education as examples in our schools). Underlying this practice is the assumption that students' needs exist in discrete groupings and that discrete groupings for service delivery will thus meet students' needs optimally. In reality, student needs exist more on a continuum. Some students need more or fewer services than others both within and across different "typologically labeled" groups.

The solution to this situation is to create ways that service intensity can be varied in direct proportion to individual student needs both within and outside special education boundaries. This situation is desirable from a student-learning standpoint and cost efficient from a resource-allocation standpoint. Instead of waiting for students to fall so far behind that their performance qualifies them for special education, resources can be expended early within a problem-solving system, when problems are less intense, in the hope of remediating the problems prior to their escalation.

One problem-solving model that accomplishes the goal of matching resources with problem intensity is the Heartland problem-solving approach. This model will be described because it is a general-case model that includes desirable characteristics from a number of different problem-solving models. Moreover, it has been implemented successfully in practice for more than

15 years, so its viability has been tested empirically.In the Heartland problem-solving approach (Figure 2), the abscissa represents the intensity of the educational problem experienced by the student. The scale ranges from low-intensity problems to high intensity problems. The ordinate represents the amount of resources necessary to resolve educational problems. The circles in the center represent the ideal match between the intensity of any given problem and the amount of resources that may be warranted to address the problem.

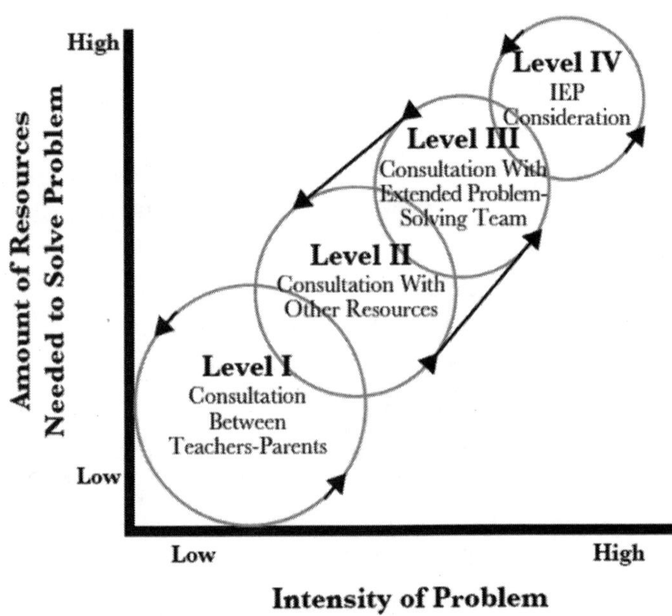

Figure 2. Heartland problem-solving approach

Parents, teachers, counselors, school nurses, principals, building assistance teams, community providers, or others having direct contact with students may express concerns and initiate problem solving. In the Heartland model, assistance can be provided to students at any of four levels. These levels vary in terms of precision of problem identification and depth of problem analysis, as well as in systematicity and amount of resources brought to bear on the problem. Level I problem solving involves parent–teacher collaboration for addressing problems. At level II, other teachers contribute expertise along with the primary teacher and parents to solve the problem. At level III, related service persons such as school psychologists guide the problem-solving process with the other participants. Level IV continues problem solving at even a more intense level, and one of the questions addressed at this level is entitlement for special education (note that level IV represents the smallest circle in the diagram, depicting that relatively few educational problems get to this level). At level IV, problem solving continues. The only administrative difference is that in some cases, special education resources may be used to address students' educational needs as part of the problem-solving process.

Problem-solving Levels

Level I: Consultation Between Teacher and Parent

Level I problem solving typically begins when a parent or teacher has concerns about an individual child's performance. Problems can arise in any educational performance domain, and there is no limit to the types of problems that might be addressed at this level. Typically, a conference will be held between the teacher and parent(s) where a plan of action will be crafted.

At level I, teachers and parents focus their attention on specific behavior(s) of concern. Typically, they discuss the nature of a problem and consider strategies that may be effective. They then determine a course of action to follow and informally monitor whether the intervention works. At level I, related services persons are not involved with defining the problem or implementing general education interventions. Indeed, level I simply acknowledges the informal problem-solving system that has been used for decades within our schools. .

Level II: Consultation With Other Resources

Level II problem solving begins when level I has not been successful or when either the parents or teacher determines there is a need for additional resources. The purpose of level II problem solving continues to be resolving the presenting problem. At level II, additional resources are brought to bear on the problem, the processes are a bit more structured, and information from level I problem solving provides the initial input into level II problem solving. Components of the level II process include (a) more systematically gathering information about the severity of the problem, (b) redefining the problem if necessary, and (c) developing and monitoring new plans to address the problem. At level II, most schools use assistance teams to address problems. These assistance teams consist of the child's parents (or caregiver) and teacher, other teachers in the school, and local support staff (such as the guidance counselor) to the extent appropriate. Additional staff from outside of the school or the student also may participate on the team if deemed desirable and appropriate by the team.

During the initial level II meeting, the assistance team discusses the concerns surrounding the performance of the child. Through this discussion, the assistance team serves as a resource to the teacher and the parent. The team helps further clarify the nature of the problem and offers strategies that the classroom teacher can use to address the problem. The parents and teacher agree upon a reasonable intervention for addressing the problem. The team then decides each member's role for assisting with the intervention and develops ideas for evaluating the intervention. The intervention is implemented, and if performance does not improve, the general education intervention is refined. This process recycles as often as needed.

Level III: Consultation With the Extended Problem-Solving Team

As illustrated in Figure 2, levels II and III of problem solving overlap and are connected. These connections illustrate that in some cases the processes and procedures used at these levels overlap. The primary distinction between levels II and III is that related service personnel with specialized expertise and techniques are significant members of the level III Extended Problem-Solving Team. School psychologists, instructional consultants, school social workers, speech and language pathologists, occupational therapists, and physical therapists, among others, all can participate in problem-solving activities at level III. At this point in the process, the purpose of the members' involvement is neither special education assessment nor programming but helping to resolve the presenting problems in general education. To this end, a systematic and structured deployment of general education resources will be undertaken by the Extended Problem-Solving Team at level III.

At level III, the team reviews all information collected at levels I and II to begin its analysis. The team examines whether the problem was identified accurately at levels I and II, and the effectiveness of interventions to date is reviewed. The team also ensures that all appropriate screenings (e.g., hearing, vision, health) have been conducted to rule in or out other plausible contributors to the problem. Based on these data, the team uses a standardized thought process to guide their next steps. The team specifies an assessment plan to guide collection of additional problem-related information.

Data then are collected to determine the nature and severity of the problem (problem identification) as well as to analyze problem etiology (problem analysis). At level III, the problem analysis will be systematic and more in depth than at levels I or II. That is, an explicitly articulated thinking process will be used in problem analysis. This thinking process involves the integration of information from multiple sources with research-derived knowledge and experience in the problem area to specify and test hypotheses regarding specific etiology of the observed problems. Based on the problem analysis, an intervention plan with a high likelihood of success can be written. As a part of this plan, specific goals are written and a progress-monitoring plan including a decision-making plan are put in place. The intervention then is implemented and its effectiveness evaluated. The most critical distinction between level III and previous levels is that level III requires practitioners to use a structured thinking process and specialized tools to assist in the problem-solving process. It is at this level that specific professional standards of quality problem solving have been defined that serve as expectations for practitioner performance.

Level IV: Problem-Solving Intervention and Entitlement Consideration

In moving to level IV, the Extended Problem-Solving Team acknowledges that special education resources may be warranted to address a student's educational problems. When taking a case to level IV, all the due process and procedural protections available under IDEA are provided. One of these protections is asking parents (or caregivers) for written permission to have their child evaluated with the intent of determining special education entitlement. It is at this point that special education entitlement becomes a consideration and thus parental notice and permission are sought.

Entitlement for special education is only one of the questions addressed at level IV. The purpose of level IV problem solving continues to be determining interventions necessary to address student needs, including whether required interventions include special education services. As a result, the focus of assessment is on direct student performance and environmental variables that are modifiable and directly related to student learning (e.g., curriculum, instruction, the learning environment). During level IV assessment, extensive record review is conducted because a large portion of the information necessary for the special education entitlement decision has been gathered throughout problem-solving levels I through III. Additional problem-solving assessments are then conducted to address additional factors related to improving the student's learning.

In addition to the use of a problem-solving approach as a resource-deployment structure in schools, problem solving is also a structured thinking process that is used to attack problems directly. It represents an important advancement of implementation of science into applied practice. In Heartland, this thinking structure is referred to as the problem-solving method. Each of the circles in Figure 2 represents one application of the problem-solving method. The problem-solving method is the same at every level of the process and recycles multiple times as interventions are carried out for an educational problem.

The Heartland problem-solving approach solved a number of important problems inherent in implementation of the problem-solving method alone.

Reengineering the Problem-Solving Approach

When Heartland's problem-solving approach was initially implemented, there were no models available to integrate special and general education using tiered systems. The impetus for changing practices for struggling students came significantly out of special education. As a result, the problem-solving model was predicated on an n 5 1 approach. That is, it was designed to work with one student at a time, from initial problem identification all the way through problem resolution, no matter where in the model that led in terms of services needed. Implementing a problem-solving approach to service delivery provided a series of advancements. It also created a series of unintended challenges that resulted from engineering the problem-solving system in a student-by-student, case-by-case manner. Some of these were practice-based challenges. Others occurred due to systems structures. Still others resulted from challenges in system engineering. Five major challenges emerged:

— Solving problems one at a time is not particularly efficient from a resource-utilization standpoint, especially when many children with educational problems have similar instructional needs.

— There is no way to deal proactively with the entire curriculum and instructional programs that were creating the educational problems seen by the problem-solving system. This statement is in no way an indictment of educational practices at the time. However, there are situations where particular combinations of curriculum, instruction, and students create student performance problems due to errors of commission (e.g., unintentionally teaching misrules) or errors of omission (e.g., leaving out or not sufficiently emphasizing critical skills or content). The problem-solving model is the recipient of school-based problems and is at the mercy of whatever problems come its way. There is no mechanism for being proactive at a school-wide or district-wide level.

— Our experience has taught us that individual teachers cannot implement more than one or two simultaneous interventions with integrity at any given time and continue teaching an entire classroom effectively. As a result, when more than two problems occur in the same classroom, the situation can become problematic for teachers as they work on varied individual interventions.

— Because the problem-solving model is still reactive to teacher-referred problems, many teachers perceive problem solving as the new way to get students into special education, which is, of course, not its purpose. These perceptions can unintentionally undermine the implementation effectiveness of general education interventions for students who teachers believe need to be in special education.

— In recent years, the possibility of reengineering the problem-solving model to incorporate recent developments in both research and practice has emerged. With the passage of No Child Left Behind (NCLB) in 2002, accountability requirements for the entire educational system have been heightened. As a result, all districts are accountable for the learning of all students, and the expectation is that all students will become proficient in basic skills. Schools are now looking for ways to effectively raise all students' achievement to at least a minimum level of proficiency, including those who historically have struggled learning basic skills. These accountability contingencies and their attendant instructional expectations (i.e., scientific research-based practices) have allowed and promoted the reengineering of the problem-solving model into a more systemwide model. That being said, it is important to point out that the science and principles underlying Heartland's original problem-solving approach were correct and remain valid.

— What has shifted is the possibility of engineering the delivery system to encompass all children, rather than only those who struggle. A series of fundamental changes have been made in the engineering of the problem-solving system. These include the following changes:

— Allowing the problem-solving model to work for all students in a system, not only those who struggle: This component typically includes conducting universal screenings in basic skills areas with all students in a school or district. These screenings identify objectively which students are potentially in need of educational interventions beyond the general education curriculum alone.

— Examination of core curriculum based on student performance data: If a sufficient percentage of students are not becoming proficient based on the core curriculum alone, data can alert the district to analyze their curriculum and instruction to determine what components may be modified to improve overall student performance. This proactive examination of the school curriculum was never possible within the original Heartland problem-solving approach.

— The ability to implement data-based group-level interventions and individual interventions, as opposed to implementing only individual level interventions: Once students are grouped based on their performance strengths and deficits, teachers can come together and design group-level supportive instruction to meet those students' needs. While this was always allowable under the original problem-solving approach, the system structures were not engineered to efficiently provide group-level data and direct group-level solutions.

One thing that has been held consistent with the old and the new systems engineering is that students with intensive instructional needs still receive individualized diagnostic evaluations of their skill strengths and weaknesses, and individualized, intensive interventions are provided to these students.

The Heartland problem-solving approach is evolving into what has been described in the literature as a three-tier model. In this model, the same descriptions provided earlier about matching resource intensity with problem intensity still hold. Indeed, all of the descriptions of the underlying logic and rationale are the same. What is different is that all students are encompassed in this new model, not just students with learning or behavioral problems. The model is designed to support school success for all learners in both academic and social–emotional areas. Also, problems in the new model are not defined based on teacher referral of struggling students in their classrooms. Instead, student problems are defined directly by performance on critical indicators of basic skills. A graphic depiction of the relationship between Heartland's problem-solving approach and a three-tier model is presented in Figure 4.

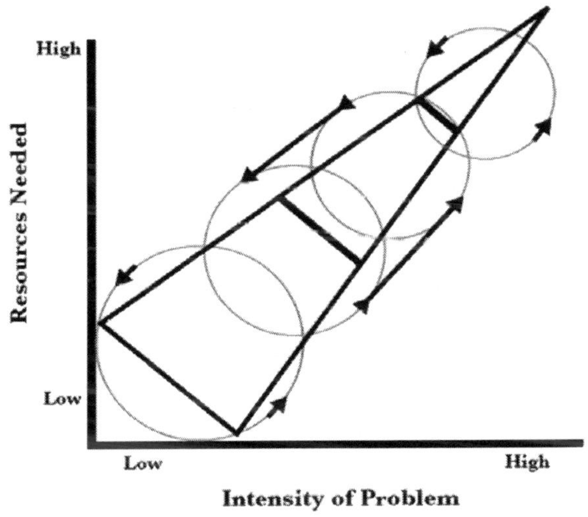

Figure 4. Relationship between the Heartland problem-solving model and a three-tier model.

With the passage of NCLB in 2002, the education landscape for all students, and all educators including school psychologists, changed precipitously. The education system is now held accountable for student learning, and there are rewards and sanctions in place as incentives. No matter what one thinks about the policy direction, the accountability provisions in NCLB had and continue to have strong bipartisan support in Congress, so it appears that though some changes may ultimately be made in the law in coming years, educators will still be held accountable for results. This shift in thinking has fundamentally rearranged the educational equation. In the old system, students were taught using the school's curriculum and the instructional methods used by the teachers in the school. Few modifications were systematically made to the curriculum or instruction as it was implemented with all students. What varied was student achievement. Most students profited and learned from the curriculum, a few excelled, and another group of students struggled to learn. These struggling students were often put in categorical programs such as special education or Title I. This situation created the familiar normal distribution of students' skills we are all so familiar with. With NCLB, the expectations have fundamentally shifted. One fundamental assumption underlying the NCLB statute is that all students will be proficient in basic academic skills (reading and mathematics) by the school year 2013–2014. The expectation is that all students will perform to at least a basic level of proficiency. To achieve this level of proficiency, it is expected that curriculum and instruction will flex and be varied based on student need. Indeed, the equation has been transposed from historical practices. NCLB even provides teachers and schools direction about what it is that they should do to accomplish total proficiency. They are to use scientific research-based practices. The words ''scientific research-based practice'' in some variation appear in the NCLB statute 111 times. It seems that Congress is trying to send a clear message.

All of these edicts work well in theory. They sound logical: Use research-based practices and students will learn. It should work. However, the statute neglects to mention that in many basic academic skills areas and for some behavioral issues, we do not as of yet have scientific research-based strategies. So, for example, if an eighth grader is struggling to comprehend what she reads because she does not understand the vocabulary in the passages she is reading, what scientific research-based vocabulary strategies are available to her teachers? Similarly, what scientific research-based practices are available to remediate a middle school student's confusion with quadratic equations? And the list goes on. Beyond not acknowledging the dearth of research-based practices in many areas, NCLB also does not acknowledge the lack of delivery mechanisms for research-based practices in schools. As noted earlier, most schools are not structured to flexibly provide access to a variety of research-based practices, and there is not a strong tradition of research-based practices in schools.

Despite these realities, NCLB has created a new context. Since 2002, schools have become avid collectors and users of data. They have learned much about data-based decision making. They have learned much about large-scale assessment. Teachers and administrators now know, with data, which students are proficient in critical basic skills areas and which ones are not. In sum, they know who is not getting it. They generally, however, do not know why they are not getting it. This information is critical to efficient remediation of students' problems. More specifically, knowledge of why students are not proficient is necessary to match instruction to specific student needs. The assessment systems in place in most schools do not allow schools to complete diagnostic assessments with sufficient specificity to help prescribe specific instruction either for groups of students or for individual students.

For example, in the current system, a school might know that a fourth grader did not pass his reading comprehension state accountability assessment. This is important information, to be sure. However, knowledge of lack of proficiency in reading comprehension provides only minimal information about what to do about it. An initial instinct in many schools is to provide strategic comprehension instruction to students like this. While this strategy might prove effective for some subset of students with comprehension problems, it is analogous to putting a person with a high body temperature in an ice bath. It may, for many students, not be treating the cause of the problem but instead is treating symptoms. A more reliable response would be to dig deeper into the student's comprehension problem using direct, skill-based assessments and then to match specific instructional strategies to the student's underlying deficits. Students with reading comprehension problems may be having comprehension problems for a variety of specific reasons. For example, the student may not comprehend because she does not understand the vocabulary in the passage she has been reading. She may not comprehend what she is reading because she is missing critical decoding (phonics) skills that cause her to misread many words. She may not comprehend because she does not have a large sight-word vocabulary. She may not comprehend because she does not read fluently enough. She may not comprehend because she is not monitoring meaning as she reads. And the list goes on.

Similar examples could be identified for social– behavioral problems. The same outward behaviors may be occurring for different reasons within the school context. These different reasons are often referred to as functions in the behavioral literature. Without understanding the underlying functions of these behaviors and matching a treatment to these functions, it is less likely that an effective treatment will be found.In sum, NCLB has taken us part of the way toward creating results-based accountability. The new context in schools is basically that all students must become proficient, schools are being held accountable for teaching them, there are rewards and sanctions associated with successful student outcomes, there is an urgency in schools about raising student achievement, and schools have become savvy at using large-scale accountability data to identify who is not proficient.

To create even more positive results at a larger scale in our schools, we must take the next steps beyond NCLB. NCLB alone is like a moped. It gets us going fast enough to get us into trouble but not fast enough to get us out. To create the additional horsepower, our next steps are to help schools understand, with data, why their students are not proficient and what to do about it. Technologies for answering these questions are becoming available, and implementing them will take us to the next level of importing science into applied practice.

Next Iteration of Science-Based Practice in Schools

When the need to import science into practice, the need to improve upon n 5 1 problem-solving models, and the need to address the new NCLB contexts for schools is combined, a need for the next evolution in importing science into practice becomes compelling. The new system needs to have all of the positive characteristics of early science-based practice implementations, it needs to maintain the positive characteristics associated with earlier problem-solving approaches, and it needs to both improve on these practices and make them available in a more efficient and broader scale.

Fortunately, an alternate model for importing science into practice has emerged in recent years. This model maintains all of the advantages of earlier problem-solving models and adds improvements that will increase effectiveness. The model has been variously referred to in the literature as the three-tier model and a school-wide model. This model has its roots in medicine, and has been translated to schools effectively in recent years. The three-tier model is often represented as a triangle.

The three-tier model is applicable to nearly any curricular area including reading, math, science, and social–emotional growth and development. One primary difference between earlier structural models (e.g., Heartland's problem-solving approach) and the three-tier model is that the three-tier model encompasses all students within a school as opposed to only students who were identified with specific learning problems. A second characteristic of the three-tier model is that it assumes all students within the triangle (which is all students) will become proficient in basic skills. The three tiers of the model each represent a group of students and a level of support that is necessary for those students to be successful.

Nature of Interventions in a Three-Tier System

In tiered systems, resources are allocated in direct proportion to student needs. Some students will achieve district- or state-defined levels of proficiency based on general education instruction (also referred to by some as core instruction). Some students will need core instruction plus something additional to achieve these proficiency levels. And a smaller number of students will need intensive instructional interventions as well. A brief description of each of these levels of intervention follows.

Tier 1: Core Instruction

Tier 1 represents students who will become successful based on the core curriculum alone. These students become academically healthy based on learning in the core curriculum. Core curriculum is generally defined as the curriculum that covers the school's standards and benchmarks that all students at a grade level receive. If a school's core curriculum is effective, approximately 80% of students should reach proficiency, based on the core curriculum alone. The 80% number is not a number set in stone and is something of an estimate based on the best evidence available. It is a logical and rational approximation of how effective core instruction should be. For example, if only 50% of students become proficient/ have their needs met through core instruction, that means that 50% of students will need either core plus supplemental instruction/intervention or core plus intensive instruction. In most public school systems, sufficient resources (time, money, and expertise) do not exist to provide this level of support to this many students. So, in this example, a prudent school's choice would be to invest significant resources in improving their core with the goal of ensuring its sufficiency for a greater number of students, in addition to working on providing effective supplemental and intensive services.

As we have said, in recent years, since passage of NCLB, schools have worked hard to adopt curricula that are scientific research-based. This is an important step that has improved curricula in schools across the country. In addition, schools are using their student performance data to guide their curricular and instruction decision making far better than was the case in previous years.

There are important considerations in addition to these features, however, that are also part of effective core curriculum programs. These include instructional match and universal screening. Tiered models assist in putting these practices in place within schools. The term instructional match refers to the process of matching the curriculum and instruction provided in a school to the needs of the student population being served. Scientific validation is a necessary but not sufficient characteristic of a curriculum. Curricula must also be matched to student need. So, for example, if a school with a very high poverty population is considering adopting a new early literacy curriculum, they may want to use the data they have collected to help steer their decision making toward one scientifically validated curriculum over another. Perhaps their data suggest the need for a very strong early language development component or the need for additional materials that parents (or caregivers) can use to work with their children. The district may then use this information to help prioritize among the various research-based curricula available.

A most important addition that tier models add to the core level of instruction is universal screening for students with learning problems. Schools routinely screen vision and hearing. In tiered systems, schools become familiar with the concept of early screening in basic academic skills as well. In the past, when our special education system was teacher-referral driven, the burden was on the teacher to perceive when students fell sufficiently far behind in order to warrant a referral for additional assessment and, potentially, additional services. There were a number of limitations to this system. First, most teachers were never given specific training about what to look for nor directed as to how bad a student's performance needed to be before they were to make a referral. Also, teachers differ in their skills at working effectively with struggling students. Moreover, the number of student needs within a classroom could limit even the best teacher's ability to work effectively with all struggling students. Finally, some students with significant learning needs simply were not detected efficiently and effectively using this referral system; that is, many students were missed. As we in the field were recognizing the limitations of our current referral system, our nation's researchers were solidifying two major findings. First, it is not efficient nor particularly effective to wait until learning problems get large to intervene; instead, it is most effective to address learning problems early when they are small. Second, the researchers identified critical indicators that could be used universally to screen all students for academic problems early, without waiting for students to fall extremely far behind their peers. Implementers using tiered models have taken what they have learned about the limitations of the historical referral system, have married them with the researchers' findings, and have come to the conclusion that universal screening must become a part of business as usual in our schools. Thus, in tiered systems, universal screenings of critical basic academic skills are used to help identify students who may need additional assessments and, potentially, additional services. Teachers still have the ability and responsibility to refer students who they are concerned about in tiered systems. There is just an additional mechanism in place to assist with the process.

In the case of early literacy, most tiered systems set forth standards for the implementation of their curricula. Many schools have adopted a 90-minute per day instructional block in grades K–3. During this time, core instruction in reading is provided to all students at a grade level. Interruptions are kept to a minimum, and teachers take their instructional responsibilities for quality delivery of the core very seriously. Student progress in the core is measured using classroom assessments, accountability assessments, grades, and periodic screening assessments.

Tier 2: Supplemental Instruction/ Interventions

In Tier 2, core plus supplemental instruction occurs. Even with very effective core curriculum and instruction in academic or social–emotional areas, there will be some students, perhaps 10–15% or so, who will need something supplemental to become proficient/have their needs met. It is important to note at this level that both core instruction and something supplemental are received by students. That supplemental can range from additional time in the core curriculum to additional opportunities and/or more time to learn, all the way through additional, strategically planned supplemental instruction. For some group of students, core plus supplemental will be sufficient for them to become proficient/have their needs met. Indeed, within the three-tier model, some students who receive supplemental instruction become successful enough that they ultimately do not require supplemental assistance and decisions can be made, based on progress-monitoring data, to move them back to core instruction alone).

Supplemental instruction is general education instruction. There is no suspicion that the student may have a disability. The student simply may need additional instruction to become proficient. There are currently two schools of thought on how to approach providing this additional instruction. One group of educators and researchers takes the position that these students need additional, supercharged balanced instruction in addition to their core instruction, with their response to this instruction continuously monitored. Research on this approach demonstrates that many children respond to this type of supplemental instruction.

A second approach is to administer additional assessments to students who do not reach desired levels of proficiency and then to provide additional, supplemental instruction focused on the areas where their skills require remediation. The idea underlying this approach is that it may be a more efficient use of resources to try to target supplemental instruction to areas where students' skills are most in need. There is less published research on this approach; however, there are data in some implementation sites documenting positive gains for students receiving intervention in this model.

No matter which approach is taken to determine the content and focus for the supplemental instruction, Torgesen has identified the following series of components that must be present in the supplemental instruction:

— Supplemental instruction must be explicit: Children with either specific or general learning disabilities, or who are poorly prepared to learn to read, must be explicitly taught most of what they need to know to learn to read. A major emphasis on word recognition is essential.

— Supplemental instruction must be more intensive than core instruction: More things must be directly taught, and children with disabilities, in particular, acquire skills more slowly and need more opportunity to apply reading and writing skills.

— Supplemental instruction must be more supportive, both emotionally and cognitively: Emotional support, in the form of encouragement, feedback, and positive reinforcement, is required because learning is more difficult and proceeds more slowly for some students needing supplemental instruction. Intellectual support, in the form of more carefully scaffolded instruction, is required because learning is more difficult.

— Supplemental instruction must include methods for student progress monitoring: This must be for both the short term and the long term.

Supplemental instruction in all cases is put in place in addition to core instruction. It does not replace it. It is usually delivered in groups of three to six students. Often, 30–45 minutes of supplemental instruction are provided to students. Usually 10 weeks of supplemental instruction might be provided in a cycle with the option of an additional 10-week cycle being available if student performance warrants it.

Tier 3: Intensive Instruction

In Tier 3, an even smaller set of students (perhaps 5% or so) will receive core plus intensive instruction. It is important to note at this level that intensive instruction does not connote special education. Special education is one service that might be brought to bear to meet some students' intensive instructional needs. However, there will be students who have intensive needs that will not qualify for nor would it be appropriate to provide them special education services. So, for example, there may be talented and gifted students who need intensive instructional services who do not qualify for special education. In another example, a student whose academic difficulties stem from the fact that he is learning English as a second language may need intensive instructional support, though he may not qualify for special education services. Tier 3 refers to the need for intensive instruction, not for a particular program.

For students with more extensive and significant needs, intensive instruction is sometimes needed. Torgesen's characteristics apply at this level of instruction as well, and both the amount and intensity of instruction at this level are even more concentrated. Intensive instruction for students is typically individualized in both type and amount. The question to answer is what type of instruction, with what type of intensity, will allow the student to learn at an acceptable rate. For many students with intensive instruction, 180 minutes of explicit, intensive instruction a day may be required. These students are already behind in the curriculum, and it is the school's objective to accelerate their learning to a rate where they potentially can begin making gains to close the gap with their peers.

An emerging evidence base suggests that implementation of a three-tiered system is effective at remediating academic and behavioral problems for a significant number of students. In addition, ongoing research is demonstrating that tiered models of service delivery can produce important improvements for special populations such as English language learners and minority populations.

References

Raimy, V. C. (Ed.). (1950). *Training in clinical psychology*. Englewood Cliffs, NJ: Prentice Hall.

Repp, A. C., & Horner, R. H. (Eds.). (1999). *Functional analysis of problem behavior*. Belmont, CA: Wadsworth.

Reschly, D. J., & Ysseldyke, J. E. (1995). School psychology paradigm shift. In A. Thomas & J. Grimes (Eds.), *Best practices in school psychology III* (pp. 17–31). Washington, DC: National Association of School Psychologists.

Thomas & J. Grimes (Eds.), *Best practices in school psychology IV* (pp. 483–501). Bethesda, MD: National Association of School Psychologists.

Ysseldyke, J., Burns, M., Dawson, P., Kelley, B., Morrison, D., Ortiz, S., et al. (2006). *School psychology: A blueprint for training and practice III*. Bethesda, MD: National Association of School Psychologists.

3

Changes and Challenges for School Psychologists

Every generation of students attends schools beset with problems that are created by the political, economic, and social forces unique to their times, challenges that also provide opportunities for those willing to recognize them. It is no different with children attending school during the last decade of the 20th century. As we rapidly approach the next millennium, we find that perhaps more than ever, the school psychologist is perfectly poised to help lead schools through current difficulties to innovative, long-term solutions, turning challenges into opportunities for positive change.

Since the 1983 report A Nation at Risk put the country on notice about the inadequacies of American education, a generation of students have attended kindergarten, grown up, and graduated from high school. For the most part, the schools they attended were not substantially different from those described in A Nation at Risk. This has led to grave failures to students:

More and more young people emerge from high school ready neither for college nor for work. This predicament becomes more acute as the knowledge base continues its rapid expansion, the number of traditional jobs shrinks, and new jobs demand greater sophistication and preparation.

Since those words were written, the school environment has become even more challenging for both student and instructor. The call for reform made in A Nation at Risk, though clearly heard by many, has yet to materialize. As school psychologists examine how best they can help transform an ailing learning environment into a model for success and pave the way to the 21st century, it may be helpful to ask, "What do today's schools now confront?"

The Changes in Today's Schools

Population Trends. Currently in the United States, 51.7 million children attend school. This represents a growth in the school-age population, known as the "Baby Boom Echo," that is straining the capacity of communities to respond to the need for additional schools and teachers. California schools will add 100,000 students per year for the next 10 years. In Clark County, Nevada, the population expands by 11,000-12,000 students every year, which is equivalent to building a new classroom every day of the year.

Declining Government Support. This expansion in student population is coming at a time of declining willingness to support education and social programs. There are now 16 million children living in poverty in this country; with welfare reform now law, it is estimated an additional one million children may fall into poverty. State and local governments, strained by disinvestment at the federal level, will be challenged to increase the services and supports they provide for children and for education. The days ahead will be difficult.

The effects are not felt by all schools and all children equally, however. Many communities in this country strive valiantly to provide a good education for their children. Others, equally committed to quality education, are unable to realize that goal because of economic circumstances. Property-rich districts by and large support quality schools; property-poor districts cannot. The problems are so extreme that at least eight states have enacted "bankruptcy laws" which allow the state to take over local school systems that fail to meet minimum standards.

Geographic and Economic Disparities. The quality of education children in this country receive varies as a function of where their schools are located. On the average, schools and schooling in the inner city, where the majority of the student population is poor and non-white, are markedly inferior to those available to white students in more affluent suburban America. Some rural areas are deeply distressed and also fail to provide adequate schooling. The net effect is a differential distribution of opportunities to learn which favors one segment of the American student population over others. The disparities are as unjust as the long-term effects are profound.

Recruitment and Training. Because the burgeoning student population is coinciding with the retirement of the first wave of the baby boom teacher generation, the demands for teachers will only increase in coming years. And yet it is becoming increasingly difficult to attract young people to the teaching profession. Only two percent of graduating college students become teachers. Colleges of education continue to be criticized for failing to prepare their graduates adequately for the reality of teaching today. And as the cultural and ethnic diversity of our society increases, the educators we are preparing neither understand these cultures sufficiently nor do they adequately represent this diversity.

Challenging Students. The student population entering America's classrooms is more challenging than at any time in our recent history. More children live in poverty, in single-parent homes, or in homes where both parents have to work long hours just to maintain a minimal standard of living. Increasing numbers of students are entering public schools without having learned basic social/socialization skills. Teachers are forced to contend with tremendous diversity in the behavior, value patterns, concepts of right and wrong, and skill levels of the students they teach. To add to these challenges, violence among young people and in schools is on the rise, with the result that too many teachers and students in many schools are preoccupied with fears for their safety. It is not surprising that many students in these schools are not learning to read, to compute, to write, or to acquire the knowledge and technical skills they will need as adults.

Mobility. Other forces contribute to instability in schools and in the classroom. These include the mobility of a large segment of the American population. With families making frequent moves, children risk receiving a disjointed education as they move from school to school, with different sites often embracing different philosophies or curriculum sequences. Schools themselves create instability and disjointedness through the use of suspension and expulsion policies as a primary means of disciplining students. Thus, the very students who most need stability and continuity of instruction are being excluded all too routinely from the classroom.

Lack of Consensus. We live in a culturally and politically diverse society, and we have vastly different ideas about the roles schools and teachers should play in the education of our young people. Some argue that the schools need to take over the functions that families no longer perform, while others argue that schools should get "back to basics." Debates over issues such as school prayer, sex education, school choice, and vouchers make it difficult to look beyond these value issues to the broader challenges of creating quality schools for all children.

While these disagreements create skirmishes which occupy the time, energy, and resources of teachers, school administrators, and school board members, the greater impact is that we have little consensus in this country on the goals of schooling. Furthermore, we have curricula and school structures that were designed many generations ago to respond to the needs of a time which has long since passed.

Technology. One of the biggest challenges facing schools is technology. For the first time in America, consumers are buying more personal computers than television sets. Using computers needs to be part of a student's education. In addition, computers are changing the way curricula are taught, from computer-based curricula on CD-ROMs to distance education and the Internet. Technology is also being used in new ways for classroom management, progress monitoring, and consultation. Bringing both students and instructors up to speed on new technology trends is one of the biggest issues that must be tackled as the next century dawns.

The Successes in Today's Schools

Universal Enrollment. While we catalog all that is wrong with schools and the distance yet to be traveled to create equal opportunities for all, it must be recognized America has done something that no other nation has even attempted: we have attained universal enrollment of children in elementary schools while seeking the twin goals of excellence and equity in education. The United States has embraced the concept of a free and appropriate education for all children regardless of race, creed, national origin, or disabilities, and many of our efforts to improve schools have been designed to meet this challenge. Schools increasingly enroll all children, and "all" is becoming increasingly diverse.

A Positive Picture. Despite the challenges, frustrations, and failure that have been met along the way, recent events give us hope. Although experts have long argued that the test scores of American students have been declining for decades and that we rate poorly on international comparisons, well-respected researchers have recently begun to argue that the picture given the American public of the status of students today is far bleaker than the reality. Many studies suggest that students are brighter than perceived, that test scores are on the rise, and that global comparisons are based on faulty premises. The United States has one of the strongest global economies and the highest productivity rate of any industrialized nation—perhaps the schools deserve some credit for these achievements.

There are schools that work well and there are children who are resilient and withstand the negative effects of poverty and disadvantage. There are professionals committed to creating schools that serve the needs of communities with multiple stressors. For example, a recent newspaper article described an elementary school in inner-city Newark, New Jersey where more than three-fourths of the student population score above grade level in reading, writing, and math, and where every classroom of the 400-student school had better than 90 percent attendance last year.

Family and Community Involvement. In addition to shining examples of schools that work, one can find many, many examples of parents who recognize that their support of education is the single most important thing they can do to ensure the success of their children. For instance, a Scientific American article a few years ago reported on the tradition of support for education among Asian-American families, with the result that this segment of the immigrant population consistently scores in the top percentiles on national scholastic achievement measures.

School Improvement Efforts. Never at any time in the history of American education has as much attention been paid to the need for educational reform and restructuring. Pick up any issue of Educational Leadership, Phi Delta Kappan Magazine, or the Harvard Review of Education, and articles describing successful efforts abound. Distinguished educators and researchers are no longer content to sermonize but are rolling up their sleeves and taking on some of the most challenging problems our schools face. Reading Recovery, Success for All, Accelerated Schools, the Coalition of Essential Schools, Project Zero, and the Paideia Group, to name but a few programs, have tackled the daunting problem of how to make school successful for all students.

American secondary schools are beginning a process of experimentation with alternative structures and programs to better meet the needs of their diverse student population. These include increasing Advanced

Placement offerings, early college entrance, mini schools-within-schools, and cooperative agreements with local colleges for gifted students as well as the development of alternative schools and expanded vocational options for non-college bound youth. Integrating technology into the classroom in ways which allow students to access the Internet, explore web sites, and create multi-media presentations is altering the shape of instruction in many schools.

Certainly we have not found all the answers to school improvement efforts. And there are those who would argue that many of our efforts are misdirected and more grandiose than they need to be. But the discussion has been joined, and there are few schools and school districts in the country which have not been touched by the call to transform education to meet the needs of today's youth and tomorrow's citizens.

Changes and Challenges for School Psychologists

School psychologists are in the crux of all these changes and are increasingly called into the most challenging school situations as front-line workers. In light of the changing context and in order to meet the needs of today's youth, school psychologists are making or being pushed to make broad changes in their role.

Increased Collaboration. Because the difficulties of many children transcend the capacity of schools to respond effectively, schools are engaged in new and deeper partnerships with parents and community agencies. These new school-family-community collaboratives are not fads; they are emerging as strong, urgently needed aspects of community development. In all of this, school psychologists have important roles to play. However, increased emphasis on interprofessional collaboration in training programs and practice is necessary.

Shift Away from Psychometrics and Labeling. It has been clear for some time that children and the schools could do well with less of categorical delivery systems which often require school psychologists to engage in simple psychometrics and child labeling. The practice of responding to diversity in the schools by creating more and more narrowly defined categorical school programs has little credibility. School psychologists have often been required to serve as the gatekeepers in this complex nonsystem. Objections to testing and labeling practices have risen to the level of fury, and school psychologists have become targets for much of this criticism.

As psychometric functions diminish in importance, school psychologists will have greater opportunities to exercise a broader and more useful version of psychology in the schools. Indeed, school psychologists' expertise in measurement, assessment, and problem solving can be used to move toward more diverse assessment of student learning and increased accountability in the schools. There are many clear instances in which school psychologists have taken the lead to improve assessment, problem solving, and intervention practices.

Focus on Success for All Students. School psychologists have played active roles in developing and implementing solutions as schools have worked hard to improve. As noted previously, we have achieved universal enrollment of all children in the schools of the nation, at least for an initial period of schooling. School psychologists are among those who helped accomplish this important goal. Along with universal enrollment comes a responsibility to help the increasingly diverse student population to successfully complete school and graduate. School psychologists have a role to play in advocating for reductions in all forms of demission—explusions, suspensions, and "drop outs"—and for increasing inclusive education options to meet the needs of all students, especially those most disenfranchised from the system.

Expanded Involvement/Broader Role. Psychology remains the most relevant of all of the disciplines and professions associated with teaching, learning, and child development. School psychologists are privileged to be in a position to deliver psychology both in schools and in the broader, emerging school-family-community framework. It is not unusual to find school psychologists who are being successful in helping design alternative schools, evaluating charter schools, assisting in creating effective school-community linkages, collaborating with the medical community to develop effective programming for students with medical problems, or participating in a long-range strategic planning effort at a district or building level.

The momentum is building. In the next few years there will be a continued refinement of our understanding of the change process and how best to bring meaningful reform to the majority of American schools. School psychologists will have an integral role in this process. It is imperative that their training give them the skills they will need to be full players in the transformation of American schools.

In addition to the influences from outside the profession, advancements within the profession that have occurred during the past decade have helped shape how school psychologists are prepared for their work and how that work is conducted. Although the following paragraphs identify separate challenges for training and practice, common themes are evident, and relevant connections between training and practice are more important than ever.

Training

Maximizing Resources. With tightening of dollars for higher education, fierce competition for resources is evident in all sectors. Within university settings, relatively high-cost school psychology programs are under increasing scrutiny from administrators who must balance budgets despite diminished resources. Training programs are faced with the challenge of maintaining quality preparation for school psychologists during an era when training content and scope are expanding and financial and staff resources are shrinking. Exploring alternative modes of instruction, such as distance learning, will be necessary as pressure to maximize resources increases.

Interdepartmental and Intersystem Collaboration. This challenge to maximize resources necessitates another change in university training programs: an increasing emphasis on collaboration with other departments and disciplines within the university and the community at large. This change has an associated risk, in that such collaboration may reduce the total number of faculty members dedicated exclusively to school psychology programs. However, potential benefits, including richness of training perspectives and reduction of redundancy and costs to the community, are apparent as well. Such interdepartmental instruction helps build inter-professional collaboration and problem solving. Intersystem collaboration provides hands-on training opportunities for students early in their training programs. It also establishes a valuable bi-directional communication link between the university and receiving systems, such as school districts and community mental health centers.

Recruitment/Retention of School Psychologists from Multicultural and Multiethnic Backgrounds. The cultural landscape of the United States and its schools continue to reflect increasing diversity. Major city schools, in particular, are settings where “minority” populations comprise the majority of the student census. As the composition of the student population changes, so too should the cultural and ethnic makeup of educators who instruct, provide models for, and counsel these youngsters. The ratio of ethnic diversity in school psychology graduate programs has remained below 10 percent for the past 15 years. This percentage has not changed despite calls for diversity and targeted financial support. This results in the existing human resources of the profession being essentially non-Hispanic White and predicted to remain so for some time to come. A major challenge facing university training programs in school psychology is the recruitment of persons from minority backgrounds to enter the field. NASP's Minority Scholarship Fund is an example of a proactive effort to address this challenge.

Instructional Validity. As school psychology practice increasingly demands broad-ranging skills over technical proficiency in administering tests, training programs must expand course offerings in these areas of practice. In addition to a broader array of course content, coursework, and broader scope of practice issues, training programs are challenged to identify and implement instructional systems that provide the kinds of modeling, feedback, and coaching essential to the development of effective process skills. Traditional vehicles for delivery of instruction at the university level may need to be replaced by or supplemented with carefully structured and supervised experiences in schools where students can observe, practice, and receive close and direct feedback, coaching, and experience in change processes. Practicum-based training opportunities under supervision, as well as other structures which link schools and universities, are vital. It is also incumbent on programs to explore more diverse, comprehensive means by which to assess the capability of students and graduates to positively impact the lives of children and youth and to evaluate and improve program effectiveness.

Practice

Acquiring & Becoming Proficient in New Skills The original Blueprint document was written at a time when the school psychologist's practice was restricted by test-label-place activities associated with implementation of the Individuals with Disabilities Education Act. Since then, a number of states have passed reforms that relax past highly prescriptive assessment practices. At the same time, concern about student outcomes and escalating violence in schools have created opportunities for school psychologists to shift from an emphasis on testing to an emphasis on designing effective academic and behavioral interventions. School psychologists are called upon to assist in developing appropriate programs and services for an increasingly heterogeneous student population. As families become alienated from public schools and disinvested in their children's education, creating home-school-community connections becomes an increasingly vital aspect of the school psychologist's role. Finally, the move to an ecological framework to help explain student performance requires school psychologists to understand and use this framework effectively. It also requires school psychologists to renegotiate informal contracts with teachers who for years were told that problems are located within students rather than in a mismatch between the characteristics of the learner and those of the instructional environment or the broader home/school context.

These examples illustrate that consumers are beginning to require different kinds of practice from school psychologists, necessitating practitioners to build upon a multitude of skills, acquire new ones, and become proficient in their use.

Examples include consultation, team process, intervention design, instructional consultation, interagency collaboration, and strategies for monitoring student progress. Many practicing school psychologists already have and demonstrate these skills, yet others who have worked their entire careers under test-label-place conditions find themselves needing to acquire and use new skills, at the same time they continue to straddle the world of special education eligibility determination.

Role Confusion/Role Release. A decade ago, school psychologists knew what they did, and so did everyone else. Today, as the gatekeeper role for school psychologists has been reduced, both practicing school psychologists and their education partners have become less clear about what they contribute that is unique to the educational system. This circumstance creates a sense of cognitive dissonance among practitioners whose once-valued work in individual diagnostic assessment is now ascribed less worth. Despite the personal conflicts that result, this situation provides a wonderful opportunity to reinvent and redefine our role, form new coalitions, and acquire and demonstrate new skills. In the future, the nature of one's work within schools will likely be defined less by title than by areas of professional skill and competence. School psychologists will less likely be restricted to a psychometric testing role and will need to cultivate other areas of practice.

A most important personal characteristic will be the ability to let go of power, to be part of a team.

Demonstrating Accountability. During an era of shrinking resources and increased market pressure, public employees must continuously demonstrate the ways in which they benefit the larger system. This is a new experience for many school psychologists whose positions have traditionally been protected and restricted by state regulations mandating the administration of intelligence tests for special education eligibility. As states eliminate or minimize such requirements, school psychology must reassert itself as a necessary profession, and individual practitioners must redefine their roles and practice within this new context. Opportunities for contributing meaningfully to the educational system are greater today than ever before. Some school psychologists have been instrumental in designing and implementing interventions to maximize student competence (e.g., social skills, mathematics, cognitive learning strategies), to ameliorate or prevent problem behaviors (e.g., anger control, conflict mediation), and to promote family-school connections. As they engage in this important work, school psychologists must collect data about valued effectiveness indicators. For example, do discipline referrals decrease as a result of anger control programs? Does attendance improve when family-school involvement is fostered? Benefit to individual students and to the system must be considered and demonstrated continually.

Serving Multiple Masters. Not all service delivery systems have rejected labels as the means to access services. As a result, school psychologists frequently find conflicts in demands and expectations from one service delivery system to another. An example is the apparently conflicting message from school administrators to spend time testing students with suspected or known disabilities in order to garner Medicaid dollars, while delivering a broader range of indirect services, such as teacher consultation and social skills interventions. Inconsistencies across and within systems can contribute to role confusion and result in professional stress and eventual burnout.

Professional Burnout. Many educators, especially those in the nation's major city districts, have conflicting and confusing job demands, work-related stress, and professional burnout. For nearly all practitioners today, the conflict between doing new things while maintaining some elements of old practices is a major source of stress. For educators in urban areas, this is compounded by other factors such as a high incidence of violent behaviors, high mobility rates of families and staff, and enormous bureaucracies that complicate the simplest decision. In spite of these difficult work conditions, there are individual practitioners in urban settings who remain excited about their work. Literature pertaining to professional resiliency can provide some insight into why this occurs. That literature suggests both internal factors (e.g., ability to reframe, sense of humor) and environmental factors (e.g., support mechanisms) are associated with triumph in stressful situations. Creating and maintaining conditions to promote resiliency among school personnel is another major challenge facing the practice of school psychology today. Since this need is shared by many educators, professional societies representing diverse disciplines (e.g., teachers, school psychologists, counselors, paraprofessionals) might collaborate to address this concern.

Data-based Decision Making and Accountability

Data-based decision making and accountability should be the organizing theme for school psychology training and practice. This should permeate every aspect of the practice: school psychologists need to be good problem solvers, able to collect information to understand problems, to make decisions about appropriate interventions, to assess educational outcomes, and to help others become accountable for the decisions they make. School psychologists always have been responsible for collecting considerable data on individual students and educational programs; increasingly, they are responsible for gathering data on school systems and classroom environments as well. They do so through assessment— a process of testing, observing, and interviewing to collect data for the purpose of making decisions about children and youth. School psychologists should be well versed in a variety of assessment methods, including formal and informal test administration, behavioral assessment, curriculum-based measurement, interviews, ecological or environmental assessment, as well as assessment methodologies to define a student's problems and needs, to assess current status, and to measure the effects of a problem-solving process. They need to provide leadership in identification of those instructional environments (school and home), as well as cognitive, emotional, social, and behavioral factors that have a significant impact on school achievement and the development of personal competence, and be able to use this information for the promotion of student competence or the prevention of student difficulties/disabilities. School psychologists should be adept at assessing the components of the instructional environment that facilitate or impede learning/behavioral change for students, and they should know how environmental factors and student characteristics interact to affect academic and behavioral outcomes. School psychologists should be expected to be called upon by school administrators to help in assessment practices designed to meet general public accountability responsibilities.

Interpersonal Communication, Collaboration, and Consultation

School psychologists must have the positive interpersonal skills necessary to facilitate communication and collaboration with students and among teams of school personnel, community professionals, agencies, and families / schools. They must be prepared to listen, adapt, deal with ambiguity, and be patient in difficult situations. They must understand the vital importance of collaboration and know how to do this well. Not only must they be able to communicate, but they must be able to clearly present and disseminate information to diverse audiences such as parents, teachers, school boards, policy makers, business leaders, and fellow school psychologists in a variety of contexts.

Consultation approaches may embrace behavioral, mental health, and/ or collaborative philosophies. At a minimum, school psychologists should have good problem-solving skills, and be proficient in systems consultation at an advanced level. School psychologists should be able to use systems consultation skills to facilitate development of harmonious school environments, to reduce the divi-siveness and disenfranchisement often found in troubled schools, and to promote the kinds of principled negotiations necessary to achieve consensus. School psychologists also function as change agents, using their skills in communication, collaboration, and consultation to promote change at the individual student, classroom, building, and district levels.

Development of Cognitive/Academic Skills

School psychologists should help schools develop challenging but achievable cognitive and academic goals for all students, with variations in standards expectations for individual students, and alternative ways to monitor or assess individual student progress toward goal or standards accomplishment. They should also be of assistance to State Education Agency and Local Education Agency personnel who design state and local accountability systems.

School psychologists should know much about the application of learning theory and cognitive strategies to the instructional process. They should know empirically de monstrated components of effective instr uction; altern a t i v e instructional methodologies, such as class-wide peer tutoring and cooperative learning; and be in a position to work with others to improve instruction. They should work directly and indirectly to facilitate student achievement as well as the development of attention, problem-solving, and study skills. School psychologists should help in assessing treatment integrity (the extent to which treatment or programs are being implemented in the ways in which they were intended). In addition, they should assist school staff in helping students become increasingly responsible for their own learning (self-regulated learning) and self-assessment. School psychologists should also be prepared to assist teachers and other educators in keeping abreast of important research on instruction.

Socialization and Development of Life Competencies

School psychologists should help schools develop challenging but achievable behavioral, affective, and adaptive behavioral goals for all students. They should know how to enhance appropriate pupil behavior and how to develop methodologies such as conflict resolution and social p roblem-solvi ng/ decision- making approaches th at will assist teachers and families in teaching pro-social behavior. School psychologists should be knowledgeable about development in social, affective, and adaptive domains and be able to identify and apply sound principles of behavior change within these domains. They should provide leadership in creating instructional environments that reduce alienation and foster the expression of appropriate behavior as well as environments in which all members of the school community—both children and adults—treat one another with respect and dignity. The following topics should be considered a minimum offering in the preservice education of school psychologists: alternative approaches to student discipline; ecological and behavioral approaches to classroom management, including management of the behavior of individual students and groups in the context of classrooms and families; and knowledge of the research on classroom climate. As with academic skills, school psychologists must be able to assess treatment integrity. They should also assist school staff in helping students become responsible for their own behavior.

Student Diversity in Development and Learning

More than ever before, students in today's schools come from a variety of racial, cultural, ethnic, experiential, and linguistic backgrounds. Their activities and talents must be acknowledged, supported, and integrated into their instructional programs. School psychologists can actively support this recognition. Experiential and linguistic differences can also result in learning difficulties and apparent disabilities. School psychologists must be effective in assisting schools in identifying what is needed for these students to succeed and what modifications are required to remedy such difficulties. They must be able to recognize their own sometimes subtle racial, class, gender, and cultural biases, and the ways in which their (and others') biases and backgrounds influence their decision making, instruction, behavior, and ultimately long-term outcomes for students.

School Structure, Organization, and Climate

School psychologists should know how to organize schools in ways that promote learning and prevent problems. This includes the design of student support teams, intervention assistance teams, programs to train paraprofessionals, instructional support, school policies on discipline and grading, communication and referral systems, development of transition programs from one aspect of schooling to another, and formation of mini-school (or schools within a school) programs.

School psychologists should provide leadership in developing schools as safe, caring, inviting places in which there is a sense of community, in which the contributions of all persons, including teachers, paraprofessionals, administrators, families, students, and related services personnel are valued, and in which there are high expectations for excellence for all students.

Prevention, Wellness Promotion, and Crisis Intervention

School psychologists need to be knowledgeable about academic, behavioral, and serious personal difficulties. They must be prepared to help in both prevention and intervention programs. They need to recognize the behaviors that are precursors to development of conduct disorders, internalizing disorders, or school dropout and know how to design programs to prevent and intervene with these problems. They need to know how to work with school personnel, students, parents, and the general community in the aftermath of crises such as suicide, death, natural disasters, murder, bombs or bomb threats, extraordinary violence, and sexual harassment. At the same time, school psychologists need to be prepared to address wellness promotion as well as diverse health issues such as substance abuse, diet, eating disorders, AIDS prevention, and stress management. While they are not expected to be experts in all of these areas, school psychologists should know how to access resources to address a wide variety of crises and how to work together with others to bring effective services to students and school staff.

Home/School/Community Collaboration

School psychologists should be prepared to help design and operate programs to promote school-family interactions. They should study and be knowledgeable about: (1) family influence on student cognitive, motivational, and social characteristics that affect classroom performance; (2) family involvement in education; (3) ways to promote partnerships between parents and educators to improve outcomes for students; and (4) cultural issues that impact home-school collaboration. They can help lead parent training programs and help establish problem-oriented drop-in centers and hot lines to assist parents. They can be expected to help educate parents for participation in IEP meetings and help schools and parents work together to design curricula and interventions for students. School psychologists should understand and promote those home factors that work to support learning and achievement in school.

School psychologists need to share in leadership roles in coordinating with other agencies and in forming linkages within the community. The move in many places to make schools less "independent" and more "collaborative"—with parents, social and health agencies, corrections authorities, local businesses, etc.—is a major and long-term development. School psychologists should be prepared to help lead and maintain the emerging collaboratives.

Research and Program Evaluation

School psychologists should know basic principles of research design, including single-subject design and qualitative design, be able to differentiate good from inadequate research, and understand measurement and statistics in sufficient depth to evaluate published research and conduct investigations relevant to their work. They should be leaders in evaluation of local school programs and in interpreting their findings to educators and to the public.

Legal, Ethical Practice and Professional Development

School psychologists should be prepared to practice in schools in ways that meet all appropriate ethical, professional, and legal standards, both to enhance the quality of services and to protect rights of all parties. They should adhere to due process guidelines in all decisions affecting students; maintain accepted standards in assessment, consultation, and general professional practice; and fulfill all legal requirements, as in response to law and court decisions.

School psychologists have a responsibility to plan and carry through a continuing program for their own development as professionals. They should maintain certification or licensure and attend continuing education functions. They should recognize their own limitations and biases, as well as those areas in which they have training and expertise. They should also work with others on the school staff to ensure that teachers and related services personnel have opportunities for continuing professional development.

Although the domains of training and practice for school psychologists are listed and defined separately, they overlap and operate together in the lives of practicing school psychologists. An example of a daily schedule for a school psychologist is presented on the next two pages. It should be noted that this example is from one school psychologist in an urban school district which has deliberately moved toward noncategorical placement and where the role of the school psychologist has been shaped intentionally over time to include many of the competency areas in which training occurred. Although the scenario is not exhaustive in its coverage of the domains of training and practice, it is a real example of how many of the domains are used on a daily basis. In addition, we realize that the domains of practice are largely dictated by the system requirements of the setting in which the school psychologist is employed.

References

American Psychological Association (1998). *Archival description of school psychology.* Washington, DC: Author

National Association of School Psychologists (2002). *School psychologists: Providing mental health services to improve the lives and learning of children and youth.* Bethesda, MD:Author.

Ysseldyke, J.E. (1985). *School psychology: The state of the art.* Minneapolis, MN: National School Psychology Inservice Training Network.

4

Education for All : A Challenge for School Psychologists

The Concept of Education For All (EFA)

In Jomtien (Thaïland) was adopted the World Declaration on Education for All. This declaration presented a broad vision of basic education, calling for a learning environment in which everyone would have the chance to acquire the basic elements that serve for further learning and enable full participation in society.

This vision implied both access to education for everybody and meeting the diverse learning needs of children, youths and adults.

In Dakar (Senegal) the World Education Forum re-affirmed this vision and adopted a Framework for Action that emphasized the need for quality in education as well as access to it.

The Six Dakar Goals

I. expanding and improving comprehensive early childhood care and education especially for the most vulnerable and disadvantaged children;

II. ensuring that by 2015 all children, particularly girls, children in difficult circumstances and those belonging to ethnic minorities have access to and complete free and compulsory primary education of good quality;

III. ensuring that the learning needs of all young people and adults are met through equitable access to appropriate learning and life skills programmes;

IV. achieving a 50 per cent improvement in levels of adult literacy by 2015 especially for women and equitable access to basic and continuing education for all adults;

V. eliminating gender disparities in primary and secondary education by 2005, and achieving gender equality in education by 2015, with a focus on ensuring girls' full and equal access to and achievement in basic education of good quality.

VI. improving all aspects of the quality of education and ensuring excellence of all so that recognized and measurable learning outcomes are achieved by all, especially in literacy, numeracy and essential life skills.

International strategy for implementing EFA

The principal actors in EFA are governments and civil society (i.e NGOs) at the national level.

The international strategy includes :

1. Planning for EFA at national/regional level (national education plans)
2. Communication and advocacy (ex: provide messages on social justice and equitable opportunity combined with stories of the impact of education on the lives of individuals and communities.
3. Financing EFA. A crucial point. In spite the Dakar forum proclaimed "no national EFA plan should be delayed for lack of financial resources", most observers have pointed out that promised money have not been provided
4. Monitoring and evaluation (EFA observatory in UNESCO Institute for Statistics.)
5. International and regional mechanisms.
    a. The EFA High level Group and the EFA Working Group are informed by the annual EFA Monitoring Report produced by an independent group of experts on a thematic basis.
    b. The Collective consultation of NGOs on EFA. This mechanism aims to facilitate civil society participation in the Dakar Follow up. The CCNGO/EFA orgaénizes regional civil society forums.
    c. The Global Campaign for Education (GCE) initiated by 3 important NGOs: Oxfam, Education International and Action Aid.

GCE lobbies for the right to education and participates in the international co-ordination mechanisms of the High Level Group and EFA Working Group.

d. The NGO Liaison Committee is the communication and liaison channel on EFA matters to the NGOs in official relationship with UNESCO.

e. The flagship programmes Under the leadership of an international Agency (i.e UNESCO; UNIEF, UNHCR…)they assist countries to achieve their EFA goals; they provide special focus for one aspect of EFA in terms of advocacy, advice and monitoring of progress.

EFA STRATEGIES AND THE SCHOOL PSYCHOLOGIST

In many countries, school psychologists are considered by administrators, policy makers, teachers and parents as experts for children with mental problems. In other words, their work is not seen as different from clinical psychologists working in mental health institution. Though this picture is partly wrong, there is some reality within it.

Even if the local legislation includes interventions on groups and school organizations, there is a critical requirement for individual assessment of children with specific needs. This child centred clinical approach,, usually founded on a medical model (FARRELL 2003-4 et 2004-1) is not very favourable to the development of a quality education for all as recommended in UNESCO orientations.A school psychology able to meet not only the individual needs of all children but also the needs of the school community as a whole should change its perspective and make a dramatic shift from a clinical point of view to an ecological point of view.

What school psychologists could do for quality education by working on the school environment ?

To change their view, they need:

1. A conceptual frame,
2. Tracks for actions
3. A support from decisions makers in education.

TRACKS FOR ACTION

Considering the 6 Dakar goals, school psychologists may play a prominent role in their achievement.

Even if school psychology has been generalized in developed countries first, its principles could be used in any country preparing a national plan of education for all. NGOs and foundations working in developing countries to implement education programmes (either in formal education or non formal) could use the expertise of school psychologists especially those who- with ISPA- have got an international and cross cultural experience.

In developed and emergent countries where school psychology does exist, there are still many needs that are not met. Countries like the USA, the UK, France, Germany have sophisticated school systems in which a lot of students have not succeeded in completing their curriculum in secondary education either they have dropped out before the end of their studies or because they could not get a final general or professional diploma. Most of these students have experienced failure early in their school life.

In these countries, school psychologists could be better used providing that their task should be organized differently. Too often, the major work of school psychologists consists in identifying individual children whose performances or behaviour are seen as symptoms of psychological troubles. Under this respect, the school psychologist does not work differently from clinical psychologists. In some cases he/she works as a therapist instead of working in improving programmes, quality of life in schools, and teachers training.

Nevertheless, in some countries, school psychologists have used their knowledge to help schools in offering more resources to their students.

In a call for contribution that was published in WGR (2004), I mentioned several topics that could be of interest for school psychologists who wish give more importance to education for all in their day to day work : among them,

1. actions to develop and promote literacy (reading, spelling) among minorities (in mother tongue or official national tongue),children (especially girls) and adults (especially women).
2. non formal education towards mothers in order to promote sound psychological development (cognitive, emotional...) for young children.
3. education in post war countries (education to peace and tolerance)
4. training of teachers in countries building or re-building their school system (for example East-European countries).

5. More generally, any programme aiming to improve basic education quality and allowing all children to have easy access to education.

The diversification of SP's activities is not really new. 15 years ago, (GUILLEMARD/MESMIN 1989) had presented a panorama of their work with the school actors.

They recommended :

1. Group discussions for parents of young children in pre-elementary schools.
2. Specific consultations for migrant families (cross cultural and ethno-psychological approach)
3. Health education and prevention of addiction (tobacco, alcohol); prevention of STD 'and HIV-Aids.
4. Information of children in primary schools about maltreatment and sexual abuse
5. Psychological training for teachers.

Professional literature (SPI,WGR…) has given numerous attempts to highlight the role of SPs as consultants of students, teachers,parents, local administrators, policy and decision makers and as resource persons to help schools in modifying disruptive behaviours by changing the class-room environment .

Some example to illustrate school psychologists actions supporting education for all:

It is not possible to mention all the examples of SPs Practices that support the improvement of school efficiency and the quality education for all. I have selected some programmes in which school psychologists have been strongly involved either as conceptors or as major participant by the 5 past years:

1. A national model : Finland (Arja Sigfrids)
2. A group discussion for Chinese parents (Rebecca Duvillié)
3. Promoting school values among families of low economical status (Nicole Bailly)

Though each country is unique,it may be interesting to consider what are "best practices in EFA". The example of Finland, a small country in Northern Europe may give a good idea of what is necessary to meet the educational need of a population in its globality.

The Finnish education system works as a whole. That means, if pedagogical matters are considered as important, they are included in a psycho-social and political context. In other words the Finnish society requests from its schools they improve the instructional quality to promote students performance. This conception of quality education (which is also the core of UNESCO orientation for the programme Education for All) was enhanced through various researches. Pianta et La Paro declare that « *the relationships that children have with adults and other children in families, child care and school programmes provide the foundation of their success in school*" and they define readiness for school as follows : "*Children are ready for school when, for a period of several years, they have been exposed to consistent stable adults who are emotionally invested in them; to a physical environment that is safe and predictable ; to regular routines and rhythms of activity; to competent peers ; and to materials that stimulate their exploration and enjoyment of the world and from which they derive a sense of mastery. These factors alone would be better indices of readiness for school than any measurable aspect of child performance.*"

All the psychosocial context is involved in the conception or education in Finland. All the children have free access to the school where their basic needs are filled. For example a warm lunch is served every day. This may appear as a trivial observation, but if we remember the hierarchical pyramid of needs by Maslow, we understand that food and security are prior to education for human beings.If these basic needs are not filled it is an illusion to believe that education could progress.

The Finnish school system is probably the most efficient in the world for literacy.100% of the children attending regular schools can read and write. It is not only because school psychologists are strongly involved in the process of reading, but in all finnish families, one or several newspapers are ordered at home every morning. This is probably the strongest motivation for a child to read.

In Finland as in most European countries, migrant and refugees families are numerous and the schools are ready to prepare their children in learning the language and the finnish way of life. It is a bit more difficult for adolescents when they arrive and cannot read in their own language, but they receive the same support as the younger ones. They are also taught in their mother tongue as first language, Finnish being taught as a second language. Adults, men and women, may also benefit of the system.

Early prevention is also well organized. Finnish children attend the kindergarden at age 3 (or even early) and regularly visit the day care centre where they meet doctors, nurses, psychologists and speech therapists. This mechanism of prevention help most children in joining the regular school (at 7) and explains the high rate of school success.

For handicapped and children with special educational needs, inclusion has been generalized. Rehabilitation teams support the child in the regular class. In some cases, handicapped children who need specific medical and therapeutic support may be orientated towards special classes or schools.

School psychologist have also an important action in the field of training and psychological information for teachers, but also for parents and students.

According to Anja Sigfrids, the recognized role of the school psychologist and his/her place in the educational staff is a factor of the quality education in Finland.However, if the ratio of SPs is high in large cities like Helsinki(1/1000 students), there are still important needs in the country where a higher number of professionals should be welcome.

The finnish model could be used in most European countries as an example of best practices and it could suggest ISPA to prepare a recommendation for EU Education committee in order that relevant suggestion should be sent to ministries of education.

Migrant children usually experience school difficulties that may lead them to school failure, dropping out and disruptive behaviours in schools and in the global society as well. Their integration in the national community is a challenge that schools are not always prepared to face. Too many teachers have a social representation of these children as condemned to failure with the social consequencies driving them towards poverty, delinquency, addiction…Several researches have shown that it was importance to make a difference between ethnic origin and economical status as factor of school difficulties. In fact, in many cases, migrants children are on a more positive way than other children. Their parents have more ambitious expectations than other families with the same socio-economical status, but they have specific barriers to overcome that are linked to misunderstanding and lack of reference of their parents in the country of migration.

From these observations, Rebecca Duvillié, school psychologist in Paris (France) has organized group discussions for migrants families. I present here the work she has proposed for Chinese families. The team she led was composed of a translater in Chinese, a social worker, the head of the school and occasional participants (like the school doctor).

Teachers in this school have expressed their distress in front of these Chinese children and their families who were not willing to consult specialists in guidance centres or hospitals and they wished that something could be organized within the school for these families and their children.

On one hand, even when they are socially integrated in the school, they remain at risk population because:

1. They are not fluent in French,
2. They usually spend when they arrive one year or more in a special class to learn basic French which delays their inclusion in a regular class and has consequences for the future of their school progress (due to the rigidity of the French school system)
3. They are good at scientific matters but rather poor at literary matters
4. They are often inhibited and even mute in the class room due to their poor French and to their Chinese education as well and they feel mugged (attacked) by the surrounding environment. The gap between the French culture at school and the Chinese culture at home is difficult to bridge over.
5. When they become fluent in French, they play a role of translator for their parents in their contacts with the French administration. this inversion of generation (they play the role of parents for their own parents) make the concept of filiation difficult to be integrated.

On the other hand,

1. They have a clear idea of their culture and of their status in the family and in the community which is secure and stimulating enough to allow them to progress.
2. Differently from other migrant communities (from Africa for example) there is a small number of children in the family (usually one sometimes two) which allows mother to be close to their child.
3. The Houang Zhou culture provides the child resources to cope with the trauma of migration and to install compensatory strategies with a rather high self esteem.

Once a month families are invited for a 2 hour session with the team in the school library of the school. Parents are seated on a circle with in the middle a play carpet with toys for younger children (infant and toddlers)brought by their mother.

Parents express their difficulties in understanding the school culture and more generally the French way of life so different from their Chinese experience. Below, the list of topics parents have discussed during the year 2003-2004:

1. China and the Houang Zhou culture, (these families come from the HouangZhou region in southern China)
2. The French school functioning and ideology: history of school in France.
3. How difficulties of pupils are treated,
4. Chinese healing versus western medicine (with the participation of the school doctor)
5. Children play in China and in France
6. Lunch time at school and Chinese cooking: memories of child food.
7. Learning French, cross cultural education,
8. Migration of HouangZhou people
9. Catholicism and Confucianism,
10. Family structures in China after the Revolution and western family structures.

A the end of the school year an international meal was organized with the participation of all ethnic groups represented in the school and children in traditional clothes dancing on local musics.

For the school psychologist, the goal of these meetings were to offer these families a recognition in and by the school in order to facilitate the social integration of their children.

The idea was :

1. to allow the parents to express their fears, misunderstanding, expectations and hope for their children,
2. to look for solution with the parents.

Finally, the discussion group in mother tongue with a translator gives sense to situations that initially are felt as nonsense by the concerned families. It also contributes to :

1. give a recognized status to these families,
2. make a link between the school institution, the families and the Chinese community;
3. help reducing the ideological rigidity of the French school.

In 1981, the french socialist government proposed a new concept, the Priority Education Area (ZEP for Zone d'Education Prioritaire). The ideology of this concept was "to give more to those who have less" and offer more resources to some schools –usually in poor suburbs of big cities but sometimes in rural areas- in order to improve educational conditions.These resources consisted in a lower ratio of students (1 teacher for 25 students and even less) A ZEP consists in a "Lycée" /senior high school (general, technical or professional), one or more "collège" (junior high school) several primary schools and pre-elementary schools (though non compulsory, pre-elementary schools-called "écoles maternelles" are attended by 100% of children, from 3 (sometimes 2) to 5. Nicole Bailly, school psychologist in a ZEP near Paris describes its contribution to an experience of work with parents of very low economical status in order to help them to become more familiar with the school culture and values and motivate their children.

If school failure is not fatal and if it remains unchanged year after year in some area of deprivation it is because everything has not been attempted, because analysis and research are not encouraged in the field. We have known for decades now, the role of family implication in the success or failure of children at school.And we also know pretty well that there is a connivance between actors belonging to the same social classes and sharing the same cultural background.The position of the school psychologist may be of major importance to attempt to bridge the gap between these families with low economical status (lower-lower class according to the anglo-saxon sociological typology) and the teachers most of them belonging to middle or upper middle class. This implies to articulate psychological, social, cultural, economical and political factors to change the relationship between the school and its users. It implies also to have time. This kind of action can be efficient on the long term only (several years) with a continuity in the work and a minimal stability of the professionals participating in the experience. A long time is necessary to prevent failure, discouragement and to refuse the imposition of a model that is another form of control of power, and of violence against these populations.

A meeting point at Chanteloup les Vignes (78). In this suburb not far from Paris, a meeting point for families has been organized in a pre-elementary school these 5 past years. Every year it is a new birth never always the same always different. This long work and co-operation between the educators and the families has allowed to develop mutual trust and mutual respect.after long hesitations each actor felt it was possible to tell one's fear, one's misunderstanding, often one's anger. It is really a cross cultural work that has been done between people supposed to belong to the same nation, living in the same country. The efforts of all to listen the others which is a rule imposed by the framework proposed by the school psychologist and the other members of the team, permit mutual trust and sometimes reveal to one or the other a feeling of communication that had never been experienced before.

The success of the experience encouraged parents whose children grew older to solicit the extension of the meeting point to elementary schools : Three new meeting points were organized with the financial support of the department of education, the local administration. This organization allowed to discharged the school staff and the school psychologist by hiring new professionals proposed by the association "School of Parents and educators"

Differently from Rebecca Duvillié, Nicole Bailly considers that what is more important and what really make the difference between pupils, in their relation with the school is not the ethnic and religious differences and the trauma of the migration but the economical situation that provoke behaviours of fight-flight, feelings of being a permanent loser, incapacity to take a personal decision ... are generated by social exclusion as a consequence of great poverty rather than cultural traditions.Even in difficult economical situations families that have maintained internal solidarities, and or have been able to use the official resources of the system are in better conditions than those who have lost or had never these network of solidarity.Bridging the gap between the school and these family is a difficult work, but when it has been done, families recover their self esteem, they have a better understanding of the school code and become unable to help their children in overcoming the cognitive barriers generated by the social conflict between their parents and the school.

To help these families experiencing great poverty and social exclusion, school may bring their children quality education by opening mechanisms like the opened meeting points described by Nicole Bailly.

Three conditions are necessary to succeed in realizing these structure:

1. Motivated and relatively permanent teams,
2. Trained staff (especially in the field of social understanding of concerned population s)
3. Close partnership with the population.

Currently, this kind of training is far from being organized either for teachers or school psychologists.

How school psychologists could contribute better to a quality education for all.?

In the current training of most school psychologists worldwide, the clinical /individual work with the child is generally emphasized. This work is important and school psychologists must be able to identify possible mental disease or severe handicap and direct these children and their families towards the specialized institutions, hospital or child guidance clinics able to give relevant care.

We have seen than in many countries, inclusive education for handicapped children and so called children with specific educational needs, begins to extend and even if improvement to provide in regular schools the support that meet their individual needs are necessary, more and more school psychologists are involved in this process of education for all.

The problem is more for school psychologists to see how they could contribute more actively in improving the quality of education in all the schools in order that children, whatever social, gender, ethnic or religious, category they belong to, may experience concretely their right to a quality education.

This implies in many country to reconsider the role and the professional identity of the psychologist working in the schools in focussing their work on education rather on healing and medical care.School and educational psychologists must be considered and consider themselves as the psychologist who have the expertise in the field of education: project and in This change in professional identity must be approved by government, professional associations and trainers in order that a new orientations should be given in the training programmes at least at the master's level and for any diploma preparing psychologist to work in educational settings.

Another important point is, how school psychologists could be implied in the development of national education plans in developing and emergent countries ?

In these countries it is not realistic to imagine to create school psychology services. It seems more relevant to train school psychologists as experts in development of projects working in universities or as consultant of ministries of education. with a small number of school psychologists it is possible to improve the training of teachers by including psychological information founded on recent researches

School psychologists may be used by NGOs who implement education programmes in various countries. These school psychologists need a specific training cross cultural psychology. This training could be included in an international practicum (several month in a given country in a multidisciplinary team either through state conventions or individual convention with NGOS.

References

American Psychological Association (1998). *Archival description of school psychology*. Washington, DC: Author.

Connecticut State Board of Education Regulation (2002). School psychology endorsement, p. 33-34. Hartford, CT: Author.

Harvey,V.S., and Struzziero, J.A. (2000). *Effective supervision in school psychology*. Bethesda, MD:Author

Jacob, S. and Hartshorne,T.S. (2003). *Ethics and law for school psychologists (4th ed.)*. Hoboken, NJ: John Wiley & Sons, Inc.

5

Professional Ethics of School Psychologists

The formal principles that clarify the proper conduct of a professional school psychologist are known as *Ethics*. By virtue of joining the Association, each New York Association of School Psychologists (NYASP) member agrees to abide by the *Ethics*, acting in a manner that shows respect for human dignity and assuring a high quality of professional service. Although ethical behavior is an individual responsibility, it is in the interest of an association to adopt and enforce a code of ethics. Following the ethical code, members will be guided toward appropriate behavior, and public confidence in the profession will be enhanced. Additionally, a code of ethics should provide due process procedures to protect members from potential abuse of the code. The NYASP *Principles for Professional Ethics* have been written to accomplish these goals.

The principles in this manual are based on the assumptions that 1) school psychologists will act as advocates for their students/clients, and 2) at the very least, school psychologists will do no harm. These assumptions necessitate that school psychologists "speak up" for the needs and rights of their students/clients even at times when it may be difficult to do so. School psychologists also are constrained to provide only those services for which they have acquired an acknowledged level of experience, training, and competency

The intent of these guidelines is to supply clarification which will facilitate the delivery of high quality psychological services in the school and community. In addition to these ethical standards, there is the ever present necessity to differentiate between legal mandate and ethical responsibility. The school psychologist is urged to become familiar with applicable legal requirements. There are several textbooks on the market, as well as state and federal websites that can address these issues. In addition, school districts typically employ legal staff that can be contacted for further clarification.

The guidance of the *Ethical Principles* is intentionally broad to make it more enduring than other documents that reflect short-term opinions about specific actions shaped by local events, popular trends, or recent developments in the field. The member must use judgment to infer the situation-specific rule from the general ethical principle. The lack of a specific reference to a particular action does not indicate permission or provide a defense against a charge of unethical practice. Therefore, one should apply *Ethical Principles* in all professional situations, realizing that one is not released from responsibility simply because another individual is not strictly a "student" or a "client."

The principles in this manual are organized into several sections, and principles discussed in one section may also apply to other sections. Every school psychologist, regardless of position (e.g., practitioner, researcher, university trainer, supervisor, state or federal consultant, administrator of psychological services) or setting (e.g., public or private school, community agency, hospital, university, private practice) should reflect upon the theme represented in each ethical principle to determine its application to her or his individual situation. At times, following these ethical

principles may require a higher standard of behavior than the prevailing policies and pertinent laws. Under such conditions, members should adhere to the *Ethics* to assure the highest standards of professional behavior are followed. Ethical behavior may occasionally be forbidden by policy or law, in which case members are expected to declare their dilemma and work to bring the discrepant regulations into compliance with the *Ethics*. To obtain additional assistance in applying these principles to a particular setting, a school psychologist should consult with experienced school psychologists and seek advice from the New York Association of School Psychologists or the National Association of School Psychologists.

Throughout the *Principles for Professional Ethics,* it is assumed that, depending on the role and setting of the school psychologist, the "client" could include children and parents, or teachers and other school personnel who are recipients of consultation services, or other professionals, trainees, or supervisees.

Since the publication of the last *Principles for Professional Ethics* in 1996, Congress created the Health Insurance Portability and Accountability Act (HIPAA), which is an attempt to streamline the information systems that support healthcare services and to protect health insurance coverage for individuals' pre-existing conditions when they change employers/residences. Though the latter will have no bearing on the work of the school psychologist, the former may indeed have some impact. Schools that receive funding for providing healthcare insurance programs such as Medicaid may be held to HIPPA standards. In addition, if your school uses electronic means to collect information regarding services and billing for healthcare services, HIPPA will probably be in effect. Individual school systems will need to examine the act in order to establish procedures for complying with its regulations.

PROFESSIONAL COMPETENCY

General

1. School psychologists strive to maintain high standards of competence. They recognize the strengths and limitations of their training and experience, engaging only in practices for which they are qualified. School psychologists enlist the assistance of other specialists in supervisory, consultative, or referral roles as appropriate in providing services. They must continually obtain additional training and education to provide the best possible services to children, families, schools, communities, trainees, and supervisees.
2. School psychologists offer only those services which are within their individual area of training and experience. Competence levels, education, training and experience are accurately represented to schools and clients in a professional manner.
3. School psychologists do not use affiliations with persons, associations, or institutions to imply a level of professional competence that exceeds that which has actually been achieved.
4. School psychologists recognize the need for continuing professional development. They remain current regarding developments in research,

training, technology and professional practices that benefit children, families, and schools.

5. School psychologists refrain from any activity in which their personal problems or conflicts may interfere with professional effectiveness. Competent assistance is sought to alleviate conflicts in professional relationships.
6. School psychologists know the *Principles for Professional Ethics* and thoughtfully apply them to situations within their employment setting or practice. Ignorance or misapplication of an ethical principle is not a reasonable defense against a charge of unethical behavior.

Professional Relationships and Responsibilities A. General

1. School psychologists are committed to the application of their professional expertise for the purpose of promoting improvement in the quality of life for children, their families, and the school community. This objective is pursued in ways that protect the dignity and rights of those involved. School psychologists accept responsibility for the appropriateness of their professional practices and consequences of their actions.
2. School psychologists respect all persons and are sensitive to individual differences, such as: physical, mental, emotional, political, economic, social, cultural, ethnic, racial, gender, sexual orientation, and religious affiliation.
3. School psychologists in all settings maintain professional relationships with children, parents, and the school community. Parents and children are to be fully informed about all relevant aspects of school psychological services in advance. The explanation should take into account language and cultural differences, cognitive capabilities, developmental level, and age so that it may be understood by the child, parent, or guardian.
4. School psychologists attempt to resolve situations in which there are divided or conflicting interests in a manner that is mutually beneficial and protects the rights of all parties involved.
5. When personal loyalties, objectives and competencies influence a professional relationship, school psychologists must inform all concerned persons of relevant issues in advance, including, when

applicable, their direct supervisor for consideration of reassignment of responsibilities.

6. School psychologists do not take advantage of clients through professional relationships or condone these actions in their colleagues. No individuals, including children, clients, employees, colleagues, trainees, parents, supervisees, and research participants, will be exposed to deliberate comments, gestures, or physical contacts of a sexual nature. School psychologists do not harass or demean others based on personal characteristics.
7. Dual relationships with clients are avoided, as inviting personal and business relations with clients may impair one's judgment and create conflicts of interest. School psychologists are aware of these situations and avoid them whenever possible.
8. School psychologists attempt to resolve suspected detrimental or unethical practices on an informal level by making direct contact with the individuals involved. If informal efforts are not productive, the appropriate professional organization is contacted for assistance, and procedures established for questioning ethical practice are followed:
    a. The filing of an ethical complaint is a serious matter. It is intended to improve the behavior of a colleague that is harmful to the profession and/or the public. Therefore, school psychologists make every effort to discuss the ethical principles with other professionals who may be in violation.
    b. School psychologists enter into the complaint process thoughtfully and with concern for the well-being of all parties involved. They do not file or encourage the filing of an ethics complaint that is frivolous or motivated by revenge.
    c. Some situations may be particularly difficult to analyze from an ethical perspective. School psychologists consult ethical standards from related fields and seek assistance from knowledgeable, experienced school psychologists and relevant state/national associations to ascertain an appropriate course of action.
    d. School psychologists document specific instances of suspected ethical violations (i.e., date, time, relevant details) as well as attempts to resolve these violations.

9. School psychologists respect the confidentiality of information obtained during their professional work. Information is revealed only with the informed consent of the child, or the child's parent or legal guardian, except in those situations in which failure to release information would result in clear danger to the child or others. Obsolete confidential information will be shredded or otherwise destroyed before disposal.
10. School psychologists discuss confidential information only for professional purposes and only with persons who have a legitimate need to know.
11. School psychologists inform children and other clients of the limits of confidentiality at the outset of establishing a professional relationship.

Students

1. School psychologists understand the intimate nature of consultation, assessment, and direct service. They engage only in professional practices that maintain the dignity and integrity of children and other clients.
2. School psychologists explain important aspects of their professional relationships in a clear, understandable manner that is appropriate to the child's or other client's age and ability to understand. The explanation includes the reason why services were requested, the uses to be made of information regarding services, persons who will receive information about the services provided, and the possible outcomes or implications of results.
3. School Psychologists recognize the obligation to the student/client and respect the student/client's right of choice to enter, or to participate, in service, voluntarily.
4. School psychologists discuss recommendations for program changes or additional services with the child/client and other appropriate individuals. This discussion includes any alternatives that may be available.

Parents, Legal Guardians, and Appointed Surrogates

1. School psychologists explain all services to parents in a clear, understandable manner. They strive to propose a set of options that takes into account the values and capabilities of each parent. Service

provision by interns, practicum students, or other trainees should be explained and agreed to in advance.

2. School psychologists recognize the importance of parental support and seek to obtain that support by assuring that there is direct parent contact prior to seeing the child on an ongoing basis (emergencies and "drop-in" self-referrals require parental notification as soon as possible; the age and circumstances under which children may seek services without parental consent varies greatly. Therefore, schools need to develop written policies to address this issue). School psychologists secure continuing parental involvement via frank and prompt reporting to the parent of findings and progress that conforms to the limits of previously determined confidentiality.
3. School psychologists encourage and promote parental participation in designing services provided to their children. When appropriate, this includes linking interventions between the school and the home, tailoring parental involvement to the skills of the family, and helping parents gain the skills needed to help their children.
4. School psychologists respect the wishes of parents who decline school psychological services and attempt to guide parents to alternative community resources.
5. School psychologists discuss with parents the recommendations and plans for assisting their children. The discussion includes alternatives associated with each set of plans, which show respect for the ethnic/cultural values of the family. The parents are informed of sources of help available at school and in the community.
6. School psychologists discuss the rights of parents and children regarding creation, modification, storage, and disposal of confidential materials that will result from the provision of school psychological services.

Community

1. School psychologists also are citizens, thereby accepting the same responsibilities and duties as any member of society. They are free to pursue individual interests, except to the degree that those interests compromise professional responsibilities and have negative impact on the profession. Awareness of such impact guides public behavior.

2. School psychologists may act as individual citizens to bring about social change in a lawful manner. Individual actions should not be presented as, or suggestive of, representing the field of school psychology or the Association.
3. As employees or employers, in public or independent practice domains, school psychologists do not engage in or condone practices that discriminate against children, other clients, or employees (if applicable) based on race, disability, age, gender, sexual orientation, religion, national origin, economic status, or native language.
4. School psychologists avoid any action that could violate or diminish the civil and legal rights of children and other clients.
5. School psychologists adhere to federal, state, and local laws and ordinances governing their practice and advocacy efforts. If regulations conflict with ethical guidelines, school psychologists seek to resolve such conflict through positive, respected, and legal channels, including advocacy efforts involving public policy.

Other Professionals/Related Professions

1. To best meet the needs of children and other clients, school psychologists cooperate with other professional disciplines in relationships based on mutual respect.
2. School psychologists recognize the competence of other professions/ professionals. They encourage and support the use of all resources to best serve the interests of children and other clients.
3. School psychologists should strive to explain their field and their professional competencies, including roles, assignments, and working relationships to other professionals.
4. School psychologists cooperate and coordinate with other professionals and agencies with the rights and needs of children and other clients in mind. If a child or other client is receiving similar services from another professional, school psychologists promote coordination of services.
5. The child or other client is referred to another professional for services when a condition or need is identified which is outside the professional competencies or scope of the school psychologist.
6. When transferring the intervention responsibility for a child or other client to another professional, school psychologists ensure that all

relevant and appropriate individuals, including the child/client when appropriate, are notified of the change and reasons for the change.

7. When school psychologists suspect the existence of detrimental or unethical practices by a member of another profession, informal contact is made with that person to express the concern. If the situation cannot be resolved in this manner, the appropriate professional organization is contacted for assistance in determining the procedures established by that profession for examining the practices in question.
8. School psychologists who employ, supervise, or train other professionals, accept the obligation to provide continuing professional development. They also provide appropriate working conditions, fair and timely evaluation, and constructive consultation.

School Psychologist Trainees, Interns and Supervised School Psychologists

1. School psychologists who supervise interns are responsible for all professional practices of the supervisees. They assure children and other clients and the profession that the intern is adequately supervised as designated by the practice guidelines and training standards for school psychologists.
2. School psychologists who conduct or administer training programs provide trainees and prospective trainees with accurate information regarding program sponsorships/ endorsements/accreditation, goals/ objectives, training processes and requirements, and likely outcomes and benefits.
3. School psychologists who are faculty members in colleges or universities or who supervise clinical or field placements apply these ethical principles in all work with school psychology trainees. In addition, they promote the ethical practice of trainees by providing specific and comprehensive instruction, feedback, and mentoring.
4. School psychology faculty members and clinical or field supervisors uphold recognized standards of the profession by providing training related to high quality, responsible, and research-based school psychology services. They provide accurate, objective and current information in their teaching and training activities; identify any limitations in information; and acknowledge disconfirming data, alternative hypotheses, and explanations.

5. School psychology faculty members and clinical or field supervisors develop and use evaluation practices for trainees that are objective, accurate, and fair.
6. School psychologists who employ, supervise and train other professionals accept the obligation of providing experiences to further their professional development. Appropriate working conditions, fair and timely evaluation and constructive consultation are provided.

Professional Practices—General principles

Advocacy

1. School psychologists typically serve multiple clients including children, parents, and systems. When the school psychologist is confronted with conflicts between client groups, the primary client is considered to be the child. When the child is not the primary client, the individual or group of individuals who sought the assistance of the school psychologist is the primary client.
2. School psychologists consider children and other clients to be their primary responsibility, acting as advocates for their rights and welfare. If conflicts of interest between clients are present, the school psychologist supports conclusions that are in the best interest of the child. When choosing a course of action, school psychologists take into account the rights of each individual involved and the duties of school personnel.
3. School psychologists' concerns for protecting the rights and welfare of children are communicated to the school administration and staff as the top priority in determining services.
4. School psychologists understand the public policy process to assist them in their efforts to advocate for children, parents, and systems.

Service Delivery/Employment Setting

1. School psychologists are knowledgeable of the organization, philosophy, goals, objectives, and methodologies of the setting in which they are employed.
2. School psychologists recognize that an understanding of the goals, processes, and legal requirements of their particular workplace is essential for effective functioning within that setting. It is their

responsibility to familiarize themselves with the system and community.

3. School psychologists accept the responsibility of becoming integral members of the client service systems to which they are assigned. They recognize the need to establish a vital role for themselves within that system.
4. School psychologists who provide services to several different groups may encounter situations in which loyalties are conflicted. To the extent possible, the stance of the school psychologist is made known in advance to all parties to prevent misunderstandings.
5. School psychologists promote changes in their employing agencies and community service systems that will benefit their clients; this may involve change in organizational structures or service models.

Assessment and Intervention

1. School psychologists maintain the highest standard of service for educational and psychological assessment and direct and indirect interventions.
2. In conducting psychological, educational, or behavioral evaluations or in providing therapy, counseling, or consultation services, due consideration is given to individual integrity and individual differences.
3. School psychologists respect differences in age, gender, sexual orientation, and socioeconomic, cultural, and ethnic backgrounds. They select and use appropriate assessment or treatment procedures, techniques, and strategies relevant to such differences. Decision-making related to assessment and subsequent interventions is primarily data-based.
4. School psychologists are knowledgeable about the validity and reliability of their instruments and techniques, choosing those that have up-to-date standardization data and are applicable and appropriate for the benefit of the child or other client.
5. School psychologists use multiple assessment methods such as observations, background information, and information from other professionals, to reach comprehensive and valid conclusions.
6. School psychologists use assessment techniques, counseling and therapy procedures, consultation techniques, and other direct and

indirect service methods that the profession considers to be responsible, research-based practice and promotes the mental health of the children served.

7. School psychologists do not condone the use of psychological or educational assessment techniques, or the misuse of the information these techniques provide, by unqualified persons in any way, including teaching, sponsorship, or supervision.
8. School psychologists develop interventions that are appropriate to the presenting problems and are consistent with data collected. They modify or terminate the treatment plan when the data indicate the plan is not achieving the desired goals. School psychologists may consult with other professionals and colleagues when appropriate.

Reporting Data and Conference Results

1. School psychologists ascertain that information about children and other clients reaches only authorized persons.
2. School psychologists adequately interpret information so that the recipient can better help the child or other clients.
3. School psychologists assist agency recipients to establish procedures to properly safeguard confidential material.
4. School psychologists communicate findings and recommendations in language readily understood by the intended recipient. These communications describe potential consequences associated with the proposals.
5. School psychologists prepare written reports in such form and style that the recipient of the report will be able to assist the child or other clients. Reports should emphasize recommendations and interpretations; unedited computer-generated reports, pre-printed "check-off" or "fill-in-the-blank" reports, and reports that present only test scores or global statements regarding eligibility for special education without specific recommendations for intervention are seldom useful. Reports should include an appraisal of the degree of confidence that could be assigned to the information. Alterations of previously released reports should be done only by the original author.
6. School psychologists review all of their written documents for accuracy, signing them only when correct. Interns and practicum students are

clearly identified as such, and their work is co-signed by the supervising school psychologist. In situations in which more than one professional participated in the data collection and reporting process, school psychologists assure that sources of data are clearly identified in the written report.

7. School psychologists comply with all laws, regulations, and policies pertaining to the adequate storage and disposal of records to maintain appropriate confidentiality of information.
8. When presenting case examples, school psychologists obtain written prior consent from the clients, or they remove identifying data from public lectures or publications.

References

Alessi, G. K., & Kaye, J. H. (1983). *Behavior assessment for school psychologists.* Washington, DC: National Association of School Psychologists

Calhoun, E. F. (1994). *How to use action research in the self-renewing school.* Alexandria, VA: Association for Supervision and Curriculum Development.

National Association of School Psychologists. (2000). *Guidelines for the provision of school psychological services.* Bethesda, MD: Author

Shinn, M. R. (Ed.). (1989). *Curriculum-based measurement: Assessing special children.* New York: Guilford Press.

6

School Counsellor: Roles and Responsibilities

A school counselor is a counselor and an educator who works in elementary, middle, and high schools to provide academic, career, college access, and personal/social competencies to K-12 students. The interventions used include developmental school counseling curriculum lessons and annual planning for every student, and group and individual counseling.

Older, dated terms for the profession were "guidance counselor" or "educational counselor" but "school counselor" is preferred due to professional school counselors' advocating for every child's academic, career, and personal/social success in every elementary, middle, and high school. In the Americas, Africa, Asia, Europe, and the Pacific, the terms school counselor, school guidance counselor, and guidance teacher are also used with the traditional emphasis career development.

Countries vary in how a school counseling program and school counseling program services are provided based on economics (funding for schools and school counseling programs), social capital (independent versus public schools), and School Counselor certification and credentialing movements in education departments, professional associations, and national and local legislation. The largest accreditation body for Counselor Education/ School Counseling programs is the Council for the Accreditation of Counseling and Related Educational Programs (CACREP). International Counselor Education programs are accredited through a CACREP affiliate, the International Registry of Counselor Education Programs (IRCEP)

In some countries, school counseling is provided by educational specialists (for example, Botswana, China, Finland, Israel, Malta, Nigeria, Romania, Taiwan, Turkey, United States). In other cases, school counseling is provided by classroom teachers who either have such duties added to their typical teaching load or teach only a limited load that also includes school counseling activities (for example- India, Japan, Mexico, South Korea, Zambia). The IAEVG focuses primarily on career development with some international school counseling articles and conference presentations.

Elementary School Counselling

The elementary school counselling and guidance programme is a part of the total school programme and complements learning in the classroom. It is child-centered, preventive, and developmental. The programme encourages students' social, emotional, and personal growth at each stage of their development.

The purpose of counselling with students, parents, and teachers is to help students maximise their potential. The elementary school counsellor also conducts guidance lessons; consults with parents, teachers, and other professionals; and coordinates student services in the school. This counselling and guidance programme provides elementary students with assistance in:

- Understanding self and developing a positive self-image.
- Showing respect for the feelings of others.
- Understanding the decision-making process.
- Maintaining effective relationships with peers and adults.
- Developing effective study skills.
- Being prepared to make the transition to the intermediate school.
- Gaining an understanding of the world of work.

Counselling is conducted with students and parents individually and in small groups when requested and determined appropriate. It is short-term, voluntary, and confidential. Parental permission is obtained prior to any extended individual or group counselling. Students are seen by the counsellor when:

- Parents request and indicate a need and desire that the counsellor meet with their children.

— Students request counselling.

— Teachers, administrators, or other school staff refer the student.

Parents are informed of counselling groups for children and adults. Groups counselling sessions for children focus on building self-esteem, learning how to make or keep friends, developing good study habits, improving communication skills, preparing for the intermediate school, and coping with changing family situations. Topics for parent groups include child-rearing concerns, child development, and methods parents may use to help children experience healthy development and success in school.

BENEFITS OF COUNSELLING

The elementary school counsellor works directly with students in individual and group counselling sessions as well as in classroom guidance lessons so students may:

— Be successful in school.

— Establish effective study skills.

— Adjust to a new school.

— Develop positive feelings about work, family, and society.

— Build positive feelings towards self and others.

— Develop skills in interacting and communicating with others.

— Cope with change in themselves and their surroundings.

— Identify and accept their own and others' strengths and weaknesses.

— Recognise the causes and effects of their actions.

— Become responsible for their own behaviour.

— Receive crisis intervention when necessary.

The guidance counsellor helps students become motivated learners and encourages them to discuss concerns with their parents. When students work through their social and emotional issues, with the help of their parents and the counsellor, they are able to devote attention and energy to the intellectual tasks at school.

The elementary school guidance counsellor works with parents through individual consultation, joint consultation with the children's teachers, and parent discussion groups. In these ways the counsellor assists parents to:

— Understand their children's progress in school.
— Select strategies to motivate their children.
— Develop realistic goals with their children.
— Become actively involved in their children's school life.
— Understand the educational programme K-12.

The counsellor may lead parent education and discussion groups and serve as a resource when parents study or discuss child-related issues. The counsellor consults with parents to identify students with special abilities and/or needs. In this capacity the counsellor helps parents understand the services available from other school staff such as the school psychologist, social worker, and resource teachers. The counsellor helps parents find other professionals within the school system or within the larger community when extra support is needed.

The elementary school guidance counsellor is an integral part of the total elementary school programme. The counsellor observes children; consults with teachers, psychologists, and social workers; gathers and provides resources; conducts classroom guidance lessons; collaborates on classroom intervention; conducts joint parent conferences; reviews and interprets school records; and serves on committees that plan for the individual needs of specific children. The elementary school guidance counsellor helps teachers by:

— Consulting with them concerning children.
— Planning small group and classroom activities to meet specific needs of students.
— Gathering and sharing resources.
— Observing children in the classroom or on the playground.
— Conferencing with parents.
— Reviewing student records and discussing their implications with the teachers and/or parents.
— Coordinating staff efforts to work with individual students.
— Promoting a positive school climate.
— Explaining the academic programme K-12.

The elementary school counsellor is a vital resource for the school staff. He or she coordinates and helps implement the staff's efforts to meet the needs of students individually, in small groups of students, and in entire classrooms.

The entire community benefits from the elementary school counselling and guidance programme because:

— All students in the entire school system are served.
— A clearly defined curriculum provides information about the programme to the community.
— Business, industry, and labour can participate actively in the programme.
— A potential work force is provided with decision-making skills and preemployment skills.

Counsellor Assessment Criteria

Assessment is the most controversial area within counsellor education. Knowledge needed by counsellors to obtain evidence, evaluate its usefulness, and interpret its meaning have long been and continue to be debated. An efficient, but fair assessment of counsellor performance focuses primarily on what the counsellor actually does—not on counsellor skills, training or experience, and not on student outcomes.

Assessment of prerequisite counsellor skills wastes time and effort in that it duplicates other forms of evaluation. Attempting to link student outcomes exclusively to individual counsellor performance is unfair in that many factors other than counselling influence student learning and behaviour. While accountability for student outcomes is important, it belongs to a broader programme evaluation which takes these other factors into account.

Counsellor assessment criteria must be based on clear role priorities in the current job setting—for example, developmental/preventative vs. crisis/remedial activities, counselling students vs. counselling with parents or teachers, academic/career vs. personal/social counselling, and counselling vs. administrative/clerical tasks. Once these priorities have been clarified, administrators and counsellors should define realistic expectations of time to be spent and tasks to be accomplished. This collaboration could result in guidelines for an assessment instrument which could be used by counsellors to monitor their own priorities and time.

In most counsellor performance assessments, programme administrators will want to know not only what the counsellor does, but how well he/she does it. Is accurate information given to students? Are school policies observed by the counsellor? Are tasks performed efficiently? These types of assessments often require subjective judgments which may be threatening to counsellors. Identifying very specific examples of each desired behaviour can reduce subjectivity, and obtaining counsellor input about the validity of these descriptions can reduce counsellor anxiety.

The most critical measurement issue in performance assessment is validity. Is specific "job-relatedness" built into the assessment instrument? Does it actually measure what it says it measures? There is no one instrument, either in format or in content, that can be used universally to assess school counsellor performance. To be valid in a particular setting, the instrument must reflect the priorities of the school, the district, or the state conducting the assessment. Constructing a useful counsellor performance assessment instrument does not require extensive measurement expertise.

Once the relevant participants in the assessment process agree on the job-relatedness of the tasks and behaviours to be assessed, a simple and easy-to-use instrument may be developed. The goal is to produce a tool that will actually be used, not a sophisticated measurement device for collecting research data. The form may be a simple one-page checklist, in which each item represents one major objective, or a several-page document, in which each objective is broken into specific tasks or characteristic behaviours. Similarly, the response called for by each item may be a check mark indicating the presence of a characteristic or completion of a task or a numerical rating with each number representing a specific behaviour description. Vague, low-to-high options should be avoided.

Even if the form is to be used primarily for assessing minimal competency or "adequate" job performance, it should contain item response options that address the full range of evaluation from unsatisfactory to outstanding and/or highly creative performance. This expands the potential usefulness of the assessment process as a positive strategy for facilitating ongoing counsellor growth and development.

In the 1960's, tests were viewed positively and were used primarily to identify students of outstanding abilities. However, in the early 1970's, Goldman suggested, using a well-known metaphor, that the marriage between tests and counselling had failed. At about that time, courts prohibited some established tests for certain purposes and legislatures passed bills to regulate aspects of the use of standardised tests.

The validity and practical utility of all testing and appraisal techniques were questioned and negative consequences of "labelling" were emphasised. Yet assessment remained commonplace in schools. Consider these findings in a survey by Engen, Lamb, and Prediger and reported by Zytowski: 93% of secondary schools administered at least one test to all students; 76% administered achievement test batteries; 66% administered academic aptitude or intelligent tests; and 16% administered inventories of school or social adjustment or personality tests. By the 1980's, vocational guidance, according to Zytowski, had become a unifying force between counselling and testing.

Zytowski described several changes that had been made in tests, themselves, and in their uses in counselling. One of these was an erosion of reliance on predictive validity and an accompanying emphasis on convergent and discriminant validity, along with construct validity. He also described the value of an assessment in terms of its ability to guide and motivate a professional toward seeking additional information for decision making.

De-formalising assessment, another change, included increased use of one-item measures, informed self estimates, and card sorts or inventories in which quantified outcomes are less important than is the process the client engages in. Computers had become more instrumental in testing, from primarily scoring and score reporting to actual test administration and providing immediate feedback. Availability and interest in computer testing have clearly increased in the decade since Zytowski's summary appeared. The counselling community has become more aware of ethical issues in testing.

An American Counselling Association (ACA) statement titled Responsibilities of Users of Standardised Tests (RUST), published in 1978 and revised in 1989, urges awareness of differing purposes for testing and reminds us to consider the limitations of tests for any purpose and to evaluate the costs of not testing or using alternative methods of gathering the information needed.

Assessment Skills

The roles that have been identified imply that counsellors should have certain skills related to assessment. Schafer and Mufson organised these into three areas: doing pupil assessment, doing programme evaluation, and using basic research. Doing pupil assessment includes: types of assessment; assessment systems and programmes; test administration and scoring; test reporting and interpretation; test evaluation and selection; design, analysis, and improvement in instrument development; formal and informal methods of assessment; methods for using assessment in counselling; administrative uses of assessment; computer-based applications; and ethics of using assessments.

Doing programme evaluation includes: needs assessment; formative and summative evaluation; sources of evaluation research invalidity (instrumental, internal, and external); choosing evaluation designs; choices of and computational methods for descriptive and inferential statistics; writing evaluation proposals and reports; disseminating information; and research ethics. Using basic research includes: locating and obtaining relevant research reports; reading and summarising research reports; evaluating validity of instruments and research designs; and purpose and assumptions of common inferential statistical procedures.

Test Interpretation Skills

School counsellors are often asked to administer and interpret norm-referenced tests. Certain fundamental test interpretation skills are necessary to accurately interpret and utilise test data.

Norm-referenced Tests

Norm-referenced tests are assessments administered to students to determine how they perform in comparison to others. They are often used to classify students for placement and award purposes. A student's current test performance is compared to that of a representative sample of students, known as a norm group, who were previously administered the test. Norm groups can be used to create either national norms or local norms, depending on who is included in the normative sample.

Norm-referenced tests have several strengths. For example, Dombrowski points out that norm-referenced testing often allows for reliable and objective measurement. However, with these types of assessments, it is critical to understand the composition of the norm group. It's also important to note that test scores on norm-referenced tests typically rise the longer the test is in use, likely due to changes in instruction or test preparation that are made as educators become more familiar with the form of a test.

Criterion-referenced and norm-referenced tests yield different, but complementary, pieces of information. Criterion-referenced tests, such as many of the state high school tests, help demonstrate how a student stands in relation to a given educational curriculum. The emphasis is not on comparison with other students, but rather, on mastery of specific content knowledge and skills. Criterion-referenced tests provide useful information about students' strengths and weaknesses in various curriculum areas. It is critical that the content domain of the assessment be clearly defined. Results of norm- and criterion-referenced tests should be combined with other formal and informal data collection methods, since no single set of test scores is adequate to make important educational decisions.

Properties of the Normal Curve

In norm-referenced tests, a child's test performance is compared to a norm group. The distribution of test scores generated by the norm group is normal. Therefore, understanding what a normal curve is becomes critical for norm-referenced test interpretation. First, a school counsellor should recognise that if he or she were to draw a vertical line down the center of the normal curve, the distribution would be divided into two equal halves. Because both halves are identical, statisticians classify normal curves as symmetrical.

The vertical line represents the mean, or average, performance of the norm group. With normal curves, this line also represents the median and the mode; however, this is not always true of other types of curves. Knowing the mean helps the test interpreter to identify the average performance of the norm group, but is not sufficient to correctly interpret an individual's performance on a norm-referenced test. The school counsellor also must know how the concept of standard deviation is related to the normal curve. Drummond indicates that standard deviation is a statistic that defines the spread of scores around the mean. Standard deviation helps determine how far above or below the norm group mean an individual's score falls.

For practical purposes, the normal curve is divided into three standard deviations above the mean and three standard deviations below the mean. In a normal curve, 34% of individuals fall between the mean and one standard deviation above the mean, 14% of individuals fall between one standard deviation above the mean and two standard deviations above the mean, and 2% of individual fall between two standard deviations above the mean and three standard deviations above the mean. Since the normal curve is symmetrical, the percentages are the same for the standard deviations above and below the mean.

Properties of Common Score Types

To accurately and efficiently interpret norm-referenced assessments, school counsellors need to be familiar with the properties of common scores they may encounter. Those score types are Z scores, T scores, NCE scores, and stanine scores.

— Z scores have a fixed mean of 0 and a standard deviation of 1. Thus, if a student's test performance is one standard deviation above the mean, the individual has a Z score of 1. If a student's test score is two standard deviations below the mean, his or her Z score is a -2. It is possible (and common) for students to have negative Z scores.

— T scores often have a mean of 50 and a standard deviation of 10. Thus, if a student's test performance is one standard deviation below the mean, the individual has a T score of 40. If a student's test score is at the mean, his or her T score is 50.

— NCE scores stands for normal curve equivalent scores. NCE scores have a fixed mean of 50 and a standard deviation of approximately 21. If a student's test performance is two standard deviations above the mean, the individual has an NCE score of 92. If a student's test score is one standard deviation below the mean, his or her NCE score is a 29.

— Stanine scores have a fixed mean of 5 and a standard deviation of 2. The term "stanine" stands for Standard Nine, indicating that the range of stanine scores is fixed from 1 to 9, with 9 representing the highest possible stanine score, and 1 representing the possible score. If a student's test performance is two standard deviations above the mean, the individual has a stanine score of 9. If a student's test score is three standard deviations below the mean, his or her stanine score is a 1. Five is the most commonly assigned stanine score, because it falls directly on the mean the curve. If a student is assigned a 5, he or she is performing better than half of the norm group on the content assessed on the norm-referenced test.

Difference between Percent and Percentile

School counsellors need to recognise that percent and percentile are different concepts. The term "percent" is an abbreviation of the Latin phrase per centum, which literally means "by the hundred." A percent represents the proportion of test material answered correctly out of a hundred. For example, if an individual took a 50-item test and answered 25 items correctly, the percent he or she got correct would be 50.

Percentiles, according to Drummond, are one of most common tools to help interpret norm-referenced assessments. Percentile scores range from 1 to 99 and tell the test interpreter the percentage of individuals in the norm-group that the test taker outperformed. For example, if a test taker earned a score in the 74th percentile, the interpretation would be that 74% of the norm group performed at or below the test taker's score.

Ability of Translating One Standard Score to Another

Once school counsellors have developed competency with the four skills addressed above, they will have the tools necessary to quickly and accurately translate scores from one common score type to another. This skill is particularly important when meeting with parents and students to discuss their norm-referenced test performance. School counsellors need to be cognisant that parents and students are often confused by the many different score types, the compact layout of many norm-reference score reporting sheets, and most importantly, the interpretation of the scores. This is an opportunity for the informed school counsellor to be particularly helpful. Because the score types discussed above (Z, T, NCE, stanine) are all based on the properties of the normal curve, the scores can easily be converted from one score type to another.

By performing test score conversions, the school counsellor can demonstrate to the parent(s) and student how the different score types are representative of how the test taker performed in comparison with the norm group. For example, if a student had a Z score of 1, the individual's performance is one standard deviation above the mean. Eighty-four percent of the norm group performed at or below the test taker's score. The student also had a T score of 60, an NCE score of 71, and a stanine score of 7.

All of the scores are one standard deviation above the mean. The same is true for students who have scores that fall below the mean. If a student's norm-referenced test score is two standard deviations below the mean, the corresponding Z score is -2, the T score is 30, the NCE score is 8, and the stanine is 1. Due to the increased reliance on norm-referenced tests in schools, it is essential that school counsellors be able to accurately interpret and explain test results to various stakeholders. While these five test interpretation skills do not guarantee expertise, they are intended to encourage school counsellors' minimum competency with regard to norm-referenced test interpretation.

Assessing Student Engagement Rates

Early studies of student engagement often focused on time-on-task behaviours. Student engagement has been used to depict students' willingness to participate in routine school activities, such as attending classes, submitting required work, and following teachers' directions in class.

The opposite of engagement is disaffection. Disaffected children are passive, do not tryhard, and give up easily in the face of challenges [they can] be bored, depressed, anxious, or even angry about their presence in the classroom; they can be withdrawn from learning opportunities or even rebellious towards teachers and classmates. From a different perspective, Pintrich and & De Groot associated engagement levels with students' use of cognitive, meta-cognitive and self-regulatory strategies to monitor and guide their learning processes.

In this view, student engagement is viewed as motivated behaviour apparent from the kinds of cognitive strategies students choose to use (e.g., simple or "surface" processing strategies such as rehearsal versus "deeper" processing strategies such as elaboration), and by their willingness to persist with difficult tasks by regulating their own learning behaviour. Use of cognitive and meta-cognitive strategies may be taken to indicate active task engagement, while use of shallow strategies may be taken to indicate superficial engagement.

Methods for Measuring Engagement

The most common way that student engagement is measured is through information reported by the students themselves. Other methods include checklists and rating scales completed by teachers, observations, work sample analyses, and case studies. Each of these methods is described briefly below.

Self-Reports: Students may be asked to complete surveys or questionnaires regarding their level of task engagement. Items relating to the cognitive aspects of engagement often ask students to report on factors such as their attention versus distraction during class, the mental effort they expend on these tasks (e.g., to integrate new concepts with previous knowledge), and task persistence (e.g., their reaction to perceived failure to comprehend the course material). Students can also be asked to report on their response levels during class time (e.g., making verbal responses within group discussions, looking for distractions, and engaging in non-academic social interaction) as an index of behavioural task engagement.

Affective engagement questions typically ask students to rate their interest in and emotional reactions to learning tasks on indices such as choice of activities (e.g., selection of more versus less challenging tasks), the desire to know more about particular topics, and feelings of stimulation or excitement in beginning new projects. In addition to asking the question of whether students are engaged in learning tasks, self-report measures can provide some indication of why this is the case.

Research into achievement goal orientations, for example, has indicated positive relationships between task or mastery goals, which reflect a desire for knowledge or skill acquisition, and students' use of effective learning strategies. Studies have also demonstrated positive relationships between students' perceived learning control and adaptive learning processes.

Checklists and Rating Scales: In addition to student self-report measures, a few studies have used summative rating scales to measure student engagement levels. For example, the teacher report scales used by Skinner & Belmont asked teachers to assess their students' willingness to participate in school tasks (i.e., effort, attention, and persistence during the initiation and execution of learning activities, such as "When faced with a difficult problem, this student doesn't try"), as well as their emotional reactions to these tasks (i.e., interest versus boredom, happiness versus sadness, anxiety and anger, such as "When in class, this student seems happy").

The Teacher Questionnaire on Student Motivation to Read developed by Sweet, Guthrie, & Ng asks teachers to report on factors relating to student engagement rates, such as activities (e.g., enjoys reading about favourite activities), autonomy (e.g., knows how to choose a book he or she would want to read), and individual factors (e.g., is easily distracted while reading).

Direct Observations: Although self-report scales are widely used, the validity of the data yielded by these measures will vary considerably with students' abilities to accurately assess their own cognitions, behaviours, and affective responses. Direct observations are often used to confirm students' reported levels of engagement in learning tasks. A number of established protocols are available in this area. Most of these observational studies have used some form of momentary time sampling system. In these methods, the observer records whether a behaviour was present or absent at the moment that the time interval ends or else during a specific time period.

In classwide observations, approximately 5 minutes of observational data can generally be collected on each target student per lesson. Thus, a 30-minute observation period would allow observations of approximately 5 target students, with 6 to 7 sessions being required to observe a full class. In addition, to obtain a representative sample of students' behaviour over the full course of a lesson, observations are generally rotated across students so that each student is observed continuously for only one minute at a time.

Work Sample Analyses: Evidence of higher-order problem-solving and metacognitive learning strategies can be gathered from sources such as student projects, portfolios, performances, exhibitions, and learning journals or logs. The efficacy of these methods hinges on the use of suitably structured tasks and scoring rubrics. For example, a rubric to assess the application of higher-order thinking skills in a student portfolio might include criteria for evidence of problem-solving, planning, and self-evaluation in the work.

A number of formal and informal protocols for assessing students' self-regulated learning strategies also incorporate components that focus on metacognitive skills. The Metacognitive Knowledge Monitoring Assessment and the Assessment of Cognitive Monitoring Effectiveness are more targeted measures suitable for use in classroom situations and with demonstrated sound psychometric properties in empirical evaluations.

Focused Case Studies: When the focus of an investigation is restricted to a small group of target students, it is often more useful to collect detailed descriptive accounts of engagement rates. Case studies allow researchers to address questions of student engagement inductively by recording details about students in interaction with other people and objects within classrooms. These accounts should describe both students' behaviours and the classroom contexts in which they occur. This might include, for example, the behaviour of peers, direct antecedents to the target student's behaviours (e.g., teacher directions), as well as the student's response and the observed consequences of that response.

Case studies generally attempt to place observations of engagement within the total context of the classroom and/or school, and are concerned as much with the processes associated with engagement as they are in depicting engagement levels. Teachers interested in assessing student engagement in the classroom should consider using separate measures to get at the cognitive, affective, and behavioural aspects of task engagement. Within each of these domain areas, using a range of methods can also strengthen the validity of findings and provide alternative perspectives on the results. Teachers may wish to include measures that address the question of why students do, or do not, engage with particular types of tasks.

Planning and Integrating Basic Skills

Postsecondary students are not graduating with the "basic skills" needed for success at work, at home, and in further education. What are these basic skills? The contemporary list goes far beyond the traditional Three R's to include the attitudes, knowledge, and behaviours needed to function in an increasingly self directed, interpersonal, and technological workplace. In addition to reading, writing, and computing, these skills include:

— learning to learn;

— effective verbal and nonverbal communication;

— adaptability (including creative thinking and problem solving);

— personal management (including self esteem, goal setting/motivation, and personal/career development);

— group effectiveness (including personal skills, negotiation, and teamwork);

— influence (including organisational effectiveness and leadership);

— the ability to understand technology;

— the ability to apply scientific knowledge to work situations; and

— the ability to balance and manage family and work.

Schools are being challenged to integrate these new basic skills across their curricula. This presents school counsellors with an opportunity: if they can prove their effectiveness in helping students plan for and acquire the basic skills and prepare for life after high school, they can trade their traditionally services oriented, possibly expendable positions in schools for positions of influence in matters such as school reform and restructuring.

Currently, the most promising models for helping school counsellors take this active role are "comprehensive counselling and guidance programmes." Comprehensive counselling and guidance programmes are the "umbrella programmes" of the 1990s, designed to provide all students with life competencies through personal, social, and career counselling. Abandoning the traditionally passive, service approach to counselling, comprehensive counselling and guidance programmes employ four interactive components that take the vagueness out of the school counsellor's role:

1. *The Guidance Curriculum*: counsellors provide structured, competency based activities in the classroom or in group situations, using this focused time with students to focus on content areas such as self knowledge, educational and occupational exploration, and career planning.
2. *Individual Planning*: Counsellors help students think ahead and think for themselves, teaching them how to plan rigorous and coherent sequences of courses, as well as monitor and manage their lives.
3. *Responsive Services*: Counsellors meet the immediate needs of students confronting personal or educational challenges.
4. *System Support*: Counsellors work to sustain and enhance the implementation of comprehensive counselling and guidance programmes.

An essential part of the effort to equip students with the basic skills is the integration of academic and vocational instruction. Basic competencies in these areas are prerequisites for lifetime learning. Additionally, as technology continues to become more sophisticated, the competencies with which students graduate are rapidly becoming requirements for landing and keeping good jobs with growth potential. Conversely, college-bound students can benefit from vocational methods of instruction and experiences connecting school to work. By using academic theory in real life settings, they can acquire skills needed outside the classroom.

Schools emphasising acquisition of the basic skills recognise the critical role counsellors can play in helping students plan a demanding sequence of academic and vocational courses that will prepare them both for employment and postsecondary education. School counsellors promote the idea that vocational education is better supported when vocational and academic education are seen as complementary strategies for student success, not as competing programmes of study. An example: a Pittsburgh, Pennsylvania, school district has discontinued its general education track. Students must now make specific curriculum choices early on. It is therefore necessary for guidance professionals to contact all students earlier and stay in contact with them.

To receive a diploma, each student must plan and complete a focused curriculum leading to an academic or an applied technology and career development certificate, or both. To inform the community about the methods the district is using to infuse career education into curriculum, the district sends letters to parents of all eighth graders, and requires all tenth graders to view a video explaining graduation and certificate requirements within a group guidance class. Counsellors now find it much easier to promote the merits of Pittsburgh's 40 vocational options and their relation to graduation, the workplace, and postsecondary education. This action, along with other initiatives, has significantly reduced dropout rates.

Without a comprehensive counselling and guidance programme to address the needs of all students, developmental needs are overlooked and students unable to state their needs fall through the cracks. Due to the large student to counsellor ratios, many students end up selecting courses based on availability, instructor popularity, or other criteria that may have nothing to do with career plans, learning styles or basic skill needs. Traditionally, counsellors have been rewarded for attending to students who already know their career needs and their principal's priorities. Little attention has been given to what has been called the "forgotten half".

Part of this stems from the nebulous role of school counsellors. Counsellors are expected to perform roles as varied as the schools within which they work. Some are advocates for students confronting severe family and social change, while others are saddled with large amounts of "administrivia." Many confront substance abuse, suicide, and teen pregnancy as regular parts of their day. Comprehensive counselling and guidance programmes call for counsellors' reduced involvement in administrative and clerical work. They place counsellors in fewer one-on-one counselling situations. At the same time, they strengthen counsellors' accountability for effectively helping all students prepare for the world beyond high school.

Unfortunately, implementing comprehensive counselling and guidance programmes has been a low priority in the school reform movement. This could be due to

(a) hesitancy of school counsellors to vocalise their positions,

(b) school counsellors' traditional isolation from schools' mainstream instructional programmes, or

(c) school counsellors' limited involvement in reform.

Implementing comprehensive counselling and guidance programmes on a large scale requires the revamping and greater standardisation of school counsellors' education. Preservice school counsellors need a more specific, focused programme that arms them with the essentials of professional renewal. School counsellor education should be built on a foundation of educational developmental theory and practice as well as psychological theory. Preservice school counsellors need training in several areas:

1) helping students plan their coursework and futures;
2) promoting curricula and instructional methods which integrate academic and vocational education; and
3) implementing comprehensive counselling and guidance programmes.

Performance Assessment

It is important to be open and specific about the purpose of a performance assessment. Counsellors should know if it will be used to determine promotions or pay increases, to provide constructive feedback for professional development, or simply to meet administrative requirements. They also should know what instrument will be used, who will conduct the assessment, when it will be conducted, and when they will be informed of the results. Conducting the assessment collaboratively, with counsellors and assessors responding to and discussing each item, is highly recommended.

Performance assessment can be time-consuming for both the assessor and assessee; to be cost-effective, it should serve as many people in as many ways as possible. Viewed positively and constructively, a performance assessment can go well beyond a pro forma documentation of minimal competency. It can address new and emerging areas of professional expertise and can serve as a challenge to maximise the ongoing professional development of even the most competent and experienced counsellor.

Supervision of School Counsellors

Professionally appropriate supervision is emerging as a highly effective means of nurturing school counsellors' professional development. New challenges in schools and increased understanding of the complexity of professional development dictate the need for increased attention to and use of effective supervision practices. Today's children and youth need highly skilled help in managing the complicated situations in which they live. School counsellors see an increasing number of suicidal children as well as adolescents.

The upsurge in substance abuse, gang involvement, and violence are well publicised. Increasingly, parents turn to the schools to help them solve problems that face them, including those posed by their children. In order to effectively help children in their classrooms, teachers seek consultative help from counsellors. The comprehensive guidance programmes being implemented in today's schools call for school counsellors to use all of their professional skills. Focused and constructive supervision is of benefit to all practitioners whether they are novices or experienced, highly competent or insufficiently trained. Due to reductions in caseloads, renewed commitment to elementary counselling, and retirement of counsellors who entered the field in the 1960's, the number of new school counsellors is increasing.

Although it is a relatively new discipline, supervision is compatibly defined in both education and in counselling. The purpose of supervision is the growth and enhanced effectiveness of the practitioner. "It is characterised by a cycle of feedback, practice, and additional feedback", based on interpretation of gathered data in light of established standards. Because of the emphasis on skill-based performance evaluations generated by educational reform, many states have defined school counsellors' roles and needed competencies: programme management, counselling, guidance, consulting, coordinating, student appraisal, and referral. With these behavioural standards as a basis, supervisors and counsellors operate with the same definitions for effective performance. The value of timely feedback has been reinforced in the career-ladder-related-teacher-appraisal systems, setting the climate for the same practice for all categories of educators.

Clinical, Developmental and Administrative Supervision

When competently done, supervision not only enhances the quality of counsellors' skills, but also helps hone professional judgment, "encourages greater self-awareness, and fosters an integrated professional and personal identity as a counsellor". Barret and Schmidt outlined a useful schema for distinguishing between the kinds of supervision needed for/by school counsellors: clinical, developmental, and administrative. In this distinction, the purpose of each supervision type accounts for the different procedures used by the various supervisors available in schools. The purpose of clinical supervision is enhancement of counsellors' professional skills and ethical functioning.

The data sources which support clinical supervision include observations of counsellors applying their professional skills and values. In the school setting, the typical opportunities for gathering data to support clinical supervision are available (e.g., live and/or recorded observations, case presentations, and consultations). Clinical supervisors must be counsellors who are competent in the school counsellor functions and in supervision practices. The purpose of developmental supervision is improvement of the guidance and counselling programme and counsellors' pursuit of professional development.

Data sources which support developmental supervision are recordings of goals and activities undertaken to attain goals and measures of goal attainment, programme plans and implementation calendars, self-reports, and consumer satisfaction surveys. Developmental supervision is best provided by competent school counsellors from the same system as the supervisee. The purpose of administrative supervision is assurance that counsellors have worthy work habits, comply with laws and policies, relate well with other school staff and parents, and otherwise work effectively within the school system.

Data sources supporting administrative supervision are such things as work schedules, recordkeeping and documentation systems, and evidence of team efforts. Either school counsellor supervisors or building administrators may be providers of administrative supervision.

Particularly relevant in the school setting is clarifying the place of supervision in the overall system for helping counsellors' improve their performance. Whether or how data used in supervision will apply to summative evaluation needs to be spelled out. Supervision provides opportunities for personalising the professional development processes. The combination of feedback from supervision and from performance appraisal is data which counsellors and their supervisors use as the basis for professional development goals.

The cyclical nature of the supervisory process is enhanced by the lengthy supervisor-supervisee relationships typical of elementary and secondary school settings. The multiple opportunities for supervision over significant lengths of time allow supervisory relationships to be rich ones. The primary obstacles to fully effective school counsellor supervision are caused by the insufficient number of school counsellor-competent supervisors.

Where there are such supervisors, there is little or no relevant counsellor-supervisor training available and/or no specialised certification required. Although the building principals can provide useful administrative supervision, it is unlikely that they are current in the clinical functions of counselling. Competent school counsellors are usually available to fulfil the developmental and clinical supervision roles, but they often lack training and certification in supervision. Although development of the appropriate job descriptions and provision of the relevant training at this time are the responsibility of local school districts, the Standards for Counselling Supervisors and the Curriculum Guide provide the guidelines needed.

A pool of potential clinical and/or developmental supervisors are available in many communities. Current school counsellors can fulfil roles as peer supervisors. An increasing number of mid-sized school systems employ central office-based guidance supervisors. Some intermediate education agencies and some state departments of education provide such expertise. Schools are also contracting with community-based, Licensed Professional Counsellors, or counsellor educators.

Supervision of professional practice is an effective, but perhaps underutilised means of nurturing the professional development of new and experienced school counsellors. It is a personalised vehicle for assuring that children, their families, and teachers benefit from quality services. For counsellor supervision to be practiced more universally in the nation's schools, states need to require appropriate certification, counsellor education programmes need to offer appropriate counselling supervisor training, and schools and district counselling supervisors need to report their counsellor supervision practices and findings.

Job Role Expectations of School Counsellors

In their study of skills needed by school counsellors, Schafer and Mufson reviewed job analyses conducted by five school districts in five different states. They found a natural division of the job role expectations of school counsellors into six areas: counselling (individual and group), pupil assessment, consultation, information officer, school programme facilitator, and research and evaluation. There are assessment-intensive aspects of each of these.

The counsellor's major function in the school is to counsel students individually and whenever practical in small or large groups. The counsellor also is responsible for identifying students with special needs. These activities include interpreting test scores and non-test data.

Pupil assessment includes scheduling and preparing for testing, scoring them or sending them out for scoring, recording results, and scheduling for interpretation. Counsellors are also responsible for assisting students in evaluating their aptitudes and abilities through interpreting standardised tests. They may be expected to advise teachers who need to understand psychological evaluations and who are interested in improving their content-referenced testing skills.

The third function is that of a consultant. The counsellor consults with and advises teachers, parents, and administrators in guidance matters and test score interpretation. In some schools the counsellor helps teachers with psychological evaluations and content-referenced testing and advises school committees in selection of tests.

The function of information officer includes informing parents, teachers, and staff about counselling services, informing employers and colleges about students according to school policy, and ensuring two-way communication between school and home. Many of these activities involve test interpretation.

The fifth function is administrative, including school administration and counselling administration. Within school administration, the counsellor is responsible for administering tests. Within counselling administrative functions, the counsellor is expected to analyse guidance services. Also, the counsellor is often asked to participate in decisions about the instructional curriculum.

The sixth function is research and evaluation. The counsellor may be responsible for evaluating the school guidance programme. The counsellor is also expected to read and interpret literature to apply research findings to everyday counsels' situations and to improve his or her skills continuously through evaluation of counselling techniques.

The counsellor responsibilities identified by Schafer and Mufson would likely be found in the large majority of school districts across the nation. Within the area of assessment, roles include test interpreter, test developer, evaluator of programmes, consultant, and researcher. Several studies reviewed by Schafer and Mufson were supportive of these roles.

Counselling for Children from Broken Family

Children's reactions depend on their age and developmental stage at the time the divorce occurs.

Early Latency (ages 5-8). Children between the ages of five and eight at the time of their parents' divorce tend to react with great sadness. Some may feel fearful, insecure, helpless, and abandoned by the missing parent. Younger children often express guilt and blame themselves for their parents' divorce.

Late Latency (ages 9-12). Children in late latency at the time of their parents' divorce are distinguished from younger children by their feelings of intense anger. Nine to 12-year-olds may still feel loneliness, loss, shock, surprise, and fear, but anger and possibly the rejection of one parent are the predominant reactions of this age group.

Adolescence (ages 13-18). Adolescents whose parents are divorcing also experience loss, sadness, anger, and pain. A typical adolescent reaction to parental divorce, however, often involves acting-out behaviours. Sexual promiscuity, delinquency, the use of alcohol and drugs, and aggressive behaviour have all been identified as adolescent reactions to parental divorce.

In Wallerstein and Kelly's five-year longitudinal study of 60 families and 131 children of divorce, teachers reported that two-thirds of the children showed changes in school behaviour and/or academic performance following the parental separation. Cantrell concurs that teachers frequently report observing changes in academic achievement, moods, attendance patterns, and behaviour of children adjusting to their parents' divorce.

Responsibilities of School

The school is in an excellent position to offer supportive services to children of divorce. Children spend much time in school, where the continuity and routine can offer a safe environment for interventions. Counsellors, teachers, and other school personnel are available on a daily basis and can provide help that avoids both the stigma and the expense associated with seeking help form private practitioners. Finally, the number of children in the school provides the possibility for group interventions.

The school counsellor can provide valuable assistance directly through counselling with the children and indirectly through services to school administrators, teachers, and parents. Scherman and Lepak suggest that counsellors not view divorce as a single problem with negative consequences, but focus on changes caused by divorce and their positive, negative, or neutral effects on the children.

Working with administrators: Drake identified 10 major issues facing administrators with regard to children of divorce: school territorial rights, parental access to school records, release of the child from school, school visits, medical emergencies, financial responsibility, the child's surname, retention, confidentiality of records, and parental access to school functions. Counsellors can consult with school administrators on these policy issues and help them to understand the legal implications of divorce for the school. Because kidnapping of a child by the noncustodial parent may be a concern, schools need to guard against the possibility of parental kidnapping. Burns and Brassard suggest that schools:

1. Ask parents to inform the school about custody concerns.
2. Require parents to show legal documentation of sole custody when they report a sole custody arrangement.
3. Ensure that teachers are aware of custody status
4. Maintain an office list of children and custodial parents.

Working with Teachers: School counsellors can help teachers and other school personnel by conducting in-services on the effects of divorce on children and their classroom behaviour. Counsellors can also help to sensitise teachers to the transition a child is experiencing and to the implications of that transition. Teachers may need to change their choice of words, or to adapt their curriculum and classroom resource materials to include various family types.

Working with Parents: Counsellors can make parents aware of the special needs of their child during the divorce transition. A study by Hammond of third- to sixth-graders, for example, revealed that 74 percent of the 82 children who were from separated or divorced families believed that school counsellors could help by talking with parents of children who asked the counsellor to do so. Counsellors can also assist parents by referring them to divorce support groups in the community, by recommending reading materials that deal with families of divorce, and by suggesting ways that parents can help their children adjust to divorce.

Working with Children: Intervention strategies with children will depend on each child's individual needs. Kieffer suggests an adaptation of Kelly and Wallerstein's Divorce Specific Assessment which involves determining the child's developmental achievements, interviewing the child about his/her response to the family situation, and evaluating the child's existing support systems.

Hammond's study found that over 86 percent of third- to sixth-graders interviewed thought that counsellors could best help children whose parents are divorcing by encouraging the children to talk about their feelings. Approximately the same percentage reported that counsellors could also help by providing children with books to read about divorce.

Individual Counselling. Although there exists little research testing the efficacy of individual counselling with children of divorce, clinicians report a desirable change in the child's affect as a result of individual counselling. Individual counselling is usually reserved for children with long-term, unproductive coping behaviours and for children who cannot work well in groups.

Group Counselling: Robson reports that children's groups on divorce, led by elementary school counsellors with specific strategies to meet the needs of these children, have been extremely successful. Divorce groups are a popular choice for counsellors because of their cost effectiveness and multiple benefits. Eighty-two percent of the students in Hammond's study reported that a group counselling situation for children would be beneficial.

Cantrell suggests that counsellors using group counselling with children of divorce deal with the developmental responses of the children while helping them to label and understand their feelings, realise that others are having similar feelings and experiences, understand the divorce process, learn new coping skills, and feel good about themselves and their parents. Several types of group counselling are available which could be beneficial to children of divorce:

1. Situational/transitional groups offer emotional support; catharsis; and information sharing about stress, mutual feelings, and similar experiences.
2. Structured groups can teach children how to deal with crisis situations through group discussions, role playing, and the use of drawings and collages.
3. One-day workshops for children between the ages of 10 and 17 can use sentence completion exercises, assertiveness training, and films about divorce to help group members explore values and assumptions about marriage and divorce, learn to express and cope with their own and their parents' feelings, and develop communication skills for handling difficult situations.

Valuing Diversity in the Schools

The valuing of diversity in the schools is no longer merely a social goal. With the make-up of the student body changing so rapidly, school counsellors, teachers and administrators realise that they are now required to learn new techniques and skills for understanding, motivating, teaching, and empowering each individual student regardless of race, gender, religion or creed. We are a nation of diverse populations and groups.

The future of our society depends upon our ability to effectively talk with one another, to reach mutual understanding, and to realise that in diversity there is strength. School counsellors can serve as catalysts to insure that teachers, students and others learn how to value diversity. That is, the valuing of diversity can be taught to others and should be a major part of any school's comprehensive guidance programme.

Valuing Diversity Model

The "A" in ASK stands for Awareness of self and others. Self and other awareness is a must if cultural diversity is to be appreciated in our schools and elsewhere. The "S" in ASK refers to both Sensitivity and Skills. Sensitivity to others as well as new, innovative, communication. Skills are needed by students and others if we are to learn to value diversity and intercultural communication is to improve. The "K" stands for Knowledge of cultures different from our own. Culture influences feelings, thoughts, non-verbal behaviours, ideas and perceptions and "cognitive empathy" (knowledge) of another's culture is needed to improve intercultural relationships.

Self-awareness

Self-aware individuals avoid a condescending attitude and do not patronise culturally different persons. To patronise implies the belief that we hold a superior position to them—we come across to them as being "better" than they. And members of other cultural groups view this as disrespectful. Relatedly, some Anglo Americans seem to have a characteristic that could best be described as "assumed similarity." That is, they assume that people either ought to be like them or want to be like them! Self-aware individuals do not hold such assumptions. Students of all ages can be taught, through various guidance and counselling activities, to be more aware of self and others.

Sensitivity and Communication Skills

Our sensitivity toward and willingness to understand others is a major key to effective communication with the culturally different. We need to be aware of others' thoughts and feelings, regardless of their race, creed or cultural background. Effective, multicultural communicators are aware of other persons' frames of reference, their views of the world. And, they understand that worldviews are influenced by culture. We can learn communication skills that will assist us in understanding how others view their worlds and react to them, as opposed to telling them how they should react and behave toward their own worlds! Their worldviews may be very different from ours, but they are based on their perceptions—which are their "realities." And, their reality determines how they feel, think and behave.

How sensitive are you to your own views of those who are different? Do you view other cultures as equally valuable to yours? Is your cultural group superior to another? Are you culturally sensitive to your own heritage and the possibility that you were taught (perhaps unconsciously) to be prejudiced as a part of your upbringing? Do you value and respect differences? Are you aware of your own values and biases and how they affect those who are culturally different? Do you avoid stereotyping and labelling? Do you monitor your own assumptions about those different from you? Are you willing to accept someone of a different race into your organisation, i.e., your sorority, your fraternity, your church? It is important that each of us examine ourselves concerning these questions if we hope to become culturally skilled communicators.

The emerging sense of worth of members of culturally distinct populations can no longer be neglected. Learning about their different values, attitudes, desires, aspirations, and beliefs is necessary because it affects all of us. Learning skills to help us communicate effectively with people from different cultures will speed up this necessary learning process.

Feelings, thoughts, nonverbal behaviours, and ideas are important in interpersonal communication and are culturally influenced and learned. Empathy, interest in others, caring, personal awareness, sensitivity and understanding are stressed as important to effective interpersonal communication and to learning to value diversity. However, having these core conditions present is not always enough for effective communication with a person from another race or culture. We also need "cognitive" empathy. That is, knowledge of that person's culture, or knowing "where that person is coming from" is also extremely important.

Students of all ages can be taught to be culturally skilled. A culturally skilled communicator is willing to gain cognitive knowledge about different cultures, i.e., their history, cultural values, current problems and lifestyles and how this impacts on their respective worldview. This may be the most important thing we can do in becoming more effective intercultural communicators. Having strong feelings of support for a particular culture and its participants is necessary.

However, it is not enough to truly communicate with participants from that cultural group. If we are ignorant of the values and ways of participants from cultural groups different from ours, we will certainly be less effective communicators than we would be if we operated with accurate, cognitive understanding of them. The teaching of the values and ways of other cultural groups can, and should be, central to any comprehensive school guidance programme.

Model Implementation

The professional school counsellor possesses many excellent communication skills that can, and should be, shared and taught to teachers, administrators, students, and others. The "cognitive knowledge" aspect of the above described model can easily be generalised to the school setting. There are many effective ways that students can obtain knowledge about others' cultures, e.g., outside speakers from different cultural backgrounds, culturally distinct student panels, field trips, etc. Learning about other cultures should be a major component of any guidance curriculum, regardless of the school level.

In addition, self awareness, awareness of others and sensitivity to self and others in regard to diversity can and should be a major component of any comprehensive school guidance programme. Many guidance activities can be developed and delivered by various modes with these themes in mind. School counsellors know how to communicate effectively with others regardless of their or the other person's cultural background. They are skilled in how to "tune in to" the feelings of others, how to put the speaker at ease by clarifying the content of what was just said, how to show interest in others through the use of open-ended questions, etc. And the research is clear, these skills can be taught to students of all ages, i.e., there is considerable evidence that peers can become very effective in helping other peers. And, through structured guidance and counselling approaches all students and teachers can be taught these facilitative communication skills.

Responsibilities of Secondary School Counsellors

Several influences have impacted what has been referred to as "the role" of secondary school counsellors. Among the influences are state certification standards; counsellor education training programmes; the nature of school systems; professional organisations; principals and other administrators' beliefs about counsellors; and the counsellors themselves. Principals have had a major influence on counsellors' roles. In many situations, principals have dictated "the role" by assigning the counsellor "duties"—often administrative or quasi-administrative duties that have little to do with the actual role of school counsellors or the needs of students.

School counsellors appear to be reluctant or unable to convince principals that they should perform the duties for which they have been trained. This must change if school counsellors are to have any influence in the restructured schools of the future. In this complex and troubled society, school counsellors are being asked to assume a greater role in the lives of their students and the students' families. The challenges facing counsellors and demands on their time will continue to grow during the next decade.

School counsellors must choose carefully where they spend their time and energy. But, given the challenges faced by today's students, school counsellors must focus on students' personal/social, educational, and career needs. In order to do so, counsellors need to move from a services-oriented approach (orientation, information, assessment, counselling, placement, and follow-up) to a school counselling programme approach. They must be clear about their "scope of practice"—the responsibilities for which they are trained—and not allow themselves to become assistant principals, attendance officers, substitute teachers, and clerks.

School counsellors can exert more control over their scope of practice if they commit themselves to designing and implementing developmental school counselling programmes. While crisis and remedial counselling will always be a part of the school counsellor's responsibilities, counsellors must provide assistance to as many students as possible. Emphasising developmental counselling programmes permits counsellors to be seen as contributing to the growth of all students and not just working with those "in trouble."

Developmental counselling programmes focus on meeting students' needs and lead to activities and structured group experiences for all students. They are proactive rather than reactive and when counsellors are busy implementing their programme, they are unavailable for unrelated administrative and clerical duties. Developmental Counselling Programmes include both "content" and "process" components. The content component of the programme speaks to:

1. The rationale for the programme (why the school and children need a counselling programme);
2. The personal-social, educational, and career development skills or competencies needed by children and youth; and
3. The management plan or blueprint intended to guide counsellors' management of the counselling programme.

The process component includes:

1. The activities counsellors will use to help students achieve the designated skills or competencies;
2. The counselling strategies they intend to employ, e.g., individual counselling, group counselling, classroom guidance, and/or consultation; and

3. Methods to be used to evaluate their programme and improve their effectiveness with students, staff, and parents.

In a comprehensive developmental school counselling programme, the counsellor has the following scope of practice (the responsibilities for which a school counsellor is trained and qualified):

Design. Counsellors design the content of the programme. Gysbers, refers to this content as a "guidance curriculum." The content of the programme is designed to help students gain skills or competencies in personal-social, educational, and career domains. Following is a list of skills/ competencies that one might expect to see in the content of a developmental counselling programme.

1. Personal-Social Skills. Students will:
   (a) gain self-awareness and improve self-esteem;
   (b) make healthy choices and effective decisions;
   (c) assume responsibility for their own behaviour;
   (d) respect individual differences and cooperate; and
   (e) learn to resolve conflicts.
2. Educational Skills. Students will:
   (a) acquire study and test-taking skills;
   (b) seek and use educational information;
   (c) set educational goals; and
   (d) make appropriate educational choices.
3. Career Development Skills. Students will:
   (a) analyse interests, aptitudes, and skills;
   (b) recognise effects of career stereotyping;
   (c) form a career identity; and
   (d) plan for their future careers.

Delivery. Counsellors must be involved in the delivery of this developmental programme content or curriculum that they have developed. They must allocate significant amounts of time to facilitate or team teach developmental learning activities in the classrooms. Also, they will need to set up inservices for teachers to enable them to assist in the facilitation of the activities. Counsellors need to deliver their programme content in small and large group sessions. Large group sessions may be appropriate for the information about and discussion of post-secondary or vocational education options and financial aid. Small groups may be more appropriate for interests or aptitude test interpretations.

Counsel. Counsellors must counsel students both individually and in small groups. Counsellors must not forget their unique counselling skills. While schools are not appropriate cites for "caseloads of clients," counsellors must always allot time for counselling students with personal-social problems, both individually and in small groups. In order to be as effective as possible in a limited number of sessions, counsellors should utilise newer theoretical approaches such as brief therapy.

Consult. Counsellors must consult with parents, teachers, other educators, and various community agencies to help students deal with more serious personal and educational problems, both individually and in small groups. In order to be as effective as possible, in a limited number of sessions, counsellors should utilise newer theoretical approaches such as brief therapy.

Coordinate. Counsellors must coordinate or collaborate with others who may be offering mental health-oriented programmes, e.g., substance abuse. Counsellors report that more and more community-based programmes are operating in the schools. The school counsellors should either coordinate the efforts of these programmes or collaborate in their delivery. Testing programmes are often coordinated by school counsellors. In these days of accountability, counsellors must be careful not to permit this responsibility to consume too much of their time. While counsellors should understand thoroughly all relevant interest, aptitude, and achievement tests and should be able to offer inservices to teachers on their interpretation and use, they should not be spending their time in direct administration of tests.

Manage. Counsellors must manage the school counselling programme. Directors of guidance are a dying breed. Many counsellors find themselves supervised by individuals who have more responsibilities than they can handle. Counsellors must take charge of their own programmes and encourage interaction and regular meetings of the counsellors in their district in order to assure programme progress. Managing a school counselling programme includes developing an active staff/community public relations programme.

Counsellors should orient staff and community to the counselling programme through newsletters, local media, and school and community presentations. Managing also involves pulling together advisory committees of parents and community members to gather input related to student needs. The management function is critical to the success of a school counselling programme.

Evaluate. Counsellors need to evaluate their efforts with students, staff, and community. Counsellors can gather evaluation data from several sources. One source of information is "general evaluation" data which includes number of students seen in individual or crisis counselling, number of small group counselling sessions, number of large group information sessions, number of conferences with parents, and number of phone calls to parents and community agencies. While this kind of general evaluation does not speak to the quality of counsellor contacts, it does provide the school board and administration information about the scope or breadth of the counselling programme.

"Specific evaluation" data takes more counsellor planning time. Counsellors need to plan to evaluate their work with students (particularly the delivery of the guidance activities in classrooms). Ratings scales to be completed by teachers and/or students and short surveys to determine what students gained from the guidance activities are two additional methods that can be used to evaluate the counselling programme. Programme evaluation is one of the weakest areas in school counselling. Many counsellors will need to seek assistance from nearby counsellor educators in setting up their evaluation process.

Responsibilities of Elementary School Counsellors

Our society faces challenges in accepting and benefiting from cultural diversity. Problems emanating from racism exist despite efforts aimed at educational reform. Elementary school counsellors must be aware of transmitting their own cultural values to children and of drawing erroneous conclusions about children's emotional and social well-being based on cultural differences.

Moreover, because counselling theories and techniques are not always applicable across cultures, counsellors must often look to new and creative ways to work effectively in multicultural settings. Elementary school counsellors should advocate for educational programmes that include counsellors, teachers, parents, and students working together for increased cultural understanding through role playing and other awareness activities.

The so-called traditional family has virtually disappeared in America. Divorce and single-parent homes are a fact of life confronting children. Elementary school counsellors must understand the effects of changing family structures and find ways to promote child growth and development within the context of family change. These ways will include divorce groups, training groups for single parents, guidance for latchkey children, and a variety of other important strategies.

Elementary school counsellors need to develop innovative approaches to help children and parents develop in a healthy fashion in spite of the ambiguity created by divorce and single-parent families. Counsellors should assume a proactive stance by collaborating with teachers in developing and implementing family education programmes.

Students often begin to experiment with drugs in elementary school and early experimentation frequently leads to abuse and addiction in adolescence. Moreover, educators are aware of problems coming from families made dysfunctional by alcoholism and drug addiction. Elementary school counsellors must understand the scope and implications of substance abuse and implement drug education programmes that are designed to prevent drug abuse and to help children overcome the effects of substance abuse in their families. Elementary school counsellors also need to recognise the serious effects of parents' alcoholism on children's development and implement compassionate approaches to helping these young victims receive help whether or not their parents are willing to accept help.

Child abuse and neglect are rampant in our society. Elementary school counsellors can build a positive school environment for youngsters who suffer from abuse and neglect by implementing such programmes as parent support groups to prevent physical abuse of children, programmes that help identify potential child abusers, and preventive sexual abuse programmes. Elementary school counsellors cannot work alone in preventing and treating child abuse. They need to develop close working relationships with social services and other community agencies that frequently advocate for victims of abuse and neglect.

Counsellors also need to work closely with teachers to help them thoroughly understand signs of abuse and to acquaint them with correct referral procedures. The elementary school classroom may be the most stable setting neglected and abused children experience and may provide the empathy and positive regard needed to help children cope with their ordeal. Elementary school counsellors must, therefore, become increasingly sensitive to the victims of abuse and to the need for effective counselling programmes in this troublesome area.

Many children in our schools are labelled exceptional and find it difficult to accept that they are "simply human." These children need to feel accepted and to use their exceptional characteristics in extraordinary ways. Children who are not so labelled need to learn ways of benefiting from those who are exceptional. The parents and teachers of exceptional children also need to find ways to understand and assist these youngsters. Elementary school counsellors should work to build a supportive learning environment for exceptional children. There is a need for strong ties between counselling and special education.

Counsellors should develop programmes for parents of exceptional children. Parents of gifted youngsters, for example, have unique needs resulting from misunderstandings created by myths, stereotypes, and the small number of gifted children in the population. Counsellors should also develop strategies to help teachers work more effectively with parents of handicapped children because the teacher is in a position to develop an active, ongoing relationship with parents but may lack the training to provide effective counselling support.

Technological advances have changed education, work, and leisure in our society. Although most people experience the benefits of these advances, most also know the anxiety and frustration that accompany rapid technological change as well as the alienation generated by impersonal aspects of technology. Elementary school counsellors need to help children develop emotionally and socially in the context of rapid technological change. Counsellors often need to deal first with their own concerns about technology before helping children understand the benefits and limitations of technology. Elementary school counsellors especially need to acquire competencies with computers, to overcome anxieties about using the technology, and to integrate computer technology into counselling programmes.

Elementary school counsellors face major challenges as they work with parents and teachers to introduce children to an ever-changing world of work.

The emphasis on career education, however, seems to have diminished from its peak in the 1970s when the United States Office of Education demanded high visibility for career education programmes in schools. This decline in career education at the elementary school level is unfortunate because economic, political, and social changes have brought women and minorities into the work force in large numbers and have altered how children must be prepared to enter the world of work. Elementary school counsellors need to enhance children's career awareness, prevent sex-role stereotyping through career exploration programmes, and use role models to expand children's occupational aspirations.

American society has placed increasing emphasis on the need for children to learn basic academic skills. Parents throughout the country complain that children are not learning to read, write, and perform basic mathematics. Governmental and private commissions have studied the poor academic achievement of children and are asking educators to account for the failure of our schools in this important area. If elementary school counsellors are to fulfil their mission in schools, they must collaborate with teachers, parents, and school administrators in an effort to improve children's achievement.

Elementary school counsellors can positively effect children's achievement. Counsellors, for example, can implement and evaluate a ten-session programme called "Succeeding in School". Counsellors can also consult with parents on matters related to children's academic progress, implement classroom programmes that improve the work habits of children who procrastinate with school work, and use group counselling as a means of motivating children to attend school.

Children's behaviour, both in and out of school, is an important concern of parents and educators. The popular media has documented seemingly wide-spread school absenteeism and delinquency among our nation's youth. How to change children's misbehaviour and to foster productive behaviour are concerns of elementary school counsellors. The techniques available to parents, teachers, and elementary school counsellors for managing children's behaviour are numerous and include modelling, positive reinforcement, behaviour contracting, and desensitisation. These behavioural change procedures have been thoroughly tested.

Although the application of these methods is often difficult, the collaborative efforts of elementary school counsellors, teachers, and parents in applying behavioural techniques eases some of the difficulties and increases the chances of success. Counselling interventions to improve behaviour include classroom guidance sessions, small group counselling sessions, and consultation with teachers. Students who receive a combination of these treatment procedures are likely to behave well in the classroom and elsewhere.

Children need to support each other in a world filled with conflict. They must learn and practice the interpersonal skills necessary for their present lives and also for the demands of peer pressure in adolescence. Elementary school counsellors must find ways both to challenge and support youngsters in the area of human relations. Counsellors can build positive relationships among children and between children and adults through affective education programmes in the classroom and through innovative approaches to peer counselling.

Elementary school counsellors play a major part in developing and maintaining a healthy social climate for children. This aspect of counsellors' work is important in part because children's relations with teachers, peers, and family affect learning and achievement. In addition, counsellors who strive to improve children's interpersonal skills are helping to ensure that the 1990s and beyond will be years in which society will move forward on the basis of cooperative efforts among the nation's citizens. Finally, the work of elementary school counsellors in this area will likely help to produce citizens who strive for productive relations across cultures and nations.

Responsibilities of Professional School Counsellors

Home education, also called homeschooling or home school, is the process by which children are educated at home rather than at an institution such as a public or private school. Prior to the introduction of compulsory school attendance in the 19th century, most education worldwide occurred within the family and community, with only a small proportion of the population attending schools or employing tutors.

Lyman offered the following reasons people choose homeschooling: religious values in education; worries over crime and lack of discipline in public schools; concern about the quality of education; and the belief that children are best educated by parents. Lange and Liu, in a study of homeschooling in Minnesota, found similarly that "special needs of the children, educational philosophy, parenting style and religious and ethical beliefs" were factors in choosing to homeschool.

McDowell offered a different perspective with an epidemiological approach to analysing the incidents of violence on the homeschooling movement. She determined that the influence of homeschooling along with the negative factors associated with public schools multiplied the number of persons who participated in homeschooling. Kozlowski addressed reasons for homeschooling by superintendents and parents in Alabama. The superintendents reported that shielding children from adverse social factors and inculcating morals and values were the parents' most frequent reasons for homeschooling. The parents on the other hand stated "individual attention and raising confident, caring and well-rounded people" as their reasons.

Families who homeschool their children generally can be described as religious, conservative, college educated, middle-class, two parent, and politically active. Bauman concluded that homeschooling families are most prevalent in rural and suburban areas of the West and tend to have one parent not in the labour force. Rudner revealed that about one-fourth of homeschooled students were being educated by a parent who was a certified teacher. In terms of achievement, Rudner found that about 25% of homeschoolers were performing at one or more grade levels above their peers in public and private schools.

Public schools have long had connections with the homeschool community via services such as part-time enrolment and participation in student activities. A public school in Barnstable, Massachusetts helped to pioneer the concept of assistance to homeschool families as early as 1978. In addition, the Cupertino Union School District in California provided open enrolment/alternative education beginning in 1975. One notable public school system connecting with homeschoolers is the Federal Way School District in Washington.

The Federal Way School District instituted an Internet academy that provides instruction through on-line courses, chat rooms, e-mail and phone support from supervising district teachers. Homeschool students can attend courses but also have the option to enroll for all instruction on-line. Those without computer access can utilise a school district computer lab or computers at public libraries. As school districts have opened their doors to homeschooled children in the areas of curricular and extracurricular activities, legal concerns have been raised with regard to the requests for services. Controversy has centered on the eligibility requirements for participation in sports programmes. School counsellors should be aware of the ways in which connections between public schools and the homeschool community continue to evolve.

One of the primary reasons for building partnerships with the homeschooling population is to serve students, which is consistent with the public school mission to provide "quality educational experiences for all school-aged children". Other reasons include the requirements of state legislation, funding that may be available for serving homeschooled children as a result of state guidelines, and "maintaining positive working relationships with students who may eventually re-enroll in the school". In rural settings, the appeal for school counselling services may be greater since alternative options for services may not be available.

Given the sparsity of research dedicated to the involvement of homeschooled children in school counselling programmes, the following recommendations are offered.

First, school counselling sponsored services such as college nights, career fairs, college admissions counselling, financial aid and scholarship information, standardised testing, test preparation sessions, access to Advanced Placement classes and other enrichment activities should be made available to the homeschooling population. In addition to these services, many school counselling programmes offer computerised career development programmes that could assist homeschooled students in identifying career fields and potential college majors. Not surprisingly this latter point is of interest to homeschoolers as many will seek admission to college.

Second, as a strategy to further involve the home school population within school counselling programmes, efforts can be made to include a home schooling advocate on school counselling advisory councils. Carney reported that a critical component of comprehensive competency-based guidance models is the advisory council that assists in the evaluation and enhancement of the school counselling programme. These councils usually consist of a broad range of individuals and include representation from ethnic minority groups, persons with disabilities, and persons of various ages. A homeschooling representative would help keep the public school counsellors in touch with the needs of homeschoolers.

Third, many school counselling programmes list the types of services that they provide on a school district or school website. This practice is beneficial to inform home school populations of the services offered. It also allows them to select the services that they desire. Publicising school activities and programmes in homeschooling resources would further encourage the involvement of homeschooled children.

Fourth, participation in school counselling programmes could assist homeschoolers in obtaining letters of recommendation from school counsellors. Since many of these students have to submit a detailed portfolio of experiences for college admissions in order to be recognised as a competitive applicant, the letters of recommendation from school counsellors could prove to be useful.

Fifth, counsellors can provide homeschooling parents information on child development, student learning, curriculum planning, assessment and evaluation. Other support services that would be beneficial are administering achievement tests and proctoring exams.

A trend has been established for public schools to provide services to homeschoolers. As services are extended to this new and growing population, school counsellors will be challenged to develop relationships and make positive connections with homeschoolers. These connections fit the mission of public education and also create relationships with students who may at some point become full-time clients on school counsellors' caseloads.

References

Huitt, W. (Compiler), (1992), *Philosophy and education*, Valdosta, GA: Valdosta State University.

Maccoby, Eleanor, (1974), *The psychology of sex differences*, Stanford, CA: Stanford University Press.

Marshall, H., (1998), *Teaching educational psychology: Learner-centered constructivist perspectives*. In N.M. Lambert & B.L. McCombs (Eds.) How students learn: Reforming schools through learner-centered education, Washington, DC: American Psychological Association.

McShane, John, (1991), *Cognitive development: An information-processing approach*, Cambridge, MA: Basil Blackwell.

Vygotskii, L. S, (1997), *Educational psychology*, Trans. Robert Silverman. Boca Raton, FL: St. Lucie Press.

7

School Guidance Programmes

Students of the present day are faced with a number of problems during the various styles of school life. There problems may be related to personal, behavioural, educational or vocational personality factors. Enabling students to overcome these problems and become self-reliant in future is one of the major aims of the guidance programme. However, one is also aware that the implementation of guidance programme in the prevailing schools is hardly noticeable. This situation still persists, inspite of various recommendations been made by the government since the last few decades. One of the likely causes for the non-implementation of this programme is largely due to the lack of adequate knowledge among the required or concerned staff regarding the planning and organisation of the guidance programme in schools.

A school guidance programme constitutes a cluster of activities which enable the students to overcome their educational, vocational, personal or social problems that they face during the different phases of development. It forms as an integral part of school education and is non-instructional in nature.

Guidance and the Effective Education

A new school of thought is emerging among educators and counsellors. Unlike the reform movement of the past decade, this new movement takes full account of students' personal needs in formulating educational goals. Proponents of this school of thought recognise the close relationship between students' academic development and their personal growth; accordingly, they are seeking to place guidance at the heart of the educational process.

Norm Gysbers' Comprehensive Guidance Programme Model, and Robert Myrick's Teacher Advisor Programme are both based on the idea that guidance is an integral part of a school's educational mission rather than an "ancillary" service peripheral to the curriculum. This idea in turn presupposes an enlightened humanistic conception of education, which recognises and validates the intrinsic dignity of every student, and which attends empathetically to students' personal and developmental needs. This conception forms the basis of William Purkey's Invitational Learning Model, a new paradigm for schooling that seeks to reconstitute the entire school setting—people, places, policies, programmes, and processes—so that every aspect of the school serves to "invite" students to learn by respecting them, encouraging them, and validating their unique importance and possibilities.

Comprehensive Guidance Programme Model

Since 1971, Norman C. Gysbers and his associates at the University of Missouri-Columbia have been developing, field-testing, refining, and implementing the Comprehensive Guidance Programme Model, an innovative, programme-based organisational plan that has been adopted by school districts throughout the nation. The foundation for the Model—the theoretical basis for identifying the guidance, knowledge, skills, and attitudes (competencies) that students need is called Life Career Development, defined as self-development over a person's life span through the integration of roles, settings, and events in a person's life. Accordingly, this Model emphasises three domains of human growth and development:

— Self-knowledge and interpersonal skills. Helping students to develop awareness and acceptance of themselves and others, and to develop personal standards and a sense of purpose in life

— Life roles, settings, and events. Emphasising knowledge and understanding of the interrelatedness of various life roles.

— Life career planning. Appraising personal values as they relate to prospective life career plans and decisions.

The Comprehensive Guidance Programme Model consists of three structural foundations and four interactive programme components. The structural foundations—definition, rationale, and assumptions—emphasise the centrality of guidance to the total education programme, and define the relationship between guidance and other aspects of the curriculum. The four programme components delineate the major activities, and the roles and responsibilities of personnel involved in the guidance programme:

- — Guidance curriculum, or structured classroom activities, organised around the three domains of student competencies;
- — Individual planning, including activities designed to assist students in monitoring and understanding their own growth and development;
- — Responsive services, such as information seeking, crisis counselling, and teacher/parent/specialist consultation; and
- — System support, activities geared toward programme management and operations.

One principal rationale behind the Comprehensive Guidance Programme Model is to enable counsellors to regain control of their time on the job by allocating 100 percent of their time to the four programme components discussed above—guidance curriculum, individual planning, responsive services, and system support. The Comprehensive Guidance Programme Model is oriented above all toward student development; it is a programmematic framework which allows counsellors to devote their primary attention to guidance activities and structured group experiences for all students.

Teacher Advisor Programme (TAP)

The assumption behind Robert D. Myrick's Teacher Advisor Programme (TAP) is that each student needs a friendly adult in the school who knows and cares about him or her in a personal way. The advisors help their advisees deal with the problems of growing up and getting the most out of school. A teacher-advisor is usually responsible for an advisee's cumulative folder, work folders, teacher-student conferences, parent conferences, group guidance experiences and follow-up on academic progress reports. Advisors also consult with other teachers, school counsellors, and support personnel about their advisees.

TAP is designed to provide an opportunity for all the students in a school to participate in a small and cohesive group of 15 to 25 peers led by a sensitive and caring teacher who promotes and monitors individual students' educational and developmental experiences as they progress through school. Teacher-advisors meet with their advisees on a regular basis through a "homeroom" or "homebase" group. This becomes, in effect, the students' home within the school, where they have a supportive teacher and group of peers with whom they can explore personal interests, goals, and concerns. The guidance curriculum varies from one school to another, but it generally addresses personal, social, and academic concerns.

Some of the personal and social skills addressed include getting acquainted, self-esteem, and time management. Academic topics might include policies and procedures from the school handbook and computing grade point averages. Career and educational planning topics include career exploration and choices, employability skills and the job market. Since many high school teachers have never had a guidance course and many are unsure of how to lead a group discussion with adolescents, teachers may need special preparation in how to work with their students and how to build guidance units for their groups.

Counsellors can therefore assist teachers in developing guidance units, or they can work together as a team in developing and delivering a guidance curriculum, with counsellors taking over homebase groups on occasion. It is important, therefore, to establish a cooperative and supportive relationship between teachers and counsellors so that they can define their respective roles and differentiate responsibilities. To enlist the support of a school's faculty for TAP and developmental guidance, it is essential that all teachers understand the philosophy of TAP and commit adequate time to it.

Counsellors should therefore provide a developmental guidance curriculum guide to establish guidance objectives and provide activities, but allow teachers to choose or discard suggested activities according to their needs. Since most teachers need more training in how to help students solve personal problems or get them working cooperatively in small groups, counsellors also may need to assist teachers in developing guidance and interpersonal skills. Administrative support and periodic evaluation are also essential.

Invitational Learning

The Invitational Learning concept, developed by William W. Purkey, offers a blueprint of what counsellors, teachers, principals, supervisors, superintendents, and others can do to enrich the physical and psychological environments of institutions and encourage the development of the people who live and work there. Invitational Learning is based on four value-based assumptions regarding the nature of people and their potential and the nature of professional helping:

— *Respect*: People are able, valuable, and responsible and should be treated accordingly;

— *Trust*: Education should be a collaborative, cooperative activity where process is as important as product;

— *Optimism*: People possess untapped potential in all areas of human endeavor; and

— *Intentionality*: Human potential can best be realised by places, policies, programmes, and processes that are specifically designed to invite development, and by people who are intentionally inviting with themselves and others, personally and professionally.

In a school or any other organisation, everything is connected to everything else. And so, in applying Invitational Learning, everything counts in creating an environment that invites individuals to reach their potential:

— *Places*: Creating an attractive and inviting physical setting is the easiest way to begin the process of incorporating the Invitational Learning concept into a school or other organisation.

— *Policies*: Professional counsellors can assist schools in developing policies that encourage student responsibility and participation rather than those that create pervasive anxiety, mistrust, and mindless conformity.

— *Programmes*: Programmes that incorporate the assumptions of Invitational Learning include incentive programmes such as peer counselling for dropout prevention, faculty mentoring, and other collaborative programmes where students, teachers, and counsellors all gain by helping and encouraging one another.

— *Processes*: How we teach or counsel and how we act while doing these things are far more important in the long run than what students or clients learn. Educators and counsellors in successful schools establish behavioural norms of collegiality, professional development, mutual assistance, and ongoing discussion of instruction and curricular improvements among themselves, and they cultivate attitudes of respect for all students and attention to their needs in all of their interactions.

— *People*: The daily interaction between teachers and students, counsellors and clients, and professionals amongst themselves, ultimately determines the success or failure of Invitational Learning. Counsellors and teachers who wish to employ Invitational Learning therefore need a sound knowledge of human development.

The goal of Invitational Learning is thus to provide an optimally inviting total environment, both for professional helpers themselves and for those with whom they work. In this respect, it is fully compatible with both the Comprehensive Guidance Programme Model and the Teacher Advisor Programme. All three approaches affirm the centrality of developmental guidance to the educational process, and all are predicated on mutual respect and human dignity—for counsellors, teachers, and students alike.

Ethical and Legal Issues

Ethical decisions are usually not clear-cut; they tend to be in the "gray areas" rather than in "black and white." Furthermore, the "right" answer in one situation is not necessarily the "right" answer in a similar case at another time. As society changes, the issues change; and, indeed, as counsellors change, their perspectives change. If we understand and accept the fact that ultimately counsellors will have to struggle with themselves to determine the appropriate action in each situation, then we realise the importance of ethical and legal awareness and sensitivity.

We then also understand the need for periodic re-examination of the issues throughout our professional lives. The importance of knowing the contents of professional codes of conduct and the purposes and limitations of such codes is essential to the understanding of ethical and legal issues in school counselling. Although detailed memorisation of the ethical codes is not required, school counsellors should have at least a basic understanding of their ethical responsibilities as defined in these documents.

The ethical standards of ASCA and the American Association for Counselling and Development (AACD) present school counsellors with the behaviours to which they should aspire and give general guidelines for addressing difficult issues. They do not, however, necessarily provide answers to the many specific dilemmas that practitioners will face. When the standards do not provide enough direction, counsellors are encouraged to consult with colleagues, professional experts, and perhaps their administrative supervisors before taking action. Almost all professionals, at some point in their career, suspect or become aware of a colleague's unethical behaviour.

School counsellors are obligated to address any conduct by a colleague that could cause harm to clients. Counsellors should:

(a) try to resolve the issue by confronting the colleague directly, if possible;

(b) report the behaviour to a superior, professional association, or credentialing authority if a direct confrontation is not possible or is not effective; and

(c) take steps to protect any vulnerable clients.

Legal Standards

Legal standards of practice are different from ethical standards. Generally, legal standards are related to accepted professional practices in the community while ethical standards tend to be idealistic. Many schools have policies that differentiate between the rights of custodial and noncustodial parents, and school counsellors are often required to implement such policies. The law is clear that, barring a specific court order to the contrary, noncustodial parents have all rights regarding their children except the right to have custody of the children permanently in their homes. When federal legislation known as the 1978 Hatch Amendment was passed and revised regulations were issued in 1984, a great deal of misinterpretation occurred that inhibited the offering of school counselling services.

Eventually it was realised that the amendment's requirement of written parental consent for children to participate in certain school programmes covered only a narrow range of activities that were federally funded, were experimental in nature, and involved psychological tests or treatment. School counsellors often play a major role in administering the school's testing programme. School counsellors should provide expert advice to school policymakers regarding the appropriate use of tests. Counsellors should assist in evaluating each test to determine whether it:

(1) discriminates in any way against any segment of the school population,

(2) is valid and reliable,

(3) is appropriate for the purposes for which it is being used, and

(4) is necessary to achieve the school's objectives.

Moreover, the counsellor is responsible for interpreting test results for students in a clear and understandable manner. The laws regarding abortions for minors are changing. Generally, school counsellors may discuss a student's decision of whether to seek an abortion with the student, but they should also encourage parental involvement when possible. Each case must be decided individually based on the facts as presented.

Group counselling presents ethical issues not found in individual interventions with clients. The advantages of a comprehensive group counselling programme are numerous; however, school counsellors who direct such programmes need to be familiar with potential ethical problems. Although group counselling in general presents special problems, providing group counselling for children introduces issues not found when working with adults. Although the ASCA Ethical Standards for School Counsellors does not directly address group counselling, some specific guidelines are found in the AACD Ethical Standards. The ASGW Ethical Guidelines for Group Counsellors provides additional direction.

Special Issues

Computers: School counselling offices are increasingly utilising computers and computer products. School counsellors have made attempts to understand and utilise this modern technology, but many counsellors are still unaware of the ethical issues involved in the use of computers. It is imperative that professional associations develop ethical standards regarding computer use. Moreover, the importance of direct counsellor-client contact in conjunction with the use of computers must be stressed.

Cultural diversity: School counsellors have a responsibility to provide services for all students, including those from other cultures. The counselling profession is a Western culture phenomenon; however, school counsellors constantly interact with families and children who speak languages other than English, adhere to values different from those of the counsellor, and conform to social expectations that may seem odd to the American school environment. The unique ethical issues involved in counselling multi-cultural populations need to be addressed.

Research: There is an increasing demand for school counsellors to engage in field-based research. Documenting programme effectiveness can do more to promote school counselling than all public relations efforts combined. But even if school counsellors never conduct research themselves, they need to know the rights of students involved in research projects, the responsibilities of researchers, and other research-related ethical issues.

Sexual intimacy: Perhaps the most pressing ethical problem in the counselling profession is sexual intimacy with clients. School counsellors are involved less often in sexual relationships with clients than are their colleagues who counsel adults. Nevertheless, clients, no matter what their age, often introduce sexual dimensions into the counselling relationship. Counsellors who are faced with sex and intimacy boundary issues in their professional counselling roles must respond in a manner that is consistent with ethical guidelines.

High School Guidance Programme

High School Guidance Counsellors deliver the comprehensive guidance programme to students in grades nine through twelve in a manner that prepares students for post secondary opportunities. High School Counsellors must have the following qualifications,

— are professional educators,

— have earned a Master's Degree,

— are specifically trained in counselling techniques,

— are certified as school counsellors by the Texas Education Agency.

High School Counsellors address their continuing professional growth through:

— Inservice training

— Workshops

— Local, state and national conferences

— Continuing Education

— Inter-school counsellor meetings

— Current professional literature and media information

— Presentations to professional groups

— Technology networking

Students may see the school counsellor through...

— A student self referral

— A teacher referral

— A parent referral

— A counsellor request

— An administrator request

Students may want to see the counsellor for many reasons, including assistance with:

— Problem-solving by exploring alternatives to make appropriate decisions.
— Developing positive attitudes towards self and others.
— Establishing personal goals.
— Developing educational plans and in selecting the related courses based on individual interests and talents.
— Interpretation of results of standardised tests.

High School Counsellors across the district provide similar services tailored to the educational level and to the student and campus needs. High School Counsellors teach the guidance curriculum and assist teachers with guidance-related curricula. The following are examples of the topics that are addressed in class guidance sessions.

— Academic support
— Career pathways
— Character development
— Decision-making
— Developmental assets
— Goal-Setting
— Graduation requirements
— Study skills
— Understanding academic records
— Conflict management

High School Counsellors provide individual or group assistance with educational planning and career exploration. Sample activities include the following:

— 9-12 Pre-registration activities such as course selection and review of graduation requirements.
— Special events such as college and career days, financial aid programmes and elective fairs.
— Assistance to students with information for special programmes such as dual credit, transition/IEP needs.

— Student/parent conferences to address educational and career planning.

— Freshman Conferences to orient students to high school.

— Sophomore conferences to review student Graduation Status Report (GSR), to interpret the standardised test scores and to provide career guidance.

— Junior Conferences to review the GSR, to provide college, career and relevant testing information.

— Senior Conferences to review the GSR, provide post-secondary education admissions information, as well as scholarship and financial aid information.

High School Counsellors provide students with counselling services, either individually or in groups, to address relevant adolescent issues as a result of student, teacher, parent and/or administrator concerns, or for crisis response. Examples of concerns students may bring to the counsellor's office include the following:

— Conflict mediation

— Dropout prevention

— Financial assistance

— Peer relations

— Progress toward graduation

— Schedule issues or changes

— Social issues

— Teen parenting

— Violence and drug abuse issues

Counsellors also provide consultation services to parents and teachers. Additionally, counsellors may refer students (and when needed, their families) to other programmes for other resources or services such as:

— Safe and Drug Free Programme,

— Gifted and Talented Programme,

— Special Education Services,

— HORIZONS Programme, (perhaps link to their website)

— Other district and community resources and services.

High School Counsellors coordinate with school and community to bring together resources for students. Counsellors provide information about:

— AP Testing Schedule
— Exit Level TAAS testing schedule
— Scholastic Aptitude Test (SAT) and American College Testing (ACT) testing schedule and preparatory classes
— PSAT Test Schedule

Counsellors organise or assist with many activities on behalf of students with other campus, district and community groups. Counsellors provide consultation and training services to school staff and parents. Topics they address can include the following:

— Developmental Assets
— Multicultural/Diversity training
— Guidance programme information
New teacher training
— Signs and symptoms of substance abuse and violence

Counselling for Hispanic Students

Based on cultural stereotypes about Hispanic students, many teachers see lower potential and expect lower performance. In a study of Mexican-American students, teachers were more likely to show disapproval toward Spanish-dominant than English-dominant students and to attribute negative characteristics to students who spoke accented or nonstandard English or nonstandard Spanish.

Another study found that teachers attributed such negative characteristics as low social status, low educational attainment, and low intelligence to Hispanic students who had accents or who were nonstandard speakers. A United States Commission on Civil Rights study showed that teachers direct praise or encouragement at Anglo students 36 percent more often than at Mexican-American students; build on the spoken contribution of Anglo students 40 percent more often; and ask Anglo students 20 percent more questions than they ask Mexican-American students.

Test Performance

A number of factors clearly depress the test performance of Hispanic students. First, the lower socioeconomic and educational level of Hispanic families generally correlates with low test performance, regardless of ethnicity. Second are problems within the testing situation: cultural differences, which hinder guessing or interpretation; text anxiety; a relatively slower speed of test taking that decreases chances of test completion; unfamiliarity with the accepted nuance of test vocabulary; and, possibly, culturally different test-taking strategies. According to Duran,

Neither high school grades nor admissions test scores alone or in combination ought to bear the sole burden of evidence for making decisions to admit Hispanic-background students to college.... Admissions personnel need to be provided with a broader range of information on Hispanics' background, language, and culture in weighing admissions decisions.

Hispanic students rely less on their guidance counsellors and parents for career information than do other groups of students and, instead, resort more frequently to books, magazines, and former students, as well as classroom teachers, librarians and career specialists. Hispanics also tend to be more vulnerable to both the positive and negative influences of school personnel than are middle-class, non-Hispanic White youth. Though research on counselling Hispanics is scarce, existing research indicates that what counsellors fail to do is just as significant as what they do.

In interviews, Puerto Rican students cited counsellors' failure to explain adequately the college-going process as preventing these students from applying to colleges. High schools that are successful in getting Hispanics into college combine a number of strategies:

— High expectations and a strong academic curriculum challenge both teachers and students and have far-reaching effects.
— Early identification of college-bound students enhances chances for better preparation. But early identification should not be rigid, should avoid tracking, and the selection of college-bound students should not be left entirely to school personnel, or be based entirely on test scores and grades. Given a proper explanation of the expectations and responsibilities, students should be allowed to enter the college process at any point in their high school careers.
— A well-developed information system needs to alert students about visits from college recruiters, test deadlines, college days/nights, college fairs, college orientation days, scholarship deadlines, and other events.

Teachers need to be attuned to these activities in order to plan lessons accordingly and to provide assistance whenever necessary. Parents need to be aware in order to provide a role of support and encouragement. And counsellors need to be sensitive to the community's language preference—and to accept the fact that some information may need to be disseminated in both Spanish and English.

— An organised effort to prepare students for standardised testing, college admission, and financial aid application is essential. Students need not only information on deadlines and visits, but an understanding of their importance in getting into college. Activities should be designed to help students successfully complete each step.

— A well-defined role for resource groups, including parents, teachers, college recruiters, ex-students, and community organisations, should be creatively designed to fit the needs of the individual school.

Precollege Guidance and Counselling

Studies show that the greatest determinant of who goes to college is socioeconomic status. Parents and counsellors are the primary influences. The decision is very different for first- and second-generation college entrants. Students who are most likely to depend on the school are those whose parents have not experienced college. Lee and Ekstrom report that 56 percent of public high school students report some counsellor influence; this is particularly true for blacks, females, students in the academic track, and those who plan to attend four-year colleges.

Counsellors play a crucial role in the student's passage through the educational process. They facilitate decision-making and access to appropriate courses and experiences to help students address immediate and long-term goals. In public schools, scheduling and discipline take precedence over precollege counselling in the use of counsellors' time. Though the student to counsellor ratio limits the practical availability of counselling, Chapman and DeMasi indicate that 20 percent of counsellor time is used for college advising and that counsellors report satisfaction with this situation.

In some studies, precollege advising has come under a great deal of criticism. Though students appreciate counsellors' functioning in other spheres, Chapman and others found low-income students indifferent to the counsellor's role in assisting with postsecondary preparation. College advising by the school counsellor is especially important in low-income and minority families where parents are unable to offer first-hand information on college life, selection, and financial aid. Chapman and others and Lee and Ekstrom, however, found that counsellors often devote more time to college-bound, middle- and upper-income white students. Though blacks have significantly more counsellor contacts than others (mostly regarding financial aid), in general, low-income students do not use counsellors as much as other students do.

Family income is the major determinant of the education a student receives. Counsellors are in a position to help overcome the considerable inequities evident in education, provided that school systems give them the support and resources necessary to carry out their responsibilities.

Lee and Ekstrom, on examination of the national longitudinal database in U.S., HIGH SCHOOL AND BEYOND, found differential access to counselling by socioeconomic status, race/ethnicity, aspiration level and ability. Also pertinent were size and location of schools, school resources, and expectations of the community. Access to counselling is thus acting as a social stratifier, possibly magnifying the differences in outcomes of secondary schooling. Students planning to attend college are more likely to seek counselling for planning their high school programmes than are students without aspirations for higher education. Hispanics, whose attrition rate is particularly high and whose expectations of success in completing college are low, make less use of counselling services.

Students who lack access to counselling are more likely to be placed in the nonacademic curriculum track. Counselling for tracking is necessary at the beginning of a student's high school career, and neglect in this area has caused many students, especially minorities and low-income students, to lack adequate preparation for postsecondary education, thus perpetuating a situation of disadvantage. Choice of track is also tied into expectations. Vocational-track students presumably take coursework to match their career plans, but general track students have the least focus in their curricular programmes and require correspondingly more assistance in making wise choices regarding appropriate employment or continuation of education.

The Commission on Precollege Guidance and Counselling recommends that less talented students need to be in more flexible programmes, moving up as competency improves and is demonstrated. Counselling must interpret to all students what is necessary for postsecondary educational access in order to help students overcome socioeconomic barriers.

Guidance Programme Evaluation

To achieve accountability, evaluation is needed concerning the nature, structure, organisation and implementation of school district/building guidance programmes; the school counsellors and other personnel who are implementing the programmes; and the impact the programmes are having on students, the schools where they learn, and the communities in which they live. Thus, the overall evaluation of school district/building guidance programmes needs to be approached from three perspectives: programme evaluation, personnel evaluation, and results evaluation.

Guidance programme evaluation asks two questions. First, is there a written guidance programme in the school district? And second, is the written guidance programme the actual implemented programme in the buildings of the district? Discrepancies between the written programme and the implemented programme, if present, will come into sharp focus as the programme evaluation process unfolds. To conduct programme evaluation, programme standards are required. Programme standards are acknowledged measures of comparison or the criteria used to make judgments about the adequacy of the nature and structure of the programme as well as the degree to which the programme is in place.

To make judgments about guidance programmes using standards, evidence is needed concerning whether or not the standards are being met. In programme evaluation such evidence is called documentation. Using the standard listed above, evidence that the standard is in place might include the following:

1. A developmentally appropriate guidance curriculum that teaches all students the knowledge and skills they need to be self-sufficient and lead socially responsible lives.
2. Yearly schedule that incorporates the classroom guidance plan.

Documentation of such evidence could include:

1. guidance curriculum guides
2. teachers' and counsellors' unit and lesson plans

3. yearly master calendar for the guidance programme
4. curriculum materials

Sometimes the programme evaluation process is called a programme audit. The American School Counsellor Association, for example, uses the "term" audit in its programme evaluation materials. The Association has developed guidelines for a programme audit for secondary schools, for middle/junior high schools, and for elementary schools.

Personnel Evaluation

Personnel evaluation begins with the organisational structure and activities of the guidance programme in a school district. A major first step is the development of job descriptions that are based directly on the structure and activities of a school district's guidance programme.

Using the Missouri Comprehensive Guidance Programme framework for example, the job description of a school counsellor would include the following key duties: implementing the guidance curriculum; counselling individuals and small groups concerning their educational and occupational plans; counselling individuals and small groups with immediate needs and specific problems; consulting with parents and teachers; referring students to appropriate community agencies; coordinating, conducting, and being involved with activities that improve the operation of the school; evaluating and updating the guidance programme; and continuing professional development.

Guidance programme personnel evaluation is based directly on their job task descriptions and usually has two parts: a formative part (supervision) and a summative part (evaluation). The job task description identifies the performance areas to be supervised and evaluated. Gysbers and Henderson have developed an extensive listing of job task descriptors for school counsellors grouped under the basic guidance programme components of guidance curriculum, individual planning, responsive services, and system support plus the areas of professional relationships and professional responsibilities.

Having established that a guidance programme is operating in a school district through programme evaluation, and having established through personnel evaluation that school counsellors and other guidance programme personnel are carrying out the duties listed on their job descriptions 100%

of the time, it now is possible to evaluate the results of the programme. Johnson suggested that there are long-range, intermediate, immediate, and unplanned-for results that need consideration. According to Johnson, long-range results focus on how programmes affect students after they have left school.

Usually long-range results are gathered using follow-up studies. Intermediate results focus on the knowledge and skills all students may gain by graduation from participating in the guidance programme. Immediate results are the knowledge and skills students may gain from participating in specific guidance activities. Finally, the possibility of unplanned-for results that may occur as a consequence of guidance activities conducted as a part of the guidance programme also need to be taken into account.

Immediate Evaluation

Do students master guidance competencies? Johnson outlined the following procedures to answer this question for immediate results. First the competencies to be mastered need to be identified. Second what results (what students should be able to write, what they may be able to talk about, or what they may be able to do) are specified. Then who will conduct the evaluation is decided. This is followed by when the evaluation is done. Then criteria are established so that judgments can be made about students' mastery of guidance competencies. Finally, how all of this is done is specified.

Do students master guidance competencies? Another way to conduct immediate evaluation, to measure mastery of guidance competencies, is the use of a confidence survey. In this format, guidance competencies are listed and students are asked to rate how confident they are that they have mastered these competencies. The confidence survey can then be used as a pre-post measure. Gain scores can be obtained and related to such measures as academic achievement and vocational identity.

Intermediate Evaluation

Do students develop and use career plans? In making judgments concerning the career plans of students, criteria need to be identified as to what makes good plans. Four criteria are recommended; plans need to be comprehensive, developmental, student-centered and student-directed, and competency based. Based on these criteria, one way to evaluate students' career plans is to judge the extent to which the activities included in the Individual Planning Component of the guidance programme lead to the development of plans that meet these criteria. A second way is to make judgments about the adequacy of the plan contents. Finally, a third way is to judge their use.

References

Cerbin, W., (1992), *A learning centered course portfolio for educational psychology*, Unpublished manuscript.

Eggen, P., & Kauchak, D., "The teaching of educational psychology: A research agenda", *Paper presented at annual meeting of the American Educational Research Association*, San Francisco.

Sherman, L., (1995), "A post modern, constructivist pedagogy for teaching Educational Psychology, assisted by computer mediated communications", *Paper presentation to the CSCL95 Conference*, Bloomington Indiana.

8

Mental Health Services for Students

Good mental health is important for everyone. Mental health is as important as physical health to our quality of life. Mental health is not simply the absence of mental illness, but also means having the skills necessary to cope with life's challenges. If ignored, mental health problems can interfere with children's learning, development, relationships, and physical health.

School psychologists are mental health professionals who help children and youth overcome barriers to success in school, at home, and in life.

All youngsters face mental health issues from time to time. According to studies, one in five children and adolescents will experience a significant mental health problem during their school years. Some problems are more serious than others, but all children face challenges that can affect their learning and behavior. These can include:

- Stress and anxiety
- Worries about being bullied
- Problems with family or friends
- Loneliness or rejection
- Disabilities
- Depression
- Thoughts of suicide or hurting others
- Concerns about sexuality
- Academic difficulties

— Dropping out
— Alcohol and substance abuse
— Fear of violence, terrorism and war

School psychologists can help prevent or reduce the immediate and long-term effects of children's mental health problems.

Children are remarkably resilient when they get the help they need. Children and youth thrive when they feel safe and supported. Parents and teachers sometimes need help in their effort to provide a system of support that meets each child's individual needs. Effective support systems include:

— Love and encouragement of parents and family
— Guidance of teachers and other important adults
— Consistent expectations and support
— Access to mental health and other helping professionals
— Services that respect and respond to personal and cultural differences
— School psychologists support parents and teachers in their efforts to help children to achieve their best.

Mental health services for children and youth must be accessible. Schools are ideal settings to provide mental health services to children and youth. Virtually every community has a school and most youngsters spend six hours a day there with trained, caring professionals.

The school environment is:

— Tailored to learning and development
— A natural context for prevention and intervention
— Connected to community resources
— Familiar and accessible to students and parents
— Designed to promote communication between home and school

School psychologists provide mental health services that address needs at home and school to help students succeed academically, emotionally, and socially.

School psychologists are specially trained to link mental health to learning and behavior. School psychologists work in schools, clinics, and other health and education settings. They are often the only school mental health professionals trained in child psychology, learning, and development as well as school systems and classroom environments. They use research and results based strategies to promote:

— Good mental health
— High academic achievement
— Positive social skills and behavior
— Tolerance and respect for others
— Safe, supportive learning environments

School psychologists work with parents, educators, and other mental health services providers to help youngsters develop resiliency, competence, and self-esteem.

School psychologists work to find the best solution for each child and each situation. School psychologists use many different strategies to address individual student needs, as well as enhance systems that support students on the school building and district-wide levels. They lower barriers to healthy learning and behavior through:

— Intervention/Treatment to help children and youth overcome mental health problems.
— Help families and schools deal with crisis and loss
— Work directly with children and families to address barriers to academic and social success
— Help students develop skills to solve conflicts and problems independently
— Teach students social skills, self-management, and coping strategies
— Consult with teachers on classroom interventions
— Prevention/Early Intervention to prevent or minimize the occurrence of mental health problems.
— Work with parents and educators to create positive school environments
— Increase awareness of mental health stressors and strategies
— Teach parents and educators skills to address behavior problems
— Screen for mental health and learning problems
— Develop suicide awareness and prevention programs
— Develop school-wide programs to prevent bullying and aggression
— Foster tolerance and understanding of diversity

Assessment/Diagnosis to provide accurate information on the nature of a child's problem and the best approach to address it. School psychologists use individual, group, and systems level tools to evaluate:

— Psychological and social competence
— Personality and emotional development
— Academic skills and learning aptitudes
— School climate related to positive behaviors and learning
— Effectiveness of intervention strategies
— Consultation/Case Management to promote more effective, coordinated support for children's mental health needs.
— Advocate for the needs of individual students both within and outside of the school setting
— Help teachers and parents understand and effectively address a child's problem
— Help families access community resources
— Facilitate coordination between parents, schools, and community services
— Establish and review outcomes of interventions
— Adjust strategies to improve outcomes
— Advocacy/Interagency Collaboration to promote research-based public policies and programs that improve academic and social outcomes for children and youth.
— Develop and maintain collaborative relationships with community mental health services
— Develop coordinated school/community crisis response
— Consult with policymakers on and advocate for mental health and education legislation
— Seek funding for integrated school/community services
— Link research-based practices to mental health policies and programs
— Provide in-service training for parents, educators, and community members
— School psychologists conduct research and develop "best practices" to support the mental health needs of children and youth.

Counselling for Gifted Students

The concept of an underachieving gifted student may seem inherently contradictory if intellectually gifted students are seen only as those who excel in school at high levels of academic achievement. However, since the new federal definition was formulated in the early 1970s, there has been growing support in the field for defining intellectual giftedness as exceptional potential for high academic achievement, whether or not it has been demonstrated at school. It is assumed that the gifted underachiever has exceptional potential. A student may be gifted in one or many areas of learning or cognitive processing; however, few mentally gifted students have the capability of truly excelling in all subjects and on all kinds of academic tasks.

Gifted underachievers manifest three patterns of behavioural responses to the school setting:

(a) non-communicative and withdrawn,

(b) passively complying to "get by," and

(c) aggressive/disruptive "problem" students.

Behaviour patterns of all three groups tend to reflect feelings of low self-esteem, a lack of belief in their ability to influence outcomes in school, an unrealistic self-concept, and negative attitudes toward school. Generally, these students tend to be loners who have difficulty making or maintaining friendships.

Increasing numbers of intellectually gifted students who have not been recognised and served as gifted because of relatively low patterns of achievement have been discovered over the last two decades as a result of three significant changes in educational practices. First, there has been an increase in the use of tests and sophisticated assessment procedures. Second, there has been an increase in teacher referrals for special education services because of learning or behavioural problems. Third, there has been an increased effort to recognise and develop the potential abilities of culturally different and minority children.

Gifted underachievers are also identified as a result of parental accounts of out-of-school behaviours that show advanced interests and skills. The most disconcerting group of gifted underachievers are those who are not recognised while in school. Awareness of this group has developed primarily through the identification of adults with superior intellectual abilities whose school records show mediocre or poor academic performance.

Identification of Gifted Underachievers

The first reason is obvious—the loss of potential contributions to society from that individual. The second reason is not so obvious—the underachiever's vulnerability to significant mental health and social problems. Often the gifted underachiever becomes a disturbing behavioural problem both at home and at school. This problem is a natural consequence of the conflict between the individual's personal psychological needs and the lack of opportunities for appropriate learning provided by the school. The third reason is that early identification permits a better chance for reversing patterns of underachievement.

Causes of Underachievement

— Lack of motivation. Many highly gifted and creative children have learning styles that are incompatible with prevailing instructional methods. Furthermore, the level of instruction may be inappropriate for these students and the restrictions on learning in the classroom discourage their full participation.

— Values Conflict. Students may not want to participate in school because of conflicts between the values of the school or the gifted programme and the values held by the individuals and/or the cultures from which they come; for example, female students from cultures in which a college education or a career is not expected may underachieve.

— Lack of environmental nurturance of intelluctual potential. Low socioeconomic status families often fail to provide exposure that stimulates the development of higher level thinking skills. Enriching experiences such as travel, educational activities, and shared problem solving may be neglected. Such students may be from isolated rural settings, economically disadvantaged urban sites, or specific ethnic or cultural minorities that do not encourage intellectual development.

— Developmental delays or chronic poor health. These students are characterised by relatively low energy levels or interfering hyperactivity. They may have a mild delay in perceptual motor skill development, or a general immaturity in all areas. Often these students have entered school as the youngest in their class.

— Specific disabilities. Impairment due to specific learning disabilities, brain damage/cerebral dysfunction or neurological impairment, or lack of normal hearing or visual perception may be the cause of underachievement. Some of these students are in fact dyslexic or neurologically disabled. It is not the disability that produces that underachievement but the lack of appropriate programming. These students frequently are not adequately challenged or encouraged to develop their intellectual abilities because of low expectations and a narrow curriculum.

— Specific or general academic skill conflicts. These students may have difficulty with writing, reading, math, or higher level skills necessary for subject matter mastery and high achievement.

Successful approaches to reversing patterns of underachievement have been based on a view that the problem behaviour has been shaped by forces within the school experience that can be altered. These forces essentially are:

(a) the social messages conveyed by the teacher and peers that invite or discourage the student to participate and

(b) the degree to which the curriculum and instruction is appropriate for the learning style and performance level of the student. Successful interventions create positive forces to shape achievement behaviour.

Programming for gifted underachievers must address three critical areas:

(a) an understanding of self—the nature of and problems related to being gifted;

(b) development of constructive ways of coping with the inevitable conflict and frustration created by the significant gap between cognitive ability and performance level; and

(c) development of a healthier, more realistic self-concept and higher self-esteem.

Effective programming for reversing patterns of underachievement can occur in self-contained classrooms, in resource rooms that provide supplementary services, or through the development of an individual educational plan that may involve a mentor in the school or community. Regardless of the structure, there are five programming components that need to be addressed:

1. The teacher(s) must accept the fact that the student is intellectually gifted, does not want to underachieve or fail, has low self-esteem, and

needs to develop constructive coping skills and self-understanding. The teacher(s) must be skilled in guidance techniques, accurate in understanding the nature of giftedness, and positive in emotional response to the challenge of working with this type of student.

2. The curriculum must be challenging, personally meaningful, and rewarding to the gifted underachiever. There must be a balance between basic skill development and more advanced exploration through the arts and sciences. Career exploration and the development of personal interests are also critical motivating elements, and all learning experiences should be designed for maximum challenge and success.
3. The instruction must require minimal memorisation and drill/practice activity and provide maximal opportunity for inquiry, scientific investigation, and creative production. Self-directed learning activities should be encouraged and the students' self-discipline nurtured. The climate created by the instructional style of the teacher should be one of excitement, anticipation, personal satisfaction, and low pressure.
4. The peer group must include at least a few other gifted students, possibly other underachievers, who may become special friends. The group must be accepting of diversity and individual differences.
5. Special services should be provided as needed for handicapped students, for those in need of remedial instruction, or for group counselling. Supplementary psychological and medical services, including family counselling, may also be needed.

Stress Management

Many gifted youngsters have a heightened sensitivity to their surroundings, to events, to ideas, and to expectations. Some experience their own high expectations for achievement as a relentless pressure to excel. Constant striving to live up to self-expectations—or those of others—to be first, best, or both can be very stressful. With every new course, new teacher, or new school, questions arise about achievement and performance, since every new situation carries with it the frightening risk of being mediocre.

Striving becomes even more stressful when unrealistic or unclear expectations are imposed by adults or peers. The pressure to excel, accompanied by other concerns such as feeling different, self-doubt (the "imposter" syndrome), and the need to prove their giftedness can drain the energy of gifted students and result in additional stress. Stress occurs even when everything is going well. Youngsters get tired from their constant efforts and may secretly fear that next time they will not be as successful.

Many gifted students accept responsibility for a variety of activities such as a demanding courseload; leadership in school activities, clubs, or sports; and part-time jobs. Even if it were humanly possible, doing everything well would be physically and emotionally stressful. Vacations may be stressful if students are comfortable only when achieving and succeeding. Taking time off may make them feel nervous and lacking control.

Gifted students need intellectual challenge. Boring, monotonous busy-work is very stressful for individuals who prefer thinking and reasoning activities. Boredom may result in anger, resentment, or, in some cases, setting personal goals for achievement and success that significantly exceed those of parents or school. Some gifted students value independence and leadership, yet the separation they feel from their peers results in loneliness and fewer opportunities to relieve stress. Finding a peer group can be difficult, particularly for adolescents. Some experience a conflict between belonging to a group and using their extraordinary abilities.

Gifted students are complex thinkers, persuasively able to argue both sides of any question. This ability, however, may complicate decisions. Students may lack information about and experience with resources, processes, outcomes, or priorities that help tip an argument toward a clear solution. Furthermore, not every problem has one obviously correct answer. Compromise and accommodation are realities in the adult world, but they are not easily perceived from a young person's viewpoint. Thus, decision making may be a very stressful process.

During the early years, school may be easy, with minimum effort required for success. If students are not challenged, they conclude that "giftedness" means instant learning, comprehension, and mastery, and that outstanding achievement follows naturally. As years pass, however, schoolwork becomes more difficult. Some students discover that they must work harder to earn top grades and that they have not developed productive study habits.

Many suspect they are no longer gifted, and their sense of self-worth is undermined. Stress can hamper the very abilities that make these students gifted. Stress clouds thinking, reduces concentration, and impairs decision making. It leads to forgetfulness and a loss of ability to focus keenly on a task, and it makes students overly sensitive to criticism. Under these conditions, they perform less well and are more upset by their failures.

Abundant gifts and the potential for success in many different subjects and careers may increase opportunities and lead to complex choices. Limiting options is a confusing and upsetting process because it means saying "no" to some attractive alternatives. A person cannot prepare to become an architect and a financial planner, or an advertising executive and a scientist. At some point, the education needed for one career splits from that needed for the other. To set career goals, students must know themselves well as individuals. They must understand their own personalities, values, and goals and use self-awareness as a guide for making decisions. These activities are all stressful. Some ways of coping with stress are healthy; others are not. Some healthy ways of handling stress include the following:

— Change the source of the stress. Do something else for a while. Put down those study notes and jog for an hour.
— Confront the source of the stress. If it is a person, persuade him or her to remove the stress. Ask the teacher for an extension on a project. Sit down with the person driving you crazy and talk about ways you might better work together.
— Talk about the source of stress. Rid yourself of frustration. Find a good listener and complain. Talk through possible solutions.
— Shift your perspective. Tell yourself that each new situation or problem is a new challenge, and that there is something to be learned from every experience.

Learn skills and attitudes that make tasks easier and more successful. Practice effective organisation and time-management skills. For example, large projects are easier and less overwhelming when broken down into manageable steps. Learn to type and revise assignments on a word processor. Learn about yourself and your priorities, and use the information to make decisions. Learn how to say "no" gracefully when someone offers you another attractive (or unpleasant) task about which you have a choice. Tell yourself that this unpleasantness will be over soon and that the whole process will bring you closer to reaching your goal. Mark the days that are left on the calendar, and enjoy crossing out each one as you near the finish.

Take time out for enjoyable activities. Everyone needs a support system. Find friends, teachers, or relatives with whom you have fun. Spend time with these people when you can be yourself and set aside the pressures of school, work, or difficult relationships. As a reward for your efforts, give yourself work breaks. Listen to your favourite music, shoot baskets, or participate in some other brief activity that is mentally restful or fun.

Ignore the source of the stress. Practice a little healthy procrastination and put a pleasant activity ahead of the stressful one. This, is, of course, only a short-term solution. Get regular physical exercise and practice sound nutrition. Physical activity not only provides time out, but also changes your body chemistry as you burn off muscle tension built up from accommodating stress. Exercise also increases resistance to illness.

Nutritious food and regular meals help regulate your body chemistry and keep you functioning at your sharpest. Eating healthy and attractively prepared food can be an enjoyable activity on its own. The following are some unhealthy ways students cope with stress:

— Escaping through alcohol, drugs, frequent illness, sleep, overeating, or starving themselves. These strategies suggest a permanent withdrawal or avoidance rather than a time out.

— Selecting strategies to avoid failure. Gifted students closely link their identities to excellence and achievement. Failure, or even the perception of failure, seriously threatens their self-esteem. By not trying, or by selecting impossible goals, students can escape having their giftedness questioned. Only their lack of effort will be questioned.

— Aiming too low. This reduces stress by eliminating intense pressure or possible feelings of failure. Dogged procrastination in starting projects, selecting less competitive colleges or less rigorous courses, or dropping out of school rather than bringing home poor grades allows students to avoid feelings of failure in the short run. Sadly, this sets the stage for long term disappointment caused by a destructive coping style.

— Overscheduling daily life with schoolwork and extracurricular activities, selecting impossibly demanding courseloads, or fussing endlessly over assignments in vain attempts to make them perfect. With this strategy, it is possible to succeed only through superhuman effort; thus the student can save face by setting goals too high for anyone to achieve.

Not all gifted youngsters are stressed by the same events. Individual responses to stress also differ. Younger students do not tend to respond to stress in the same way that teenagers do. Since each student is unique, parents and teachers will have to watch carefully to know whether a child is stressed to the point of constructive excitement or to the point of damaging overload. The following checklist includes many, but not all, symptoms of burnout:

- Student is no longer happy or pleasantly excited about school activities, but, rather, is negative or cynical toward work, teachers, classmates, parents, and the whole school- and achievement-centered experience.
- Student approaches most school assignments with resignation or resentment.
- Student exhibits boredom.
- Student suffers from sleeplessness, problems in falling asleep, or periodic waking.
- Student overreacts to normal concerns or events.
- Student experiences fatigue, extreme tiredness, low energy level.
- Student exhibits unhappiness with self and accomplishments.
- Student has nervous habits such as eye blinking, head shaking, or stuttering.
- Student has physical ailments such as weekly or daily stomachaches or headaches.
- Student is frequently ill.
- Student exhibits dependency through increased clinging or needing and demanding constant support and reassurance.
- Student engages in attention-getting behaviours such as aggressive or acting-out behaviours.
- Student has a sense of being trapped or a feeling or being out of control.
- Student is unable to make decisions.
- Student has lost perspective and sense of humour.
- Student experiences increased feelings of physical, emotional, and mental exhaustion in work and activities that used to give pleasure.

Role of Parents, Teachers and Counsellors for Stress Reduction

Help each gifted student understand and cope with his or her intellectual, social, and emotional needs during each stage of development. In some ways, the needs of gifted students mirror those of more typical children. Giftedness, however, adds a special dimension to self-understanding and self-acceptance. If gifted youngsters are to develop into self-fulfilled adults, the following differential needs must be addressed:

(a) the need to understand the ways in which they are different from others and the ways in which they are the same;

(b) the need to accept their abilities, talents, and limitations;

(c) the need to develop social skills;

(d) the need to feel understood and accepted by others; and

(e) the need to develop an understanding of the distinction between "pursuit of excellence" and "pursuit of perfection."

Help each gifted student develop a realistic and accurate self-concept. Giftedness does not mean instant mastery or winning awards. Parents and teachers need to set realistic expectations for efforts and achievements and help the student choose appropriate goals. It is important to recognise and appreciate efforts and improvement. On the other hand, giftedness permits people to learn and use information in unusual ways.

Given parental support and encouragement, personal motivation, and opportunities to learn and apply their knowledge, gifted students may enjoy the process of creating new ideas, especially if they believe that it is all right to think differently than age-mates. Help each gifted student be a whole person. Gifted youngsters are children first and gifted second. While their learning styles may be special, they are individuals with emotions, likes and dislikes, and unique personalities. They will not wake up one day and be "not gifted." They should not feel responsible for solving world problems, nor does the world owe them tribute. It is up to each student to make life meaningful. Understanding these realistic limits to the bounty of giftedness can reduce stress on confused students. Gifted students have strong emotions that give personal meaning to each experience. Emotions should be recognised, understood, and used as a valid basis for appropriate behaviours.

Show patience. Let students select and strive toward their own goals. Do not compare them or their achievements to others. Some gifted students are intensely curious and may have less tolerance for ambiguity and unpredictability than their age-mates. Help them develop patience with themselves.

Show acceptance and encouragement. Encourage students to work purposefully, thoughtfully, and thoroughly and do the best they can. It is not necessary to excel in every situation. Help them develop priorities to decide which tasks require the best efforts and which require simply "good enough." Accept and reward efforts and the process of working on tasks. Sincere effort is valuable in itself and deserves reinforcement. The means may be more deserving of merit than the ends.

Efforts are within the gifted students' control; the outcomes (high grades, prizes, honors, etc.) are not. Show love and acceptance, regardless of the outcome. These youngsters need to be cherished as individuals, not simply for their accomplishments. They must know that they can go home and be loved—and continue to love themselves—even when they do not finish first or best. Encourage flexibility and appropriate behaviour. Curiosity is frequently mentioned as a characteristic of gifted learners.

Many individuals agree that gifted students seem to question rules automatically, asking "How come?" Concerned adults can reduce stress on gifted students by helping them distinguish between hard-and-fast rules that should be followed and those that can safely be questioned or altered and helping them understand why rules sometimes change from time to time. Many people recognise that new ideas come from reshaping and discarding old notions of right and wrong and want students to be inquiring, creative, and resourceful thinkers. But society, schools, teachers, and academic subjects have rules.

In our society, flagrant rule breakers may be penalised and shut out of opportunities for further growth and enrichment. Our students will become better thinkers by learning that rules are man-made guides to behaviour, not perfect or divine, but they are to be learned, understood, and followed appropriately in certain situations. For instance, not every student will like every teacher, but showing respect is appropriate behaviour even if the student privately thinks otherwise. Wise adults can model problem-solving methods that result in workable solutions and help gifted students learn when and how to use their novel perceptions, creativity, and independent thoughts appropriately and effectively.

Understanding and following rules does not mean conforming to every situation. There are some occasions when gifted students should not be expected to accommodate others. For example, a severe mismatch between a youngster's ability level and a school programme may be very stressful. Altering the student's curriculum may solve the problem. Some parents unintentionally send mixed messages regarding behaviour. When children are rude or uncooperative and offend teachers, other adults, or peers, their parents behave as though giftedness somehow excuses such behaviour and the offending actions highlight their child's specialness. Some even seem pleased.

These parents do their children a great disservice by denying them the opportunity to learn empathy, teamwork, and tolerance for individual differences. Let students live their own lives. Caring adults support, encourage, and celebrate students' efforts and successes, but they stand back a bit from these efforts and achievements. They let students select and master activities for personal enjoyment. Unfortunately, some students wonder whether their efforts and gains are for personal satisfaction or to please overly involved parents, teachers, or others. When these students wish to give up an activity that no longer brings pleasure or interest, they fear they will disappoint others, and they are likely to feel trapped.

Be available for guidance and advice. Some gifted students appear to be more mature than their chronological age indicates. They have advanced verbal skills and can talk a good line. Nevertheless, they are still children and need realistic, clearly stated guidelines about limits, values, and proper behaviour. These young people may not have enough information or experience to make wise and effective decisions. They may not understand decision-making processes, and they need wise adults to listen and guide as they talk through the problem, the alternatives, and the pro's and con's and try out choices.

Knowing that they can be independent and still talk through their thoughts with others without losing face reduces stress for these students. Gifted students need to hear adults openly state some of their perspectives to understand expectations and acceptable limits. While these students are very perceptive, they cannot read minds. Gifted students may know more facts about their interest area than do their parents and other adults. However, they have not lived longer; they need loving concern and guidance.

Attention Deficit Hyperactivity Disorder (ADHD)

Gifted children whose attention deficits are identified later may be at risk for developing learned helplessness and chronic underachievement. ADHD children whose giftedness goes unrecognised do not receive appropriate educational services. It is recommended that children who fail to meet test score criteria for giftedness and are later diagnosed with ADHD be retested for the gifted programme. As a group, ADHD children tend to lag two to three years behind their age peers in social and emotional maturity.

Gifted ADHD children are no exception. This finding has important implications for educational placement. As a group, gifted children without ADHD tend to be more similar in their cognitive, social, and emotional development to children two to four years older than children their own age. When placed with other high ability children without the disorder, ADHD children may find the advanced maturity of their classmates a challenge they are ill prepared for.

Also, gifted children without the disorder may have little patience for the social and emotional immaturity of the gifted ADHD student in their midst. This is not to say that gifted ADHD students should not be placed with other gifted students. The research is clear that lack of intellectual challenge and little access to others with similar interests, ability, and drive are often risk factors for gifted children, contributing to social or emotional problems.

It is difficult to differentiate true attention deficits from the range of temperament and behaviour common to gifted children. There is concern in the literature that clinicians err on the side of pathologising normal gifted behaviour. Common characteristics of gifted children can be misconstrued as indicators of pathology when the observer is unfamiliar with the differences in the development of gifted children. This difficulty can be exacerbated when the gifted child in question spends considerable time in a classroom where appropriate educational services are not provided.

The intensity, drive, perfectionism, curiosity, and impatience commonly seen in gifted children may, in some instances, be mistaken for indicators of ADHD. The creatively gifted child may appear to be oppositional, hyperactive, and argumentative. Gifted children with some kinds of undiagnosed learning disabilities will be very disorganised, messy, and have difficult social relations. Ideally, a diagnosis of ADHD in gifted children should be made by a multidisciplinary team that includes at least one clinician trained in differentiating childhood psychopathologies and one professional who understands the normal range of developmental characteristics of gifted children.

Since as many as two thirds of children with ADHD have coexisting conditions such as learning disabilities or depression, assessment must include an evaluation for these disorders as well. School personnel rarely have the training needed to differentially diagnose ADHD, and few clinicians are aware of the unique developmental characteristics of gifted children. Accurate assessment must be a team effort. One of the reasons parents may be hesitant to comply with treatment recommendations for their children is because they aren't convinced their child has the disorder. Parents want a thorough evaluation, and parents of gifted children want assurance that their child's giftedness has been taken into consideration when evaluations are conducted. When parents see that their child has been properly evaluated, they may be more willing to participate in a treatment plan.

Attention Deficit Disorder without Hyperactivity (ADD)

Attention Deficit Disorder without Hyperactivity (ADD) or with Hyperactivity (ADHD) continues to be a misunderstood diagnosis by many. Some parents and teachers still hold a perception that the label simply provides an excuse for disruptive behaviour; however, studies continue to support a biochemical or organic basis to the disorder. Presentation of symptoms can be affected by family interactions, school expectations, and other demands placed on the individual child. Part of the reason that attention deficit is usually diagnosed in school age children (e.g., first to third grade) is attributable to the demands placed on the child when beginning school (American Psychiatric Association [APA]).

The structure at school differs from that in the home or preschool environment. Typical predisposing factors within the individual, as well as in the family history, are being identified in the literature. For example, a history of alcoholism, smoking, or depression in parents can be predisposing factors. Certain physiological markers, such as frequent early ear infections, have also been associated with the presentation of attention deficit.

Physical complications can be a factor in the development of language and reading disabilities that are associated with attention deficit for between 45% and 60% of those diagnosed. Attention Deficit Disorder presents in a slightly different way for each individual, partially due to the factors noted above. Although there is a cluster of symptoms usually associated with the disorder, the individual presentation can be just as varied as the predisposing factors.

Diagnosis in children and adults is usually made by history, self-report, and observation from significant others in the person's life. Central to diagnosis in children are the symptoms in the general areas of inattention, impulsivity, and hyperactivity. In adults, the most prominent symptom is inattention.

Symptoms of attention deficit can be mimicked by emotional disorders, e.g., reaction to abuse, depression or anxiety. If therapy is not successful in addressing underlying emotional concerns, medication may be used with positive results just as in the case of more classic symptoms of ADHD. In those cases where early abuse or neglect has been instrumental in affecting the neurology of the individual, the actual outcome, and thus treatment, may not differ significantly from other cases of ADHD. Difficulty sleeping is often seen with attention deficit, particularly for those with hyperactivity. Sleep problems can also be exacerbated by medication use.

Other disorders may co-occur with Attention Deficit Disorder. Those commonly observed include: Tourette's, Obsessive-Compulsive Disorder, Depression, Autism, Oppositional Defiant Disorder (ODD), or Conduct Disorder (CD). The relationship between ADHD, ODD, and CD is often presented on a continuum or as a progressive relationship. Symptoms of ADHD often present initially, followed by ODD, and ultimately CD for a small percentage of those with initial attention problems. Individual characteristics, family factors, and life experiences all interact to push some individuals through this continuum to more serious behavioural concerns.

The comorbidity of other disorders or symptoms often makes successful treatment more difficult. Other features of ADHD include differences in level of executive functioning between those who present with hyperactivity and those who do not. Deficits in executive functioning are associated with greater hyperactivity and impulsivity. These differences in executive functioning include an inability to self-monitor and self-control. Prevalence estimates for ADHD and ADD are between 3 to 7% of school age children.

Treatment

Effective treatment usually combines medication and therapy, including behavioural interventions aimed at increasing structure at home and school. Parents and teachers are active participants in successful treatment efforts. Stimulants are the most commonly used medications, with some use of anti-depressants, for co-morbid conditions of depression and anxiety. Other interventions include parent training and family therapy, individual therapy, support groups, and social skills training.

Providing structure for these individuals, and helping children learn to provide structure for themselves, are at the core of successful interventions. Although medication is often part of a successful treatment approach, school personnel are usually not directly involved in recommending a prescription. Diagnoses and prescriptions can only be provided by the family physician, pediatrician, or psychiatrist. Even the process of referral can expose a school to liability for financial responsibility, so the counsellor needs to be aware of the manner in which any conversation about medication or referral takes place.

Role of Counsellor

The counsellor's role in enhancing the academic performance of students with ADD or ADHD often involves consultation with teachers around classroom interventions, as well as providing support and education to parents. In addition to basic behavioural interventions, coping skills, social skills, and self-monitoring skills are important tools that can be reviewed through various modalities, including individual counselling, group sessions, or classroom guidance modules.

Providing workshops in the evening with separate sessions for parents and children can be a resource welcomed by parents. Such efforts may be jointly offered with community support groups. Parents often need information about appropriate expectations for behaviour and school work, positive parenting techniques, and support groups at the school or in the community, such as CHADD (a support group for children and adults with attention deficit disorder). For example, a counselling newsletter to parents can provide descriptions of ADD, such as the fact that disruptive behaviours observed at school may not be observed at home, or that behaviour can be inconsistent—at times under the child's control, and impulsive at others.

Information and support can help parents in making the decision to seek an evaluation. Typical challenges for students with ADD or ADHD include:

1) organisational problems;
2) problems with transitions;
3) acting as if rules don't apply to them;
4) adopting a negative attitude out of frustration in academic tasks, social interactions, or as a defence against low self esteem;
5) experiencing isolation or exclusion from peers;
6) poor grades as a result of rushing through assignments, incomplete work, or distractibility in class;
7) impulsive behaviour;
8) difficulty sustaining attention;
9) different learning styles; or
10) disruption of sleep or appetite, as a result of ADD or medication.

These students often describe feeling bored at school, and may appear oppositional. Motivation around academic tasks or conforming to rules can be a challenge for these students. A simple intervention that has proven successful includes "chunking" or organising assignments into smaller sections. This makes successful completion a more likely outcome, and if applied to in-class assignments, allows the student a legitimate reason to get up and walk to the teacher's desk. Even such a small amount of movement can help discharge energy that is so critical for these students.

It is for this reason that a common consequence for not completing homework (i.e., losing recess) is actually counter-productive with overactive children. It is also important to remember the lack of self-monitoring ability as being central for many of these individuals. Teachers and parents can help children and adolescents develop this skill. Mechanisms to increase self-awareness include external monitoring systems such as checklists in the classroom.

Additionally, the teacher can provide verbal cues such as asking the class to, "Stop and check—where is your mind?" Or the teacher can use physical monitoring cues for particular students, e.g., a simple tap on the shoulder to help them self-monitor. These cues are general enough to ensure that students don't feel ostracised by their use.

Depression in Children

Within the past three decades, it has become evident that mood disorders are common among children and adolescents. In children and adolescents, the most frequently diagnosed mood disorders are major depressive disorder, dysthymic disorder, and bipolar disorder. These are briefly described below.

Major Depressive Disorder: Major depressive disorder is a serious condition characterised by one or more major depressive episodes. In children and adolescents, an episode lasts an average of seven to nine months. Depressed children are sad and lose interest in activities they used to enjoy. They feel unloved, pessimistic, or even hopeless; they think that life is not worth living; and they may think about or threaten suicide. They are often irritable, which may lead to disruptive or aggressive behaviour. They may be indecisive, have problems concentrating, and lack energy or motivation. They may neglect appearance and hygiene, and their normal eating and sleeping patterns may be disturbed.

Dysthymic Disorder: Dysthymic disorder has fewer symptoms, but is more persistent. The child or adolescent is depressed for most of the day on most days, and symptoms may continue for several years, the average dysthymic period being approximately four years. Seventy percent of children and adolescents with dysthymia eventually experience an episode of major depression. When this combination of major depression and dysthymia occurs, the condition is referred to as double depression.

Bipolar Disorder: In bipolar disorder, episodes of depression alternate with episodes of mania. The depressive episode usually comes first, with the first manic features becoming evident months or even years later. Adolescents with mania feel energetic and confident; may have difficulty sleeping but do not tire; and talk a great deal, often speaking very loudly or rapidly. They may complain of racing thoughts. They may do schoolwork quickly and creatively, but in a chaotic, disorganised way. In the manic stage, they may have exaggerated or even delusional ideas about their capabilities and importance, become overconfident, and be uninhibited with others. They may engage in reckless behaviour (e.g., fast driving or unsafe sex). Sexual preoccupations are increased and may be associated with promiscuous behaviour.

Approximately two-thirds of children and adolescents with major depressive disorder also have another mental disorder, such as anxiety disorder, conduct disorder, oppositional defiant disorder, psychoactive substance abuse or dependence, or phobias. Authorities have also noted that children with medical problems often face extreme and/or chronic stress, which places them at risk for depression. Estimates of depression among youngsters with medical problems range from 7% in general medical patients to 23% in orthopedic patients.

Depression has also been linked to a variety of other medical conditions, including endocrinopathies and metabolic disorders (e.g., diabetes and hypoglycemia), viral infections (e.g., influenza, viral hepatitis, and viral pneumonia), rheumatoid arthritis, cancer, central nervous system disorders, metal intoxications, and disabling diseases of all kinds. Some of these conditions may be temporary, but some may be diagnosed as primary disabilities in youngsters with health impairments.

Depression and Suicide

A number of studies have confirmed that children and adolescents with depression are at high risk for suicidal behaviour. Because mood disorders substantially increase the risk of suicide, suicidal behaviour is a matter of serious concern for parents, educators, and clinicians who deal with the mental health problems of children and adolescents. Over 90% of children and adolescents who commit suicide have a mental disorder.

The precise causes of depression are not known. Research on adults with depression generally points to both biological and psychosocial factors, but there has been considerably less research on children and adolescents.

— *Family and genetic factors*: Between 20% and 50% of depressed children and adolescents have a family history of depression. It is not clear whether the relationship between parent and childhood depression derives from genetic factors or if depressed parents create an environment in which children are more likely to develop mental disorders.

— *Biological factors*: Biochemical and physiological correlates of depression have been studied by medical researchers, with results that generally point to a chemical imbalance in the brain as a causal factor. Most of these studies have been conducted with adults, so the findings may not apply to children and adolescents.

— *Cognitive factors*: For several decades there has been considerable interest in the relationship between a pessimistic mindset and a predisposition to depression. Pessimistic individuals generally react more passively, helplessly, and ineffectively to negative events than optimistic individuals. The specific origins of pessimistic mindset have not been established but are topics of current research interest.

Recent research has focused on the development and validation of checklists and protocols to be used by mental health professionals along with clinical interviews and medical tests. An accurate diagnosis of depression is a complex task, extremely difficult for even highly skilled physicians and other clinicians. It requires a careful examination of physical, mental, emotional, environmental, and cultural factors related to the child or adolescent, his/ her family, and the environment. Teachers, counsellors, and other school personnel are not expected to diagnose depression in young people; the major roles of educators are to detect the symptoms of depression and make appropriate referrals.

Treatment

Treatment approaches for children and adolescents include psychosocial interventions (e.g., cognitive behaviour therapy) and medication, as well as traditional psychotherapy. Two forms of cognitive therapy (i.e., self-control therapy for prepubertal children and coping skills for adolescents) have been judged as probably effective. A number of medications are commonly prescribed for children and adolescents with depression, but many of these have not yet been subjected to sufficient study. Effective treatment requires intervention by both medical and mental health professionals, with support from all others who come in contact with the young person; and is therefore not within the purview of the school alone.

School Intervention

The educator's most important contribution is the provision of a positive and supportive environment, components of which include satisfaction of basic needs, caring relationships with adults, and physical and psychological security. Any inclusion in a student's programme that serves to enhance feelings of self-worth, self-control, and optimism has the potential for ameliorating feelings of depression. Aversive techniques (e. g., punishment and "get tough" approaches) should be avoided to the extent possible. Educators must use instructional strategies that are both positive and effective so that the student will achieve success and enjoy the learning process.

Examples include direct instruction with positive reinforcement, thematic instrucional units with varied levels of classroom assignments, learning strategies (e. g., mnemonic devices) and utilisation of the principles of universal design for leaning, which promote access to the general curriculum for students with learning problems. Some protective factors have been addressed in published curicula (e. g., preventing alienation, enhancing self-esteem, and learning self-control). Other interventions that have implications for school programmes (e. g., phototherapy and exercise) have been found to have value in reducing symptoms of depression in adults, but have not yet been subjected to sufficient study with children and adolescents.

Problems of Disabled Students

Career and technical education (CTE) can provide significant benefits to disabled students. CTE teachers need to be aware of the rights of students with disabilities and of the planning process involved in meeting their needs. In addition, CTE teachers must know what role they play both in planning and in providing instruction. CTE teachers often need background information on the details of disabilities and the accommodations required.

Research shows that students with disabilities in secondary CTE programmes were less likely to drop out and more likely to be employed, to have paid competitive jobs, and to work full time after high school. However, CTE that included only simulated work experience in classroom settings did not appear to lead to optimal employment outcomes. Students with disabilities who had paid or unpaid work experience in high school had better employment outcomes—higher wages, more hours, more continuous employment.

Furthermore, students with disabilities mainstreamed into regular CTE or academic classrooms obtained paid competitive jobs more often and felt better prepared to keep their jobs. Qualitative studies reviewed by Eisenmann imply that integration of academic and vocational curricula promoted meaningful engagement and inclusion of students with disabilities by increasing persistence, academic achievement, and postsecondary engagement.

Rights of Disabled Students

Four key federal laws define the rights of students with disabilities. Two federal civil rights laws, the Americans with Disabilities Act of 1990 and

Section 504 of the Rehabilitation Act of 1973, require access for students with disabilities to all federally funded programmes and prohibit discrimination based on disability in any aspect of public education programmes. The 1998 Perkins Act requires equal access for special populations, including students with disabilities, to all vocational programmes, services, and activities and prohibits discrimination based on special population status.

The Individuals with Disabilities Education Act (IDEA), as amended in 1997, establishes the right of students with disabilities to a free appropriate public education, including special education, related services, and transition services. The Individualised Education Programme (IEP) mandated by IDEA draws on the results of a comprehensive evaluation of the student's educational needs at least once every 3 years. The IEP must identify the student's current level of educational performance; measurable goals and objectives; special education, related services, and other accommodations to be provided; and the extent of participation with nondisabled students.

The IEP must also specify how the student's progress will be measured, how parents will be informed of progress, and the extent of modification in state- and districtwide tests. Beginning at age 14, the IEP must include a statement of transition services the student will need to reach postschool goals; beginning at age 16, the IEP must include a statement of transition services to help the student prepare for leaving school. IDEA requires that six participants be involved in the IEP meeting: the student (if appropriate); a parent (and family if desired); at least one of the student's special education teachers (or related services provider, if appropriate); at least one of the student's regular education teachers; a representative of the local educational agency; and other agency personnel with knowledge or expertise to meet the student's needs.

The planning process involved in IEP development includes three steps.

— the abilities, needs, interests, and preferences of the individual student are determined.

— individual postschool goals are developed based on abilities, needs, interests, and preferences.

— instructional activities and accommodations, modifications, and supports appropriate to the student's postschool goals are identified.

A variety of individuals must work together in an effective IEP team, including special education, CTE, and academic teachers, programme support staff, guidance counsellors, and school administrators. Other personnel are included as appropriate to meet the individual student's needs—for example, speech, occupational, or physical therapists; adult service providers such as rehabilitation or independent living counsellors; and employers or postsecondary education representatives. Effective planning for activities and services that benefit students with disabilities and improve postschool outcomes involves several broad practices.

Planning should be proactive, focused on individual students, and driven by students and parents; it should involve student assessment, life skills development, and accommodations. Planned educational activities should focus on school- and work-based experiences linking high academic and workplace standards, with integrated academic and vocational curricula for employment skills and specific occupational instruction. Family involvement should be facilitated by training to increase parents' knowledge and skills in advocacy, planning, support, and legal issues.

Business, labour, and government and community agencies should be actively involved to provide resources, training sites, and mentoring for students and educators. Finally, programme policy and structure should support needed partnerships, philosophy, planning, evaluation, and human resource development.

Role of CTE Teacher

CTE teachers are only one member of the team that plans and provides educational activities and accommodations for students with disabilities. In IEP development and transition planning, CTE teachers' role is to provide information, support, and assistance to others who lead the process. However, CTE teachers play a primary role in providing instruction through school- and work-based experiences and activities linking the two and in integrating academic and vocational instruction; in that role, CTE teachers should receive support and assistance from others.

Special educators typically play the primary role in identifying educational activities and accommodations that suit students' interests, aptitudes, abilities, and postschool preferences. Trained vocational assessors, if available, may use formal assessment tools, or special educators can conduct informal assessments using data in school records; interviews with students, families, and previous instructors; or published interest, aptitude, or skills instruments.

CTE teachers may be able to provide programme inventories or assessment tools to establish a student's readiness for specific occupational courses. CTE teachers can also provide information on the instructional demands (e.g., prerequisite basic, interpersonal, reasoning, and learning-to-learn skills) and setting demands (e.g., independent work, self-monitoring, ability to stay on task). In particular, CTE teachers can provide CTE-specific information. That information would include occupationally specific courses of study, cooperative education, apprenticeship, and career guidance and counselling services.

CTE teachers would also provide any formal programme entry criteria (e.g., prerequisite courses or entry-level skills along with tests to assess them). Although students with disabilities must meet standard programme entry requirements, entry testing must allow any accommodations listed in a student's IEP for test-taking (e.g., extended time, use of a reader).

CTE teachers have a larger responsibility in providing instruction for students with disabilities, particularly school-based experiences. CTE teachers must plan and provide school-based instructional activities that correspond with the goals and objectives of students' IEPs, including classroom and lab activities to teach occupationally specific skills and work-related behaviours. Planning activities that integrate academic and occupational instruction requires collaboration and coordination between CTE and academic teachers.

CTE teachers must also evaluate and grade students' attainment of the IEP objectives on which instruction is based. In addition, CTE teachers must either provide the instructional accommodations and modifications specified in each student's IEP or work with special education personnel who do so. CTE teachers also have an important role to play in providing effective work-based experiences for students with disabilities, which can include field trips, job shadowing, school-based enterprises, career-related camps, apprenticeships, internships, cooperative education, work-study, and part-time job placement.

CTE teachers may share responsibility for contacting local employers; arranging sites and experiences that meet employer and student needs; orienting employers to work-site roles (coaches for instruction, mentors for social initiation and inclusion); visiting sites to observe student work; and monitoring student progress, work, and difficulties. Perhaps most important, CTE teachers must plan and provide the connecting activities that link school- and work-based learning—feedback sessions, discussions, journal writing, student presentations, projects, or portfolios, for example.

To meet the needs of students with disabilities, CTE teachers need background information on students' disabilities and on appropriate accommodations. Accommodations can include modified instructional methods (e.g., repeat and summarise key points, use audiovisual aids, conduct oraltesting or alternative assessments) or equipment (e.g., hand or foot controls, adjustable tables); curriculum objectives might be adapted or supplemented to meet specific student needs.

CTE teachers should identify the assistance available from special educators, tutors, paraprofessionals, or volunteers (e.g., providing print materials in alternative formats, monitoring student work, answering questions, developing teaching aids). So in a nutshell, CTE teachers are one member of the team that helps students with disabilities participate fully and meaningfully in high-quality educational programmes. They play a key role in providing a strong mix of all school programmes—academic, functional, occupational—carefully linked to each other and to work experience, delivered with customised accommodations to meet students' individual needs, and embodying the same high expectations they have of all students.

Guidance for Abused Children

Child abuse is the physical or psychological maltreatment of a child by an adult often synonymous with the term child maltreatment or the term child abuse and neglect.

Recognising the Abused Child

Sexual abuse is an uncommonly common thing. It knows no cultural, economic, social or religious barriers. It rears its ugly head in the best of families. Although there is no "typical" victim, those who have suffered this kind of abuse certainly share many behaviours and feelings.

Sexually abused children do not understand their feelings and seldom realise that their ways of behaving are abnormal and/or inappropriate. How the many different kinds of behaviours resulting from incest and sexual abuse manifest themselves often depends on the personalities of individual children and the kinds of experiences that took place. The more traumatised the child is, the more bizarre his or her behaviour will be—and the more extreme the reaction to social interactions.

Because Jeff wanted a more comprehensive list of warning signals, these are:

— extreme reclusiveness, fearfulness, or nonresponsiveness to peer interactions;

— physical and/or emotional difficulties or complaints (nightmares, phobias, stomach pains, venereal infections, etc.);

— violent or highly aggressive behaviours;

— low self-esteem and low self-image;

— vacillation between being pseudo-adult and ultra-immature;

— regressive behaviours (thumb-sucking, clinging, infantile postures, baby talk);

— bedwetting which is not an organic or developmental problem.

Although any one of these symptoms may not, in itself, indicate sexual abuse, all do show that the child is experiencing some kind of physical, emotional or psychological discomfort, and should be checked out. Sexual abuse, whether it occurs "only once or twice" or many times, usually has a critical impact on personality development. Self-esteem suffers immediately, and this is quickly followed by guilt, feelings of helplessness, depression and repressed emotionality.

Academic problems are common among abused children, as are difficulties with concentration and social interactions. Extreme passivity or aggressiveness may be manifested. Their attitudes are often quite punitive and self-destructive. They have experienced a betrayal and a personal violation which should not be, but often is, ignored or discounted in some way. The victimised child adjusts and copes with the situation by assuming responsibility for what has happened. Feelings of shame and self-incrimination have a profound affect on all of his or her future relationships.

Trusting becomes a lifelong problem. It is important for counsellors to provide structure and consistency when dealing with their young clients. Additionally, they give the children explicit permission to be honest in expressing their feelings, and that the counsellors in turn be open and accepting of all that is shared with them. It is important that counsellors, parents and religious leaders alike learn how to identify the various indicators of sexual abuse.

The term "sexual abuse" covers a wide range of behaviours. Some, like an obscene phone call or exhibitionism, are shocking and annoying. Others—incest, rape, child pornography or child prostitution—are more tragic and traumatising. Chronic or ongoing sexual abuse by someone close to the family (a relative, friend or neighbour) can disrupt a child's psychosocial developmental tasks.

Victimised children often develop poor social skills with peers, though they may camouflage this lack by becoming overly gregarious. They are often unable to form anything but very superficial relationships. These children find it extremely difficult to trust people, and are confused as to their sexual roles and identities. Suicide, drugs and alcohol may become avenues of escape for them. Many parents mistakenly believe that their children would never fall for molesters' advances or ploys. But child molesters are highly skilled manipulators and usually mislead adults as well as children.

We have all told our children, "Don't talk to strangers!" But molesters are often not strangers, but relatives, neighbours, family friends or church acquaintances. We need to remember that the sexual abuser is usually known or familiar to the child. A child who is molested by a stranger will probably tell someone about it shortly after it has happened. This child will usually be believed and protected from further abuse. But the victims of ongoing abuse are not so lucky.

Children are taught compliance at an early age. They are instructed to do what an adult or authority figure demands. Most children are awed or intimidated by adults. Perpetrators often convince children that what is going to occur is something very special. Most children do not know that it is wrong or abnormal behaviour. They may feel uncomfortable or sense that what is happening is not OK, but they will usually believe the abuser and discount their own feelings. Once the abuse has begun, the child is hooked into secrecy.

The brighter children are, the more stressful the experience will be for them when they realise that they have been duped. They will feel guilt, shame, helplessness and anger. A statement we often hear from such children is, "I should have known better." Yet how can we expect our children to "know" unless we teach them the skills needed to protect themselves from sexual abuse, just as we teach them other forms of safety? We need to recognise the signs of abuse and to be willing to become advocates for children who are hurting.

We need to listen to our children and to talk to them about sexual abuse. We need to protect them without unduly alarming or scaring them. Parents are not the only ones who find it difficult to talk to children about such abuse. Counsellors, educators, clergy and other clinicians often shy away from asking children—and adults—questions about it. Research indicates that we should be wary of the motives of adults who show an acute interest in our children, and who want to spend a lot of time alone with them. Churches must carefully screen those who work with children. Another precaution is to have co-leaders for youth work. At least one of them should be selected by the congregation, since molesters tend to choose other molesters as their assistants.

In addition, we can educate congregations, Sunday school teachers and other youth personnel about sexual abuse. Children can be taught the difference between "good touch and bad touch," what "private" areas are, and what "lures" child molesters may use. They can learn how to resist getting hooked into something bad that sounds so good! Sexual abuse is not a pleasant topic. It is not a pleasant experience. Guilt, shame, shattered spirits and self-destructive behaviours are its legacy.

Abused children can be found in every city, in every neighbourhood, in every congregation. To deny this or to ignore the warning signs is to help perpetuate the cycle of abuse. Our eyes must be opened and our ears must be trained to hear the silent pleas of the hurting children among us.

Counselling for Abused Children

Counselling abused children is a challenging task for practitioners. The incidence of reported and substantiated child abuse and neglect has risen dramatically since the "discovery" of the Battered Child Syndrome in the sixties, and subsequent mandatory reporting laws. The nation has moved through stages of public awareness about the phenomenon. Currently practitioners have become aware of the widespread sexual abuse of girls (estimated at one in four females) and are developing increasing awareness of the sexual abuse of boys.

Rapid changes in the knowledge base demand that counsellors keep abreast of the indicators of maltreatment, the laws for reporting suspected abuse, and the ways in which children can best be served to overcome effects of a negative family experience. All fifty states require that helping professionals report suspected child abuse to the child protection agency or the police. Many counsellors experience difficulty with reporting requirements for fear of violating the trust of a child, or creating mistrust with the child's parents. Such reporting to Children's Protective Services has saved the lives of many children, and brought help to families.

Although children are still removed from their families and placed in foster homes when it is necessary for their protection, the emphasis has shifted to serving children in their own homes, and providing services to help the family overcome the situations which lead to abuse or neglect. Counsellors should be familiar with child abuse reporting laws in their own states. Typically counsellors and school personnel are required to report suspected abuse, and are granted immunity from liability because they are presumed to be acting in good faith. Many states also have criminal or civil penalties established for mandated professionals who fail to report.

Types of Maltreatment

A common theme underlying most forms of maltreatment—physical abuse, neglect, or sexual abuse and exploitation—is that of emotional hurt. The child who is physically abused often suffers emotionally from inconsistent parenting and fear. The sexually abused child suffers from the lack of affection or supervision which leaves him/her vulnerable to the subtle advances of the perpetrator; and the neglected child becomes anxious or apathetic about a life in which basic needs aren't met. One general consequence of child maltreatment is developmental fixation or "freezing." The child who comes to the attention of the counsellor due to difficulties in the classroom or poor social adjustment may very well be a maltreated child.

Neglect

Neglect accounts for more deaths than the physical abuse of children. In a national study of reported child maltreatment, only 4% experienced major physical injury, while 60% experienced a type of physical neglect. Neglect was associated with 56% of child deaths. All types of neglect are essentially a failure by the parents to provide something needed for the child's healthy growth and development. The concept of neglect includes the assumption that some harm must befall the child as a result of the parents' failure to provide.

Physical Abuse

Physical abuse is usually defined as the intentional or nonaccidental inflicting of injury on a child by a caregiver. It manifests as bruises, welts, broken bones, burns, lacerations, or even death. It may occur through hitting, striking, beating, kicking, biting, slapping or other forms of violence directed at a child. Many, if not most, parents who abuse children have been reared in an environment in which some form of maltreatment occurred. Physical abuse appears in all socioeconomic classes, but is correlated with the stresses of poverty.

Sexual Abuse

Child sexual abuse is the adult (or older child) exploitation of the normal childhood development process, through the use of sexual activity. Examples of the types of sexual activity might include touching, kissing, fondling, manipulations of the genitals with the fingers, and actual sexual intercourse. In examining patterns of sexual abuse and exploitation, it is important to keep in mind that the knowledge base is changing rapidly. While earlier belief was that sexual abuse perpetrators were almost always men, McCarty studied female perpetrators and found both accomplices who aided male perpetrators, and independent abusers, who had come from a background of bad childhoods, unhappy marriages and earlier sexual victimisation.

Within the last decade it has been acknowledged that male children are also sexually victimised and are at great risk. It currently appears that female children are more likely to be sexually abused in an incestuous situation, while more male children are sexually abused outside the home.

Emotional Neglect

Emotional neglect generally implies a consistent indifference to the child's needs and covers a range of behaviour, from the parent who never speaks to the child and doesn't remove the child from a crib, to the psychotic parent unable to acknowledge the reality of the child's world, or that the child actually exists. Emotional abuse, on the other hand, implies an active rejection or persecution of the child by the parent. Chronic verbal abuse erodes the child's self-esteem. The use of confinement or excessive punishment is also a form of emotional abuse. Emotional abuse or neglect is usually accompanied by other forms of maltreatment such as sexual abuse or physical abuse. Clearly, children who are being maltreated are not getting their developmental needs met.

Children who have been maltreated are usually unwilling or unable to reveal their situation to a counsellor because of parental threats, or a feeling of loyalty to the family. While sensitive interviewing may help to unearth details of maltreatment, counsellors need to be aware of non-verbal ways in which the message of abuse may be communicated. The presence of one indicator alone does not necessarily mean that maltreatment has occurred. The counsellor looks rather for configurations of indicators. If there are a number of indicators, the counsellor has reason to suspect maltreatment, even if the child has not confided in the counsellor. When abuse is suspected, the counsellor is obligated, under law, to report this concern to Children's Protective Services.

Counselling, in and of itself, cannot ensure the safety of a maltreated child. There will be many professionals involved in working with maltreated children. Typically, a Children's Protective Services worker may coordinate the intervention. Medical personnel will be involved. This may include a coordinating pediatrician who will follow the child's growth and development, several specialists and other health practitioners such as a physical therapist or public health nurse who has worked with the family.

If the child must be removed from the home, the team may include a foster parent. Educators and school personnel are also an important part of the team. They can help to monitor a child's day-to-day safety and progress, and can build programmes to help the child's self-esteem and enhance cognitive development. In dealing with situations where there is risk to a child, the counsellor will find that a team approach accomplishes more for the child than the single intervention of offering counselling.

Child Counselling

One of the primary purposes of counselling the maltreated child is to provide a safe place and safe relationship within which the child may experiment with new adaptations to a safer world, and in which the child's arrested development may become "unstuck." Counsellors cannot literally replace the requisite parental bonding which helps children to grow and develop, but have an opportunity to help the child develop a trusting relationship with an adult. The key to understanding the maltreated child is to look at the developmental stage rather than the chronological age.

The counsellor will be able to identify adaptations which the child made to the maltreatment and teach the child more appropriate ways of interacting. Children often reveal in play the traumatic events of their earlier years. They may also show to the counsellor maladaptive behaviour which puts them at risk of further maltreatment. In the counselling relationship, working with maltreated children requires many techniques other than talking and listening. Using structured or unstructured play situations and artwork, music or clay provide a safe way for children to release tension and express themselves. Younger children do well with dolls and dollhouses to act out family issues for the counsellor.

Many maltreated children have not had normal play opportunities and benefit greatly from free play in the counsellor's office. Using puppets, reading stories, or acting out role plays are ways in which abused children can try out new approaches to relationships. Abused children also do well when counsellors work with them in groups. Younger children do well with developmental play groups, while older children and youth can benefit from activity groups as well as treatment-oriented groups. Group counselling can be especially useful with children and youth who have been sexually abused by reducing their feelings of shame and differentness and helping them to learn how to protect themselves.

Counselling abused children is challenging in that it can arouse many complex feelings within the counsellor. Anger with the child's parents, uneasiness over the child's acting out, or feelings of frustration and sadness are not uncommon for counsellors to face. Anxiety about protecting the children from further maltreatment may be a predominant theme for the counsellor. It is important for counsellors working with the sensitive issues of maltreatment to seek consultation, supervision, or even treatment for themselves when they become overwhelmed with feelings.

Recognising one's professional limitations can also be helpful. It is important to remember that counselling alone cannot protect children, and that any effective long-term intervention will require a concerted team approach and a community which cares enough to offer adequate resources for families. Children will be healed and protected as families are helped.

References

Good, T. & Brophy, J. (2002). *Looking in classrooms, 9th edition.* Boston: Allyn & Bacon.

Kazdin, A. E. (Ed.) (2002). *Encyclopedia of psychology.* New York: Oxford University.

Jones, V. & Jones, L. (2006). *Comprehensive classroom management: Creating communities of support and solving problems, 6th edition.* Boston: Allyn & Bacon.

Woolfolk, A. E., Winne, P. H., & Perry, N. E., (2006). *Educational Psychology,* Toronto, Canada: Pearson.

Vygotskii, L. S, (1997). *Educational psychology*, Trans. Robert Silverman. Boca Raton, FL: St. Lucie Press.

9

Supporting Children's Learning

Each person has an individual profile of characteristics, abilities and challenges that result from learning and development. These manifest as individual differences in intelligence, creativity, cognitive style, motivation, and the capacity to process information, communicate, and relate to others. The most prevalent disabilities found among schoolage children are attention-deficit hyperactivity disorder (ADHD), learning disability, dyslexia, and speech disorder. Less common disabilities include mental retardation, hearing impairment, cerebral palsy, epilepsy and blindness.

Although theories of intelligence have been discussed by philosophers since Plato, intelligence testing is an invention of educational psychology, and is coincident with the development of that discipline. Continuing debates about the nature of intelligence revolve on whether intelligence can be characterised by a single, scalar factor, multiple factors, or whether it can be measured at all. In practice, standardised instruments such as the Stanford-Binet IQ test and the WISC are widely used in economically developed countries to identify children in need of individualised educational treatment. Children classified as gifted are often provided with accelerated or enriched programmes. Children with identified deficits may be provided with enhanced education in specific skills such as phonological awareness.

Learning and Cognition

Two fundamental assumptions that underlie formal education systems are that students (a) retain knowledge and skills they acquire in school, and (b) can apply them in situations outside the classroom. Research has found that, even when students report not using the knowledge acquired in school, a considerable portion is retained for many years and longterm retention is strongly dependent on the initial level of mastery. There is much less consensus on the crucial question of how much knowledge acquired in school transfers to tasks encountered outside formal educational settings, and how such transfer occurs. Several perspectives have been established within which the theories of learning used in educational psychology are formed and contested. These include behaviourism, cognitivism, social cognitive theory, and constructivism.

Behaviour Perspective

Applied behaviour analysis, a set of techniques based on the behavioural principles of operant conditioning, is effective in a range of educational settings. For example, teachers can improve student behaviour by systematically rewarding students who follow classroom rules with praise, stars or tokens exchangeable for sundry items. Despite the demonstrated efficacy of awards in changing behaviour, their use in education has been criticised by proponents of self-determination theory, who claim that praise and other rewards undermine intrinsic motivation. There is evidence that tangible rewards decrease intrinsic motivation in specific situations, such as when the student already has a high level of intrinsic motivation to perform the goal behaviour. But the results showing detrimental effects are counterbalanced by evidence that, in other situations, such as when rewards are given for attaining a gradually increasing standard of performance, rewards enhance intrinsic motivation.

Cognitive Perspective

Among current educational psychologists, the cognitive perspective is more widely held than the behavioural perspective perhaps because it admits causally related mental constructs such as traits, beliefs, memories, motivations and emotions. Cognitive theories claim that memory structures determine how information is perceived, processed, stored, retrieved and forgotten. Among the memory structures theorised by cognitive psychologists are separate but linked visual and verbal systems described by Allan Paivio's dual coding theory. Educational psychologists have used dual coding theory and cognitive load theory to explain how people learn from multimedia presentations.

The spaced learning effect, a cognitive phenomenon strongly supported by psychological research, has broad applicability within education. For example, students have been found to perform better on a test of knowledge about a text passage when a second reading of the passage is delayed rather than immediate. Educational psychology research has confirmed the applicability to education of other findings from cognitive psychology, such as the benefits of using mnemonics for immediate and delayed retention of information.

Problem solving, regarded by many cognitive psychologists as fundamental to learning, is an important research topic in educational psychology. A student is thought to interpret a problem by assigning it to a schema retrieved from long term memory. When the problem is assigned to the wrong schema, the student's attention is subsequently directed away from features of the problem that are inconsistent with the assigned schema. The critical step of finding a mapping between the problem and a pre-existing schema is often cited as supporting the centrality of analogical thinking to problem solving.

Social Cognitive Perspective

Social cognitive theory is a highly influential fusion of behavioural, cognitive and social elements. The theory identifies several factors that determine whether observing a model will affect behavioural or cognitive change. These factors include the learner's developmental status, the perceived prestige and competence of the model, the consequences received by the model, the relevance of the model's behaviours and consequences to the learner's goals, and the learner's self-efficacy. The concept of self-efficacy, which played an important role in later developments of the theory, refers to the learner's belief in his or her ability to perform the modeled behaviour.

An experiment was conducted to study grade 2 students who had previously experienced difficulty in learning subtraction. One group of students observed a subtraction demonstration by a teacher and then participated in an instructional programme on subtraction. A second group observed other grade 2 students performing the same subtraction procedures and then participated in the same instructional programme. The students who observed peer models scored higher on a subtraction post test and also reported greater confidence in their subtraction ability. The results were interpreted as supporting the hypothesis that perceived similarity of the model to the learner increases self-efficacy, leading to more effective learning of modelled behaviour. It is supposed that peer modeling is particularly effective for students who have low self-efficacy.

Over the last decade, much research activity in educational psychology has focused on developing theories of self-regulated learning (SRL) and metacognition. These theories work from the central premise that effective learners are active agents who construct knowledge by setting goals, analysing tasks, planning strategies and monitoring their understanding. Research has indicated that learners who are better at goal setting and self-monitoring tend to have greater intrinsic task interest and self-efficacy; and that teaching learning strategies can increase academic achievement.

Constructivist Perspective

Constructivism is a category of learning theories in which emphasis is placed on the agency and prior knowledge of the learner, and often on the social and cultural determinants of the learning process. Educational psychologists distinguish individual constructivism, identified with Piaget's learning theory, from social constructivism.

One view is that behaviour, skills, attitudes and beliefs are inherently situated, that is, bound to a specific sociocultural setting. According to this view, the learner is enculturated through social interactions within a community of practice. The social constructivist view of learning has spawned approaches to teaching and learning such as cognitive apprenticeship, in which the tacit components of a complex skill are made explicit through conversational interactions occurring between expert and novice in the setting in which the skill is embedded.

Psychology of Teaching and Learning

In the past two decades teaching has changed significantly, so much in fact that schools are not what some of us may remember from our own childhoods. The changes have affected both the opportunities and the challenges of teaching, as well as the attitudes, knowledge and skills that it takes to prepare for a teaching career. There are four new trends in education, at how the trends have changed what teachers do, and at how you will therefore need to prepare yourself to teach.

— *The first trend is toward diversity*: students today are more diverse in many ways. The diversity has made teaching more fulfilling as a career, but also made instructional planning more challenging in certain respects.

— *The second trend is toward instructional technology*: classrooms, schools, and students use computers today than in the past for research, writing, communicating, and keeping records. The use of technology has created new ways for students to learn, but in the process has altered how teachers can teach most effectively, and even raised issues about what constitutes "true" teaching and learning.

— *The third trend is toward accountability in education*: both the public and educators themselves are paying much more attention than in the past to how to assess (or provide evidence for) learning and good quality teaching. The attention has increased the importance of education to the public (a good thing) and also improved educational choices for some students. But it also may be creating new constraints on what teachers teach on what students learn.

— The fourth trend is toward increased the professionalism of teachers. Now more than ever, teachers are in positions to assess the quality of their own work as well as that of colleagues, and to take steps to improve it when or if it is necessary. This change gives teachers more opportunity to use their professional expertise, but it also creates higher standards of commitment and of practice and therefore greater worries about teaching "well enough."

Teachers' Perspectives on Learning

For teachers, learning usually refers to things that happen in schools or classrooms, even though every teacher can of course describe examples of learning that happen outside of these places. In particular, teachers' perspectives on learning often emphasize three ideas, and sometimes even take them for granted:

— curriculum content and academic achievement,

— sequencing and readiness, and

— the importance of transferring learning to new or future situations.

Learning on Curriculum and Academic Achievement

When teachers speak of learning, they tend to emphasize whatever is taught in schools deliberately, including both the official curriculum and the various behaviours and routines that make classrooms run smoothly. In practice, defining learning in this way often means that teachers equate learning with the major forms of academic achievement—especially language and mathematics—and to a lesser extent musical skill, physical coordination, or social sensitivity.

The imbalance occurs not because the goals of public education make teachers responsible for certain content and activities (like books and reading) and the skills which these activities require (like answering teachers' questions and writing essays). It does happen not because teachers are biased, insensitive, or unaware that students often learn a lot outside of school.

A side effect of focusing learning on curriculum and academics is that classroom social interactions and behaviours become issues for teachers—become something that they need to manage. In the small space of a classroom, no other viewpoint about social interaction makes sense. Yet in the wider world outside of school, learning often does happen incidentally, "accidentally" and without conscious interference or input from others: I "learn" what a friend's personality is like, for example, without either of us deliberately trying to make this happen.

As teachers, we sometimes see incidental learning in classrooms as well, and often welcome it; but our responsibility for curriculum goals more often focuses our efforts on what students can learn through conscious, deliberate effort. In a classroom, unlike in many other human settings, it is always necessary to ask whether classmates are helping or hindering individual students' learning.

Dependence of Learning on Teaching

Focusing learning on changes in classrooms has several other effects. One, for example, is that it can tempt teachers to think that what is taught is equivalent to what is learned—even though most teachers know that doing so is a mistake, and that teaching and learning can be quite different.

Sequencing and readiness

The distinction between teaching and learning creates a secondary issue for teachers, that of educational readiness. Traditionally the concept referred to students' preparedness to cope with or profit from the activities and expectations of school. A kindergarten child was "ready" to start school, for example, if he or she was in good health, showed moderately good social skills, could take care of personal physical needs, could use a pencil to make simple drawings, and so on. At older ages (such as in high school or university), the term readiness is often replaced by a more specific term, prerequisites. To take a course in physics, for example, a student must first have certain prerequisite experiences, such as studying advanced algebra or calculus. To begin work as a public school teacher, a person must first engage in practice teaching for a period of time.

Transfer as a crucial part of learning

Still another result of focusing the concept of learning on classrooms is that it raises issues of usefulness or transfer, which is the ability to use knowledge or skill in situations beyond the ones in which they are acquired. Learning to read and learning to solve arithmetic problems, for example, are major goals of the elementary-school curriculum because those skills are meant to be used not only inside the classroom, but outside as well. We teachers intend, that is, for reading and arithmetic skills to "transfer"—even though we also do out best to make the skills enjoyable while they are still being learned.

In the world inhabited by teachers, even more than in other worlds, making learning fun is certainly a good thing to do, but making learning useful as well as fun is even better. Combining enjoyment and usefulness, in fact, is a "gold standard" of teaching: we generally seek it for students, and even though we may not succeed at providing it all of the time.

Theories and Models of Learning

Several ideas and priorities, then, affect how teachers think about learning, including the curriculum, the difference between teaching and learning, sequencing, readiness, and transfer. The ideas form a "screen" through which to understand and evaluate whatever psychology has to offer education. As it turns out, many theories, concepts, and ideas from educational psychology do make it through the "screen" of education, meaning that they are consistent with the professional priorities of teachers and helpful in solving important problems of classroom teaching. In the case of issues about classroom learning, for example, educational psychologists have developed a number of theories and concepts that are relevant to classrooms, in that they describe at least some of what usually happens there and offer guidance for assisting learning.

It is helpful to group the theories according to whether they focus on changes in behaviour or in thinking. The distinction is rough and inexact, but a good place to begin. For starters, therefore, consider two perspectives about learning, called behaviourism (learning as changes in overt behaviour) and constructivism, (learning as changes in thinking). The second category can be further divided into *psychological constructivism* (changes in thinking resulting from individual experiences, and *social constructivism,* (changes in thinking due to assistance from others).

Behaviourism

Behaviourism is a perspective on learning that focuses on changes in individuals' observable behaviours—changes in what people say or do.

— *Respondent Conditioning*: Learning New Associations with Prior Behaviours

— *Operant Conditioning*: New Behaviours Because of New Consequences

Constructivism

Behaviourist models of learning may be helpful in understanding and influencing what students do, but teachers usually also want to know what students are thinking, and want to enrich what they are thinking. For this aspect of teaching, some of the best help comes from constructivism, which is a perspective on learning focused on how students actively create (or construct) knowledge out of experiences.

Learning Tactics and Strategies

A learning strategy is a general plan that a learner formulates for achieving a somewhat distant academic goal. Like all strategies, it specifies what will be done to achieve the goal, where it will be done, and when it will be done.

A learning tactic is a specific technique that a learner uses to accomplish an immediate objective. As you can see, tactics have an integral connection to strategies. They are the learning tools that move you closer to your goal. Thus, they have to be chosen so as to be consistent with the goals of a strategy.

If you had to recall verbatim the preamble to the Indian Constitution, for example, would you use a learning tactic that would help you understand the gist of each stanza or one that would allow for accurate and complete recall? It is surprising how often students fail to consider this point.

Types of Tactics

Most learning tactics can be placed in one of two categories based on each tactic's intended primary purpose.

One category, called memory-directed tactics, contains techniques that help produce accurate storage and retrieval of information.

The second category, called comprehension-directed tactics, contains techniques that aid in understanding the meaning of ideas and their interrelationships.

Within each category there are specific tactics from which one can choose.

The first two, rehearsal and mnemonic devices, are memory-directed tactics. Both can take several forms and are used by students of almost every age.

The last two, notetaking and self-questioning, are comprehension-directed tactics and are used frequently by students from the upper elementary grades through college.

Rehearsal

The simplest form of rehearsal, rote rehearsal, is one of the earliest tactics to appear during childhood and is used by most everyone on occasion. It is not a particularly effective tactic for long-term storage and recall because it does not produce distinct encoding or good retrieval cues.

Most five- and six-year-olds do not rehearse at all. Seven-year-olds sometimes use the simplest form of rehearsal. By eight years of age, instead of rehearsing single pieces of information one at a time, youngsters start to rehearse several items together as a set.

A slightly more advanced version, called cumulative rehearsal, involves rehearsing a small set of items for several repetitions, dropping the item at the top of the list and adding a new one, giving the set several repetitions, dropping the item at the head of the set and adding a new one, rehearsing the set, and so on.

By early adolescence rehearsal reflects the learner's growing awareness of the organisational properties of information. When given a list of randomly arranged words from familiar categories, 13-year-olds will group items by category to form rehearsal sets.

Mnemonic Devices

A mnemonic device is a memory-directed tactic that helps a learner transform or organise information to enhance its retrievability.

Such devices can be used to learn and remember individual items of information, sets of information, and ideas expressed in text.

These devices range from simple, easy-to-learn techniques to somewhat complex systems that require a fair amount of practice. Since they incorporate visual and verbal forms of elaborative encoding, their effectiveness is due to the same factors that make imagery and category clustering successful—organisation and meaningfulness.

Self-questioning

Since students are expected to demonstrate much of what they know by answering written test questions, self-questioning can be a valuable learning tactic.

The key to using questions profitably is to recognise that different types of questions make different cognitive demands. Some questions require little more than verbatim recall or recognition of simple facts and details.

If an exam is to stress factual recall, then it may be helpful for a student to generate such questions while studying. Other questions, however, assess comprehension, application, or synthesis of main ideas or other high level information.

Since many teachers favour higher-level test questions, we will focus on self-questioning as an aid to comprehension. Much of the research on self-questioning addresses two basic questions:

1) Can students as young as those in fourth grade be trained to write comprehension questions about the content of a reading passage?
2) And does writing such questions lead to better comprehension of the passage in comparison to students who do not write questions?

The answer to both questions is yes, if certain conditions are present. Research on teaching students how to generate questions as they read suggests that the following conditions play a major role in self-questioning's effectiveness as a comprehension-directed learning tactic:

1) The amount of prior knowledge the questioner has about the topic of the passage.

2) The amount of metacognitive knowledge the questioner has compiled.
3) The clarity of instructions.
4) The instructional format.
5) The amount of practice allowed the student.
6) The length of each practice session.

Notetaking

As a learning tactic, notetaking comes with good news and bad.

The good news is that notetaking can benefit a student in two ways. First, the process of taking notes while listening to a lecture or reading a text leads to better retention and comprehension of the noted information than just listening or reading does.

Second, the process of reviewing notes produces additional chances to recall and comprehend the noted material. The bad news is that we know very little at the present time about the specific conditions that make notetaking an effective tactic.

Components of a Learning Strategy

As noted, a learning strategy is a plan for accomplishing a learning goal. It consists of six components: metacognition, analysis, planning, implementation of the plan, monitoring of progress, and modification.

Metacognition

In the absence of some minimal awareness of how we think and how our thought processes affect our academic performance, a strategic approach to learning is simply not possible.

We need to know, at the very least, that effective learning requires an analysis of the learning situation, formulation of a learning plan, skilful implementation of appropriate tactics, periodic monitoring of our progress, and modification of things that go wrong.

In addition, we need to know why each of these steps is necessary, when each step should be carried out, and how well prepared we are to perform each step.

Without this knowledge, students who are taught one or more of the learning tactics mentioned earlier do not keep up their use for very long, nor do they apply the tactics to relevant tasks.

Analysis

Any workable plan must be based on relevant information. By thinking about the type of task that one must confront, the type of material that one has to learn, the personal characteristics that one possesses, and the way in which one's competence will be tested, the strategic learner can generate this information by playing the role of an investigative journalist and asking questions that pertain to what, when, where, why, who, and how.

In this way the learner can identify important aspects of the material to be learned (what, when, where), understand the nature of the test that will be given (why), recognise relevant personal learner characteristics (who), and identify potentially useful learning activities or tactics (how).

Planning

Once satisfactory answers have been gained from the analysis phase, the strategic learner then formulates a learning plan by hypothesizing.

Implementation of the plan

Once the learner has formulated a plan, each of its elements must be implemented skilfully.

A careful analysis and a well-conceived plan will not work if tactics are carried out badly. Of course, a poorly executed plan may not be entirely attributable to a learner's tactical skill deficiencies.

Part of the problem may be a general lack of knowledge about what conditions make for effective use of tactics (as is the case with notetaking).

Monitoring of progress

Once the learning process is under way, the strategic learner assesses how well the chosen tactics are working.

Possible monitoring techniques include writing out a summary, giving an oral presentation, working practice problems, and answering questions.

Modification

If the monitoring assessment is positive, the learner may decide that no changes are needed.

If, however, attempts to memorise or understand the learning material seem to be producing unsatisfactory results, the learner will need to reevaluate and modify the analysis. This, in turn, will cause changes in both the plan and the implementation.

There are two points we would like to emphasize about the nature of a learning strategy.

The first is that learning conditions constantly change. Subject matters have different types of information and structures, teachers use different instructional methods and have different styles, exams differ in the kinds of demands they make, and the interests, motives, and capabilities of students change over time.

Accordingly, strategies must be formulated or constructed anew as one moves from task to task rather than selected from a bank of previously formulated strategies. The true strategist, in other words, is very mentally active.

The second point is that the concept of a learning strategy is obviously complex and requires a certain level of intellectual maturity.

Thus, you may be tempted to conclude that, although you could do it, learning to be strategic is beyond the reach of most elementary and high school students. Research evidence suggests otherwise, however. A study of high school students in Scotland, for example, found that some students are sensitive to contextual differences among school tasks and vary their approach to studying accordingly.

Reciprocal Teaching

A study of strategy training aimed at improving reading comprehension is the reciprocal teaching (RT) programme.

Students learn certain comprehension skills by demonstrating them to each other. A small group of seventh graders, whose reading comprehension scores were at least two years below grade level, were trained to use the techniques of summarising, self-questioning, clarifying, and predicting to improve their reading comprehension. These four methods were chosen because they can be used by students to improve and monitor comprehension.

During the early training sessions, the teacher explained and demonstrated the four methods while reading various passages. The students were then given gradually increasing responsibility for demonstrating these techniques to their peers, with the teacher supplying prompts and corrective feedback as needed.

Eventually, each student was expected to offer a good summary of a passage, pose questions about important ideas, clarify ambiguous words or phrases, and predict upcoming events, all to be done with little or no intervention by the teacher.

This produced two general beneficial effects. First, the quality of students' summaries, questions, clarifications, and predictions improved. Early in the programme students produced overly detailed summaries and many unclear questions. But in later sessions concise summaries and questions dealing explicitly with main ideas were the rule. For example, questions on main ideas increased from 54 percent to 70 percent. In addition, the questions were increasingly stated in paraphrase form rather than as verbatim statements from the passage.

Second, RT-trained students scored as well as a group of average readers on tests of comprehension and much better than a group taught how to locate information that might show up in a test question.

Most impressively, these levels of performance held up for at least eight weeks after the study ended and generalised to tests of social studies and science.

Information Processing Approach to Cognition

Cognitive psychology represents the dominant approach in psychology today. A primary focus of this approach is on memory, a subject that has been of interest for thousands of years. The most widely accepted theory is labelled the "stage theory," based on the work of Atkinson and Shriffin. The focus of this model is on how information is stored in memory; the model proposes that information is processed and stored in three stages. In this theory, information is thought to be processed in a serial, discontinuous manner as it moves from one stage to the next.

In addition to the stage theory model of information processing, there are three more that are widely accepted. The first is labelled the "levels-of-processing" theory. The major proposition is that learners utilise different levels of elaboration as they process information. This is done on a continuum from perception, through attention, to labeling, and finally, meaning. The key point is that all stimuli that activate a sensory receptor cell are permanently stored in memory, but that different levels of processing contribute to an ability to access, or retrieve, that memory. Evidence from hypnosis and forensic psychology provide some interesting support for this hypothesis. It is not only how the information is processed, but how the information is accessed. When the demands for accessing information more closely match the methods used to elaborate or learn the information, more is remembered.

Two other models have been proposed as alternatives to the Atkinson-Shiffrin model: parallel-distributed processing and connectionistic. The parallel-distributed processing model states that information is processed simultaneously by several different parts of the memory system, rather than sequentially as hypothesized by Atkinson-Shiffrin. Work done on how we process emotional data somewhat supports this contention. The stage-theory model shown below differs slightly from the original Atkinson-Shriffin model in order to incorporate this feature.

The connectionistic model extends the parallel-distributed processing model. It is one of the dominant forms of current research in cognitive psychology and is consistent with the most recent brain research. This model emphasizes the fact that information is stored in multiple locations throughout the brain in the form of networks of connections. It is consistent with the levels-of-processing approach in that the more connections to a single idea or concept, the more likely it is to be remembered.

General Principles

Even though there are widely varying views within cognitive psychology, there are a few basic principles that most cognitive psychologists agree with.The first is the assumption of a limited capacity of the mental system. This means that the amount of information that can be processed by the system is constrained in some very important ways. Bottlenecks, or restrictions in the flow and processing of information, occur at very specific points.

A second principle is that a control mechanism is required to oversee the encoding, transformation, processing, storage, retrieval and utilisation of information. That is, not all of the processing capacity of the system is available; an executive function that oversees this process will use up some of this capability. When one is learning a new task or is confronted with a new environment, the executive function requires more processing power than when one is doing a routine task or is in a familiar environment.

A third principle is that there is a two-way flow of information as we try to make sense of the world around us. We constantly use information that we gather through the senses and information we have stored in memory in a dynamic process as we construct meaning about our environment and our relations to it. This is somewhat analogous to the difference between inductive reasoning and deductive reasoning. A similar distinction can be made between using information we derive from the senses and that generated by our imaginations.

A fourth principle generally accepted by cognitive psychologists is that the human organism has been genetically prepared to process and organise information in specific ways. For example, a human infant is more likely to look at a human face than any other stimulus. Given that the field of focus of a human infant is 12 to 18 inches, one can surmise that this is an important aspect of the infant's survival. Other research has discovered additional biological predispositions to process information.

For example, language development is similar in all human infants regardless of language spoken by adults or the area in which they live. All human infants with normal hearing babble and coo, generate first words, begin the use of telegraphic speech, and overgeneralise at approximately the same ages. The issue of language development is an area where cognitive and behavioural psychologists as well as cognitive psychologists with different viewpoints have fought many battles regarding the processes underlying human behaviour. Needless to say the disussion continues.

Stage Model of Information Processing

One of the major issues in cognitive psychology is the study of memory. The dominant view is labelled the "stage theory" and is based on the work of Atkinson and Shiffrin.

Sensory memory (STSS). Sensory memory is affiliated with the transduction of energy. The environment makes available a variety of sources of information, but the brain only understands electrical energy. The body has special sensory receptor cells that transduce this external energy to something the brain can understand. In the process of transduction, a memory is created. This memory is very short.

It is absolutely critical that the learner attend to the information at this initial stage in order to transfer it to the next one. There are two major concepts for getting information into STM:

1) Individuals are more likely to pay attention to a stimulus if it has an interesting feature. We are more likely to get an orienting response if this is present.
2) Individuals are more likely to pay attention if the stimulus activates a known pattern. To the extent we have students call to mind relevant prior learning before we begin our presentations, we can take advantage of this principle.

Short-term memory (STM). Short-term memory is also called working memory and relates to what we are thinking about at any given moment in time. In Freudian terms, this is conscious memory. It is created by our paying attention to an external stimulus, an internal thought, or both. It will initially last somewhere around 15 to 20 seconds unless it is repeated at which point it may be available for up to 20 minutes. The hypothalamus is a brain structure thought to be involved in this shallow processing of information. The frontal lobes of the cerebral cortex is the structure associated with working memory. For example, you are processing the words you read on the screen in your frontal lobes. However, if I ask, "What is your telephone number?" your brain immediately calls that from long-term memory and replaces what was previously there.

Another major limit on information processing in STM is in terms of the number of units that can be processed an any one time. Because of the variability in how much individuals can work with it is necessary to point out important information. If some students can only process three units of information at a time, let us make certain it is the most important three.

There are two major concepts for retaining information in STM: organisation and repetition. There are four major types of organisation that are most often used in instructional design:

1) *Component (part/whole)*—classification by category or concept (e.g., the components of the teaching/learning model);
2) *Sequential* — chronological; cause/effect; building to climax (e.g., baking a cake, reporting on a research study);
3) *Relevance* — central unifying idea or criteria (e.g., most important principles of learning for boys and girls, appropriate management strategies for middle school and high school students);
4) *Transitional (connective)* — relational words or phrases used to indicate qualitative change over time (e.g., stages in Piaget's theory of cognitive development)

A related issue to organisation is the concept of chunking or grouping pieces of data into units. For example, the letters "b d e" constitute three units of information while the word "bed" represents one unit even though it is composed of the same number of letters. Chunking is a major technique for getting and keeping information in short-term memory; it is also a type of elaboration that will help get information into long-term memory.

Repetition or rote rehearsal is a technique we all use to try to "learn" something. However, in order to be effective this must be done after forgetting begins. Researchers advise that the learner should not repeat immediately the content, but wait a few minutes and then repeat. For the most part, simply memorising something does not lead to learning. We all have anecdotal evidence that we can remember something we memorised, but just think about all the material we tried to learn this way and the little we are able to remember after six months or a year.

Long-term memory (LTM). Long-term memory is also called preconscious and unconscious memory in Freudian terms. Preconscious means that the information is relatively easily recalled (although it may take several minutes or even hours) while unconscious refers to data that is not available during normal consciousness. It is preconscious memory that is the focus of cognitive psychology as it relates to long-term memory. The levels-of-processing theory, however, has provided some research that attests to the fact that we "know" more than we can easily recall. The two processes most likely to move information into long-term memory are elaboration and distributed practice.

There are several examples of elaboration that are commonly used in the teaching/learning process:

a) imaging — creating a mental picture;

b) method of loci (locations)—ideas or things to be remembered are connected to objects located in a familiar location;

c) pegword method (number, rhyming schemes)—ideas or things to be remembered are connected to specific words (e.g., one-bun, two-shoe, three-tree, etc.)

d) Rhyming (songs, phrases)—information to be remembered is arranged in a rhyme (e.g., 30 days hath September, April, June, and November, etc.)

e) Initial letter—the first letter of each word in a list is used to make a sentence (the sillier, the better).

Organisation (types) of Knowledge

As information is stored in long-term memory, it is organised using one or more structures: declarative, procedural, and/or imagery.

Declarative memory

a) *Semantic memory*— facts and generalised information (concepts, principles, rules; problem-solving strategies; learning strategies).

b) *Schema / Schemata* — networks of connected ideas or relationships; data structures or procedures for organising the parts of a specific experience into a meaningful system.

c) *Proposition* — interconnected set of concepts and relationships; if/then statements.

d) *Script* — "declarative knowledge structure that captures general information about a routine series of events or a recurrent type of social event, such as eating in a restaurant or visiting the doctor".

e) *Frame* — complex organisation including concepts and visualisations that provide a reference within which stimuli and actions are judged.

f) *Scheme* — an organisation of concepts, principles, rules, etc. that define a perspective and presents specific action patterns to follow.

g) *Program* — set of rules that define what to do in a particular situation.

h) *Paradigm* — the basic way of perceiving, thinking, valuing, and doing associated with a particular vision of reality.

i) *Model* — a set of propositions or equations describing in simplified form some aspects of our experience. Every model is based upon a theory or paradigm, but the theory or paradigm may not be stated in concise form.

j) *Episodic memory*— personal experience.

k) *Procedural memory* — how to

l) Imagery — pictures

Concept Formation

One of the most important issues in cognitive psychology is the development or formation of concepts. A concept is the set of rules used to define the categories by which we group similar events, ideas or objects. There are several principles that lend themselves to concept development:

1) Name and define concept to be learned (advance organiser)
    a) reference to larger category
    b) define attributes
2) Identify relevant and irrelevant attributes (guided discovery)
3) Give examples and nonexamples (tie to what is already known — elaboration)
4) Use both inductive (example/experience —> definition) and deductive reasoning (definition —> examples)
5) Name distinctive attributes (guided discovery)

Learning Styles

Learning styles are, simply put, various approaches or ways of learning. They involve educating methods, particular to an individual, that are presumed to allow that individual to learn best. It is commonly believed that most people favour some particular method of interacting with, taking in, and processing stimuli or information. Based on this concept, the idea of individualised "learning styles" originated in the 1970s, and has gained popularity in recent years. It has been proposed that teachers should assess the learning styles of their students and adapt their classroom methods to best fit each student's learning style. The alleged basis for these proposals has been extensively criticised.

Models

David Kolb's model

The David Kolb styles model is based on the Experiential Learning Theory (ELT), as explained in David A. Kolb's book *Experiential Learning: Experience as the source of learning and development*. The ELT model outlines two related approaches toward grasping experience: Concrete Experience and Abstract Conceptualisation, as well as two related approaches toward transforming experience: Reflective Observation and Active Experimentation. According to Kolb's model, the ideal learning process engages all four of these modes in response to situational demands. In order for learning to be effective, all four of these approaches must be incorporated. As individuals attempt to use all four approaches, however, they tend to develop strengths in one experience-grasping approach and one experience-transforming approach. The resulting learning styles are combinations of the individual's preferred approaches. These learning styles are as follows:

1) Converger
2) Diverger
3) Assimilator
4) Accomodator

Convergers are characterised by abstract conceptualisation and active experimentation. They are good at making practical applications of ideas and using deductive reasoning to solve problems.

Divergers tend toward concrete experience and reflective observation. They are imaginative and are good at coming up with ideas and seeing things from different perspectives.

Assimilators are characterised by abstract conceptualisation and reflective observation. They are capable of creating theoretical models by means of inductive reasoning.

Accommodators use concrete experience and active experimentation. They are good at actively engaging with the world and actually doing things instead of merely reading about and studying them.

Anthony Gregorc's model

Gregorc and Butler worked to organise a model describing how the mind works. This model is based on the existence of perceptions-our evaluation of the world by means of an approach that makes sense to us. These perceptions in turn are the foundation of our specific learning strengths, or learning styles.

In this model there are two perceptual qualities: concrete and abstract; and two ordering abilities: random and sequential.

Concrete perceptions involve registering information through the five senses, while abstract perceptions involve the understanding of ideas, qualities, and concepts which cannot be seen.

In regard to the two ordering abilities, sequential involves the organisation of information in a linear, logical way and random involves the organisation of information in chunks and in no specific order.

Both of the perceptual qualities and both of the ordering abilities are present in each individual, but some qualities and ordering abilities are more dominant within certain individuals.

Sudbury model

Some critics of today's schools, of the concept of learning disabilities, of special education, and of response to intervention, take the position that every child has a different learning style and pace, and that each child is unique, not only capable of learning but also capable of succeeding.

Sudbury Model democratic schools assert that there are many ways to study and learn. They argue that learning is a process you do, not a process that is done to you; That is true of everyone. It's basic.

The experience of Sudbury model democratic schools shows that there are many ways to learn without the intervention of teaching, to say, without the intervention of a teacher being imperative. In the case of reading, for instance in the Sudbury model democratic schools, some children learn from being read to, memorising the stories and then ultimately reading them. Others learn from cereal boxes, others from games instructions, others from street signs.

Some teach themselves letter sounds, others syllables, others whole words. Sudbury model democratic schools adduce that in their schools no one child has ever been forced, pushed, urged, cajoled, or bribed into learning how to read or write, and they have had no dyslexia. None of their graduates are real or functional illiterates, and no one who meets their older students could ever guess the age at which they first learned to read or write. In a similar form students learn all the subjects, techniques and skills in these schools.

Describing current instructional methods as homogenisation and lockstep standardisation, alternative approaches are proposed, such as the Sudbury Model of Democratic Education schools, an alternative approach in which children, by enjoying personal freedom thus encouraged to exercise personal responsibility for their actions, learn at their own pace and style rather than following a compulsory and chronologically-based curriculum. Proponents of unschooling have also claimed that children raised in this method learn at their own pace and style, and do not suffer from learning disabilities.

Assessment Methods: Learning Style Inventory

The Learning Style Inventory (LSI) is connected with Kolb's model and is used to determine a student's learning style. The LSI diagnoses an individual's preferences and needs regarding the learning process. It does the following: (1) allows students to designate how they like to learn and indicates how consistent their responses are; (2) provides computerised results which show the student's preferred learning style; (3) provides a foundation upon which teachers can build in interacting with students; (4) provides possible strategies for accommodating learning styles; (5) provides for student involvement in the learning process; (6) provides a class summary so students with similar learning styles can be grouped together.

Evidence or Lack of Evidence

Learning-style theories have been criticised by many. Some psychologists and neuroscientists have questioned the scientific basis for these models and the theories on which they are based. Many educational psychologists believe that there is little evidence for the efficacy of most learning style models, and furthermore, that the models often rest on dubious theoretical grounds.

Applications: Learning Styles in the Classroom

Various researchers have attempted to provide ways in which learning style theory can take effect in the classroom. Learners are affected by their: (1) immediate environment (sound, light, temperature, and design); (2) own emotionality (motivation, persistence, responsibility, and need for structure or flexibility); (3) sociological needs (self, pair, peers, team, adult, or varied); and (4) physical needs (perceptual strengths, intake, time, and mobility). Not only can students identify their preferred learning styles, but that students also score higher on tests, have better attitudes, and are more efficient if they are taught in ways to which they can more easily relate. Therefore, it is to the educator's advantage to teach and test students in their preferred styles.

Although learning styles will inevitably differ among students in the classroom, teachers should try to make changes in their classroom that will be beneficial to every learning style. Some of these changes include room redesign, the development of small-group techniques, and the development of Contract Activity Packages. Redesigning the classroom involves locating dividers that can be used to arrange the room creativel, clearing the floor area, and incorporating student thoughts and ideas into the design of the classroom.

Small-group techniques often include a "circle of knowledge" in which students sit in a circle and discuss a subject collaboratively as well as other techniques such as team learning and brainstorming. Contract Activity Packages are educational plans that facilitate learning by using the following elements: (1) clear statement of what the students needs to learn; (2) multisensory resources (auditory, visual, tactile, kinesthetic) that teach the required information; (3) activities through which the newly-mastered information can be used creatively; (4) the sharing of creative projects within small groups of classmates; (5) at least three small-group techniques; 6) a pre-test, a self-test, and a post-test.

Methods for visual learners include ensuring that students can see words written down, using pictures when describing things, drawing time lines for events in history, writing assignments on the board, using overhead transparencies/handouts, and writing down instructions.

Methods for auditory learners include repeating difficult words and concepts aloud, incorporating small-group discussion, organising debates, listening to books on tape, writing oral reports, and encouraging oral interpretation.

Methods for tactile/kinesthetic learners include providing hands-on activities, assigning projects, having frequent breaks to allow movement, using visual aids and objects in the lesson, using role play, and having field trips. By using a variety of teaching methods from each of these categories, teachers are able to accommodate different learning styles.

Instructional Strategies

There are two broad categories of instruction, sometimes called direct instruction and student-centered instruction. Each of these approaches to teaching is useful for certain purposes. Although instructional strategies differ in their details, they all function to encourage certain major forms of learning and thinking, each with distinctive educational purposes. The forms sometimes overlap, in the sense that one form of thinking may contribute to a student's success with another form. There are three complex forms of thinking that are common goals of classroom learning:

— critical thinking,

— creative thinking, and

problem-solving.

Critical Thinking

Critical thinking is the mental skill for analysing the reliability and validity of information, as well as an attitude or disposition to do so. The skill and attitude may be expressed or displayed with regard to a particular subject matter or topic, but in principle it can occur in any realm of knowledge or living. A critical thinker does not necessarily have a negative attitude in the everyday sense of being critical of someone or something. Instead he or she can simply be thought of as astute: the critical thinker asks key questions, evaluates the evidence for ideas accurately, reasons about problems logically and objectively, and expresses ideas and conclusions clearly and precisely. Last, the critical thinker can apply these habits of mind in more than one realm of life or knowledge, though he or she may not always do so in fact.

With such a broad definition, it is not surprising that educators have nominated a wide variety of specific cognitive skills as contributors to critical thinking. In one study, for example, the researcher found that critical thinking about a published article was stimulated by annotation—writing questions and comments in the margins of the article. In this study students who were initially instructed in ways of annotating reading materials. Later, when the students completed additional readings for assignments, it was found that some students in fact used their annotation skills much more than others—some simply underlined passages, for example, with a highlighting pen. When essays written about the readings were later analysed, the ones written by the annotators were found to be more well-reasoned—more critically astute—than the essays written by the other students.

But the skills comprising critical thinking are not just written ones. In another study, for example, a researcher found that critical thinking can also involve oral discussion with classmates of personal issues or dilemmas. In this study, students were asked to describe to classmates a recent personal incident that disturbed them. Classmates then discussed the incident together in order to identify the precise reasons why the incident was disturbing to the individual, as well as the assumptions that the student had made in thinking about the incident.

The original student—the one who had first told the story—then used the results of the group discussion to frame a topic for a research essay. In one story of a troubling incident, for example, a student told of a time when a store clerk has snubbed or rejected the student during a recent shopping errand. Through discussion, classmates decided that an assumption underlying the student's disturbance was her suspicion that she had been a victim of racial profiling based on her skin color. The student then used this idea as the basis for a research essay on the topic of "racial profiling in retail stores." The group discussion thus stimulated critical thinking in the student and the classmates, but it also relied on their prior critical thinking skills at the same time.

Notice that in both of these research studies, as in others like them, what made the thinking "critical" was students' use of metacognition—strategies for thinking about thinking and for monitoring the success and quality of one's own thinking. There we pointed out that when students acquire experience in building their own knowledge, they also become skilled both at knowing how they learn, and at knowing whether they have learned something well. These two defining qualities of metacognition are part of critical thinking as well. In fostering critical thinking, then, a teacher is really fostering a student's ability to construct or control his or her own thinking and to avoid being controlled by ideas unreflectively.

How best to teach the skills of critical thinking, however, remains a matter of debate. One issue is whether to infuse critical skills into existing courses or to teach them through separate, freestanding units or courses. The first approach has the potential advantage of demonstrating how critical thinking relates to students' entire educations. But it does so at the risk of diluting students' understanding and use of critical thinking simply because critical thinking takes on so in many different forms—its details and appearance varying among courses and teachers. The freestanding approach has the opposite qualities: it stands a better chance of being understood clearly and coherently, but by the same token its connections to other courses, tasks, and activities may not be as clear to students. Unfortunately, research to compare the infusion versus freestanding strategies for teaching critical teaching does not settle the matter; it suggests that either approach can work as long as it is implemented thoroughly and the teachers are committed to the value of critical thinking.

A related issue about teaching critical thinking is about who needs or should learn critical thinking skills the most. Should it in fact be all students? This goal seems the most democratic and therefore appropriate for educators.

Surveys of teachers have found, however, that teachers sometimes favour teaching of critical thinking to high-advantage students—the ones who already achieve well, who come from relatively high-income families, or (for high school students) who take courses intended for university entrance. Presumably the rationale for this bias is that high-advantage students can benefit and/or understand and use critical thinking better than other students. There is little evidence to support this idea, however, even if it were not ethically questionable.

Creative Thinking

Creativity is the ability to make something new that is also useful or valued by others. The "something" can be an object (like an essay or painting), a skill (like playing an instrument), or an action.

Problem-solving

Somewhere between open-ended, creative thinking and the focused learning of content lies problem solving, the analysis and solution of tasks and situations that are somewhat complex or ambiguous and that pose difficulties, inconsistencies, or obstacles of some kind.

Relationships of Major Instructional Strategies

Because the forms of thinking just described—critical thinking, creativity, and problem solving—are broad and educationally important, it is not surprising that educators have identified a lot of strategies to encourage their development. There are so many possibilities, in fact, that just keeping them all in mind—let alone choosing among them—can be difficult.

Lectures and readings

Lectures and readings are traditional staples of educators, particularly when teaching older students. At their best, they are the good examples of pre-organised information, so that the student only has to remember what was said in the lecture or written in the text in order to begin understanding it.

Mastery learning

This term refers to an instructional approach in which all students learn material to an identical, high level, even if some students require more time than others to do so. In mastery learning the teacher directs learning, though sometimes only in the indirect sense of finding, writing, and orchestrating.

Direct instruction

Sometimes this term serves as a synonym for teacher-directed instruction, but more often direct instruction refers to a relatively scripted version of mastery learning, meaning that it not only organises the curriculum into small modules or units, but it also dictates how teachers should teach, including.

Madeline Hunter's effective teaching model

Many teacher-directed strategies have been combined by Madeline Hunter into a single, relatively comprehensive approach that she calls mastery teaching (not to be confused with the related term mastery learning) or the effective teaching model.

Student-centered models of learning

Student-centered models of learning shift some of the responsibility for directing and organising learning from the teacher to the student. Being student-centered does not mean, however, that a teacher gives up organisational and leadership responsibilities completely. It only means.

You can see that choices among instructional strategies are numerous indeed, and that deciding among them depends on the forms of thinking that you want to encourage, the extent to which ideas or skills need to be organised by you to be understood by students, and the extent to which students need to take responsibility for directing their own learning. Although you may have personal preferences among possible instructional strategies, the choice will also be guided by the uniqueness of each situation of teaching—with its particular students, grade-level, content, and purposes.

Instructional Planning

Casey Stengel, a much-admired baseball coach, was talking about baseball when he made this remark. But he could easily have been speaking of teaching as well. Almost by definition, education has purposes, goals, and objectives, and a central task of teaching is to know these are and to transform the most general goals into specific objectives and tasks for students. Otherwise, as Casey Stengel said, students may end up "someplace else" that neither they, nor the teacher, nor anyone else intends. A lot of the clarification and specification of goals needs to happen before a cycle of instruction actually begins, but the benefits of planning happen throughout all phases of teaching.

If students know precisely what they are supposed to learn, they can focus their attention and effort more effectively. If the teacher knows precisely what students are supposed to learn, then the teacher can make better use of class time and choose and design assessments of their learning that are more fair and valid.

At the most general or abstract level, the goals of education include important philosophical ideas like "developing individuals to their fullest potential" and "preparing students to be productive members of society." Few teachers would disagree with these ideas in principle, though they might disagree about their wording or about their relative importance. As a practical matter, however, teachers might have trouble translating such generalities into specific lesson plans or activities for the next day's class.

What does it mean, concretely, to "develop an individual to his or her fullest potential"? Does it mean, for example, that a language arts teacher should ask students to write an essay about their personal interests, or does it mean that the teacher should help students learn to write as well as possible on any topic, even ones that are not of immediate interest? And what exactly should a teacher do, from day to day, to "prepare students to be productive members of society" as well? Answers to questions like these are needed to plan instruction effectively. But the answers are not obvious simply by examining statements of general educational goals.

National and state learning standards

Some (but not all) of the work of transforming such general purposes into more precise teaching goals and even more precise objectives has been performed by broad national organisations that represent educators and other experts about particular subjects or types of teaching. The groups have proposed national standards, which are summaries of what students can reasonably be expected to learn at particular grade levels and in particular subjects areas. In the United States, in addition, all state governments create state standards that serve much the same purpose: they express what students in the state should (and hopefully can) learn at all grade levels and in all subjects.

Because they focus on grade levels and subject areas, general statements of educational standards tend to be a bit more specific than the broader philosophical goals. As a rule of thumb, too, state standards tend to be more comprehensive than national standards, both in coverage of grade levels and of subjects. The difference reflects the broad responsibility of states in the United States for all aspects of public education; national organisations, in contrast, usually assume responsible only for a particular subject area or particular group of students.

Either type of standards provides a first step, however, toward transforming the grandest purposes of schooling (like developing the individual or preparing for society) into practical classroom activities. But they provide a first step only. Most statements of standards do not make numerous or detailed suggestions of actual activities or tasks for students, though some might include brief classroom examples—enough to clarify the meaning of a standard, but not enough to plan an actual classroom programme for extended periods of time. For these latter purposes, teachers rely on more the detailed documents, the ones often called curriculum frameworks and curriculum guides.

Curriculum Frameworks and Curriculum Guides

The terms curriculum framework and curriculum guide sometimes are used almost interchangeably, but for convenience we will use them to refer to two distinct kinds of documents. The more general of the two is curriculum framework, which is a document that explains how content standards can or should be organised for a particular subject and at various grade levels. Sometimes this information is referred to as the scope and sequence for a curriculum. A curriculum framework document is like a standards statement in that it does not usually provide a lot of detailed suggestions for daily teaching. It differs from a standards statement, though, in that it analyses each general standard in a curriculum into more specific skills that students need to learn, often a dozen or more per standard. The language or terminology of a framework statement also tends to be somewhat more concrete than a standards statement, in the sense that it is more likely to name behaviours of students—things that a teacher might see them do or hear them say. Sometimes, but not always, it may suggest ways for assessing whether students have in fact acquired each skill listed in the document. Teachers' need for detailed activity suggestions is more likely to be met by a curriculum guide, a document devoted to graphic descriptions of activities that foster or encourage the specific skills explained in a curriculum framework document. The descriptions may mention or list curriculum goals served by an activity, but they are also likely to specify materials that a teacher need, time requirements, for grouping students, drawings or diagrams of key equipment or materials, and sometimes even suggestions for what to say to students at different points during the activity. In these ways the descriptions may resemble lesson plans.

Formulating learning objectives

Given curriculum frameworks and guides like the ones just described, how do you choose and formulate actual learning objectives? Basically there are two approaches: either start by selecting content or topics that what you want students to know (the cognitive approach) or start with what you want students to do (the behavioural approach).

Taxonomies of educational objectives

When educators have proposed taxonomies of educational objectives, they have tended to focus on one of three areas or domains of psychological functioning: either students' cognition (thought), students' feelings and emotions (affect), or students' physical skills (psychomotor abilities). Of these three areas, they have tended to focus the most attention on cognition. The taxonomy originated by Benjamin Bloom, for example, deals entirely with cognitive outcomes of instruction.

Students as a source of instructional goals

The instructional planning has described goals and objectives as if they are selected primarily by educators and teachers, and not by students themselves. The assumption may be correct in many cases, but there are problems with it. One problem is that choosing goals and objectives for students, rather than by students, places a major burden on everyone involved in education—curriculum writers, teachers, and.

Enhancing student learning through a variety of resources

Whether instructional goals originate from curriculum documents, students' expressed interests, or a mixture of both, students are more likely to achieve the goals if teachers draw on a wide variety of resources. As a practical matter, this means looking for materials and experiences that supplement—or occasionally even replace—the most traditional forms of information, such as textbooks.

Creating bridges among curriculum goals and students' Experiences

To succeed, then, instructional plans do require a variety of resources. But they also require more: they need to connect with students' prior experiences and knowledge. Sometimes the connections can develop as a result of.

Planning for Instruction as well as for Learning

It started with the idea that teachers need to locate curriculum goals, usually from a state department of education or a publisher of a curriculum document. These authorities provide for individual classroom teachers, and how their documents can be clarified and rendered specific enough for classroom use. Instructional planning, in other words, has to be not just for students, but also by students, at least to some extent.

Assessment of Student Learning

Best practices in assessing student learning have undergone dramatic changes in the last 20 years. The tests varied little format and students always did them individually with pencil and paper. Now, however, many teachers—including mathematics teachers—use a wide variety of methods to determine what their students have learned and also use this assessment information to modify their instruction.

Assessment is an integrated process of gaining information about students' learning and making value judgments about their progress. Information about students' progress can be obtained from a variety of sources including projects, portfolios, performances, observations, and tests. The information about students' learning is often assigned specific numbers or grades and this involves measurement. Measurement answers the question, "How much?" and is used most commonly when the teacher scores a test or product and assigns numbers. Evaluation is the process of making judgments about the assessment information. These judgments may be about individual students, the assessment method used, or one's own teaching.

Assessment for learning is often called formative assessment, i.e., it takes place during the course of instruction and provides information that teachers can use to revise their teaching and students can use to improve their learning. Formative assessment includes both informal assessment involving spontaneous unsystematic observations of students' behaviours and formal assessment involving preplanned, systematic gathering of data.

Assessment *of* learning involves assessing students in order to certify their competence and to fulfill accountability mandates, which is primarily about standardized tests. Assessment of learning is typically summative, that is, administered after the instruction is completed. Summative assessments provide information about how well students mastered the material, whether students are ready for the next unit, and what grades should be given.

Using assessment to advance students' learning not just check on learning requires viewing assessment as a process that is integral to the all phases of teaching including planning, classroom interactions and instruction, communication with parents, and self-reflection. Essential steps in assessment for learning include:

Step 1: Having Clear Instructional Goals and Communicating them to Students

This may be hard for beginning teachers. For example, Vanessa, a middle school social studies teacher, might say that the goal of her next unit is, "Students will learn about the civil war." Clearer goals require that Vanessa decides what it is about the civil wear she wants her students to learn, e.g. the dates and names of battles, the causes of the civil war, the differing perspectives of those living in the North and the South, or the day-to-day experiences of soldiers fighting in the war. Vanessa cannot devise appropriate assessments of her students' learning about the civil war until she is clear about her own purposes. For effective teaching Vanessa also needs to communicate clearly the goals and objectives to her students so they know what is important for them to learn. No matter how thorough a teacher's planning has been, if students do not know what they are supposed to learn they will not learn as much.

Step 2: Selecting Appropriate Assessment Techniques

Selecting and administrating assessment techniques that are appropriate for the goals of instruction as well as the developmental level of the students are crucial components of effective assessment for learning. Teachers need to know the characteristics of a wide variety of classroom assessment techniques and how these techniques can be adapted for various content, skills, and student characteristics. They also should understand the role reliability, validity, and the absence of bias should play is choosing and using assessment techniques.

Step 3: Using Assessment to Enhance Motivation and Confidence

Students' motivation and confidence is influenced by the type of assessment used as well as the feedback given about the assessment results. Consider,

Samantha a college student who takes a history class in which the professor's lectures and text book focus on really interesting major themes. However, the assessments are all multiple choice tests that ask about facts and Samantha, who initially enjoys the classes and readings, becomes angry, loses confidence she can do well, and begins to spend less time on the class material. In contrast, some instructors have has observed that that many students in educational psychology classes like the one you are now taking will work harder on assessments that are case studies rather than more traditional exams or essays.

Step 4: Adjusting Instruction Based on Information

An essential component of assessment for learning is that the teacher uses the information gained from assessment to adjust instruction. These adjustments occur in the middle of a lesson when a teacher may decide that students' responses to questions indicate sufficient understanding to introduce a new topic, or that her observations of students' behaviour indicates that they do not understand the assignment and so need further explanation. Adjustments also occur when the teacher reflects on the instruction after the lesson is over and is planning for the next day.

Step 5: Communicating with Parents and Guardians

Students' learning and development is enhanced when teachers communicate with parents regularly about their children's performance. Teachers communicate with parents in a variety of ways including newsletters, telephone conversations, email, school district websites and parent-teachers conferences. Effective communication requires that teachers can clearly explain the purpose and characteristics of the assessment as well as the meaning of students' performance. This requires a thorough knowledge of the types and purposes of teacher made and standardized assessments and well as clear communication skills.

References

Cole, M, et al., (2005). *The Development of Children*, New York: Worth Publishers.

Crain, William C. (1985).*Theories of Development* (2Rev ed.). Prentice-Hall.

Kauchak, D., and Eggen, P. (2008). *Introduction to teaching: Becoming a professional* (3rd ed.). Upper Saddle River, NJ: Pearson Education, Inc.

Lave, J. and Wenger, E. (1991). *Situated Learning, Legitimate peripheral participation*, Cambridge: University of Cambridge Press.

10

Motivating School Children

Motivation is an internal state that activates, guides and sustains behavior. School psychology research on motivation is concerned with the volition or will that students bring to a task, their level of interest and intrinsic motivation, the personally held goals that guide their behavior, and their belief about the causes of their success or failure. As intrinsic motivation deals with activities that act as their own rewards, extrinsic motivation deals with motivations that are brought on by consequences or punishments.

A form of attribution theory developed by Bernard Weiner describes how students' beliefs about the causes of academic success or failure affect their emotions and motivations. For example, when students attribute failure to lack of ability, and ability is perceived as uncontrollable, they experience the emotions of shame and embarrassment and consequently decrease effort and show poorer performance. In contrast, when students attribute failure to lack of effort, and effort is perceived as controllable, they experience the emotion of guilt and increase effort and show improved performance.

Motivational theories also explain how learners' goals affect the way they engage with academic tasks. Those who have mastery goals strive to increase their ability and knowledge. Those who have performance approach goals strive for high grades and seek opportunities to demonstrate their abilities. Those who have performance avoidance goals are driven by fear of failure and avoid situations where their abilities are exposed. Research has found that mastery goals are associated with many positive outcomes such as persistence in the face of failure, preference for challenging tasks, creativity and intrinsic motivation. Performance avoidance goals are associated with negative outcomes such as poor concentration while studying, disorganized studying, less self-regulation, shallow information processing and test anxiety. Performance approach goals are associated with positive outcomes, and some negative outcomes such as an unwillingness to seek help and shallow information processing.

Locus of control is a salient factor in the successful academic performance of students. During the 1970s and '80s, Cassandra B. Whyte did significant educational research studying locus of control as related to the academic achievement of students pursuing higher education coursework. Much of her educational research and publications focused upon the theories of Julian B. Rotter in regard to the importance of internal control and successful academic performance. Whyte reported that individuals who perceive and believe that their hard work may lead to more successful academic outcomes, instead of depending on luck or fate, persist and achieve academically at a higher level. Therefore, it is important to provide education and counseling in this regard.

Misconceptions about Motivation

Motivation is typically defined as the forces that account for the arousal, selection, direction, and continuation of behaviour. Nevertheless, many teachers have at least two major misconceptions about motivation that prevent them from using this concept with maximum effectiveness. One misconception is that some students are unmotivated. Strictly speaking, that is not an accurate statement. As long as a student chooses goals and expends a certain amount of effort to achieve them, he is, by definition, motivated. What teachers really mean is that students are not motivated to behave in the way teachers would like them to behave.

The second misconception is that one person can directly motivate another. This view is inaccurate because motivation comes from within a person. What you can do, with the help of the various motivation theories discussed in this chapter, is create the circumstances that influence students to do what you want them to do.

Many factors determine whether the students in your classes will be motivated or not motivated to learn. You should not be surprised to discover that no single theoretical interpretation of motivation explains all aspects of student interest or lack of it. Different theoretical interpretations do, however, shed light on why some students in a given learning situation are more likely to want to learn than others. Furthermore, each theoretical interpretation can serve as the basis for the development of techniques for motivating students in the classroom.

Sometimes it is useful to think of motivation not as something "inside" a student driving the student's behaviour, but as equivalent to the student's outward behaviours. In its most thorough-going form, behaviourism focuses almost completely on what can be directly seen or heard about a person's behaviour, and has relatively few comments about what may lie behind the behaviour. When it comes to motivation, this perspective means minimising or even ignoring the distinction between the inner drive or energy of students, and the outward behaviours that express the drive or energy. The two are considered the same, or nearly so.

Equating the inner and the outward might seem to violate common sense. How can a student do something without some sort of feeling or thought to make the action happen? This very question has led to alternative models of motivation that are based on cognitive rather than behaviourist theories of learning.

Sometimes the circumstances of teaching limit teachers' opportunities to distinguish between inner motivation and outward behaviour. Certainly teachers see plenty of student behaviours-signs of motivation of some sort. But the multiple demands of teaching can limit the time needed to determine what the behaviours mean. If a student asks a lot of questions during discussions, for example, is he or she is curious about the material itself, or just wanting to look intelligent in front of classmates and the teacher? In a class with many students and a busy agenda, there may not be a lot of time for a teacher to decide between these possibilities. In other cases, the problem may not be limited time as much as communication difficulties with a student.

Consider a student who is still learning English, or who belongs to a cultural community that uses patterns of conversation that are unfamiliar to the teacher, or who has a disability that limits the student's general language skill. In these cases discerning the student's inner motivations may take more time and effort. It is important to invest the extra time and effort for such students, but while a teacher is doing so, it is also important for her to guide and influence the students' behaviour in constructive directions. That is where behaviourist approaches to motivation can help.

Operant Conditioning

The most common version of the behavioural perspective on motivation is the theory of operant conditioning associated with B. F. Skinner. The description in that chapter focused on behavioural learning, but the same operant model can be transformed into an account of motivation. In the operant model, you may recall, a behaviour being learned increases in frequency or likelihood because performing it makes a reinforcement available.

To understand this model in terms of motivation, think of the likelihood of response as the motivation and the reinforcement as the motivator. Imagine, for example, that a student learns by operant conditioning to answer questions during class discussions: each time the student answers a question, the teacher praises this behaviour. In addition to thinking of this situation as behavioural learning, however, you can also think of it in terms of motivation: the likelihood of the student answering questions is increasing because of the teacher's praise.

Many concepts from operant conditioning, in fact, can be understood in motivational terms. The decrease in performance frequency can be thought of as a loss of motivation, and removal of the reinforcement can be thought of as removal of the motivator.

Behavioural Perspectives on Motivation

As we mentioned, behaviourist perspectives about motivation do reflect a classroom reality: that teachers sometimes lack time and therefore must focus simply on students' appropriate outward behaviour. But there are none the less cautions about adopting this view. An obvious one is the ambiguity of students' specific behaviours; what looks like a sign of one motive to the teacher may in fact be a sign of some other motive to the student. If a student looks at the teacher intently while she is speaking, does it mean the student is motivated to learn, or only that the student is daydreaming? If a student invariably looks away while the teacher is speaking, does it mean that the student is disrespectful of the teacher, or that student comes from a family or cultural group where avoiding eye contact actually shows more respect for a speaker than direct eye contact?

Another concern about behaviourist perspectives, including operant conditioning, is that it leads teachers to ignore students' choices and preferences, and to "play God" by making choices on their behalf. According to this criticism, the distinction between "inner" motives and expressions of motives in outward behaviour does not disappear just because a teacher chooses to treat a motive and the behavioural expression of a motive as equivalent. Students usually do know what they want or desire, and their wants or desires may not always correspond to what a teacher chooses to reinforce or ignore. Approaches that are exclusively behavioural, it is argued, are not sensitive enough to students' intrinsic, self-sustaining motivations.

There is truth to this allegation if a teacher actually does rely on rewarding behaviours that she alone has chosen, or even if she persists in reinforcing behaviours that students already find motivating without external reinforcement. In those cases reinforcements can backfire: instead of serving as an incentive to desired behaviour, reinforcement can become a reminder of the teacher's power and of students' lack of control over their own actions.

A classic research study of intrinsic motivation illustrated the problem nicely. In the study, researchers rewarded university students for two activities—solving puzzles and writing newspaper headlines—that they already found interesting. Some of the students, however, were paid to do these activities, whereas others were not. Under these conditions, the students who were paid were less likely to engage in the activities following the experiment than were the students who were not paid, even though both groups had been equally interested in the activities to begin with. The extrinsic reward of payment, it seemed, interfered with the intrinsic reward of working the puzzles.

Later studies confirmed this effect in numerous situations, though they have also found certain conditions where extrinsic rewards do not reduce intrinsic rewards. Extrinsic rewards are not as harmful, for example, if a person is paid "by the hour" rather than piecemeal. They also are less harmful if the task itself is relatively well defined and high-quality performance is expected at all times. So there are still times and ways when externally determined reinforcements are useful and effective. In general, however, extrinsic rewards do seem to undermine intrinsic motivation often enough that they need to be used selectively and thoughtfully. As it happens, help with being selective and thoughtful can be found in the other, more cognitively oriented theories of motivation. These use the goals, interests, and beliefs of students as ways of explaining differences in students' motives and in how the motives affect engagement with school. We turn to these cognitively oriented theories next, beginning with those focused on students' goals.

Importance of Motivation

One way motives vary is by the kind of goals that students set for themselves, and by how the goals support students' academic achievement.

In addition to holding different kinds of goals-with consequent differences in academic motivation-students show obvious differences in level of interest in the topics and tasks of the classroom.

Attributions are perceptions about the causes of success and failure. Suppose that you get a low mark on a test and are wondering what caused the low mark.

In addition to being influenced by their goals, interests, and attributions, students' motives are affected by specific beliefs about the student's personal capacities. In self-efficacy theory the beliefs become a primary, explicit explanation for motivation.

Motivation is affected by several factors, including reinforcement for behaviour, but especially also students' goals, interests, and sense of self-efficacy and self-determination. The factors combine to create two general sources of motivation: students' expectation of success and the value that students place on a goal. Viewing motivation in this way is often called the expectancy-value model.

Most motivation theorists assume that motivation is involved in the performance of all learned responses; that is, a learned behaviour will not occur unless it is energised. The major question among psychologists, in general, is whether motivation is a primary or secondary influence on behaviour. That is, are changes in behaviour better explained by principles of environmental/ecological influences, perception, memory, cognitive development, emotion, explanatory style, or personality or are concepts unique to motivation more pertinent.

Motivation and Emotion

Emotion is different from motivation in that there is not necessarily a goal orientation affiliated with it. Emotions occur as a result of an interaction between perception of environmental stimuli, neural/hormonal responses to these perceptions, and subjective cognitive labeling of these feelings.

Evidence suggests there is a small core of core emotions that are uniquely associated with a specific facial expression. This implies that there are a small number of unique biological responses that are genetically hard-wired to specific facial expressions.

A further implication is that the process works in reverse: if you want to change your feelings, you can do so by changing your facial expression. That is, if you are motivated to change how you feel and your feeling is associated with a specific facial expression, you can change that feeling by purposively changing your facial expression. Since most of us would rather feel happy than otherwise, the most appropriate facial expression would be a smile.

In general, explanations regarding the source(s) of motivation can be categorised as either extrinsic (outside the person) or intrinsic. Intrinsic sources and corresponding theories can be further subcategorised as either body/physical, mind/mental or transpersonal/spiritual.

In current literature, needs are now viewed as dispositions toward action. Action or overt behaviour may be initiated by either positive or negative incentives or a combination of both. The following chart provides a brief overview of the different sources of motivation that have been studied. While initiation of action can be traced to each of these domains, it appears likely that initiation of behaviour may be more related to emotions and/or the affective area while persistence may be more related to conation or goal-orientation.

Sources of Motivational Needs

Behavioural/external

a) elicited by stimulus associated/connected to innately connected stimulus

b) obtain desired, pleasant consequences (rewards) or escape/avoid undesired, unpleasant consequences

Social

a) imitate positive models

b) be a part of a group or a valued member

Biological

a) increase/decrease stimulation (arousal)

b) activate senses (taste, touch, smell, etc.

c) decrease hunger, thirst, discomfort, etc.

d) maintain homeostasis, balance

Cognitive

a) maintain attention to something interesting or threatening

b) develop meaning or understanding

c) increase/decrease cognitive disequilibrium; uncertainty

d) solve a problem or make a decision

e) figure something out

f) eliminate threat or risk

Affective

a) increase/decrease affective dissonance

b) increase feeling good

c) decrease feeling bad

d) increase security of or decrease threats to self-esteem

e) maintain levels of optimism and enthusiasm

Conative

a) meet individually developed/selected goal

b) obtain personal dream

c) develop or maintain self-efficacy

d) take control of one's life

e) eliminate threats to meeting goal, obtaining dream

f) reduce others' control of one's life

Spiritual

a) understand purpose of one's life

b) connect self to ultimate unknowns

THEORIES OF MOTIVATION

Many of the theories of motivation address issues introduced previously in these materials. The following provides a brief overview to any terms or concepts that have not been previously discussed.

Behavioural

Each of the major theoretical approaches in behavioural learning theory posits a primary factor in motivation. Classical conditioning states that biological responses to associated stimuli energise and direct behaviour. Operant learning states the primary factor is consequences: the application of reinforcers provides incentives to increase behaviour; the application of punishers provides disincentives that result in a decrease in behaviour.

Cognitive

There are several motivational theories that trace their roots to the information processing approach to learning. These approaches focus on the categories and labels people use help to identify thoughts, emotions, dispositions, and behaviours.

The first is cognitive dissonance theory which is in some respects similar to disequilibrium in Piaget's theory of cognitive development. The implication is that if we can create the appropriate amount of disequilibrium, this will in turn lead to the individual changing his or her behaviour which in turn will lead to a change in thought patterns which in turn leads to more change in behaviour.

A second cognitive approach is attribution theory. This theory proposes that every individual tries to explain success or failure of self and others by offering certain "attributions." These attributions are either internal or external and are either under control or not under control.

In a teaching/learning environment, it is important to assist the learner to develop a self-attribution explanation of effort. If the person has an attribution of ability as soon as the individual experiences some difficulties in the learning process, he or she will decrease appropriate learning behaviour. If the person has an external attribution, then nothing the person can do will help that individual in a learning situation. In this case, there is nothing to be done by the individual when learning problems occur.

A third cognitive approach is expectancy theory which proposes the following equation:

Motivation = Perceived Probability of Success (Expectancy)

Connection of Success and Reward (Instrumentality)

Value of Obtaining Goal (Valance, Value)

Since this formula states that the three factors of Expectancy, Instrumentality, and Valance or Value are to be multiplied by each other, a low value in one will result in a low value of motivation. Therefore, all three must be present in order for motivation to occur. That is, if an individual doesn't believe he or she can be successful at a task OR the individual does not see a connection between his or her activity and success OR the individual does not value the results of success, then the probability is lowered that the individual will engage in the required learning activity. From the perspective of this theory, all three variables must be high in order for motivation and the resulting behaviour to be high.

Humanistic Theories

One of the most influential writers in the area of motivation is Abraham Maslow.

Abraham Maslow attempted to synthesize a large body of research related to human motivation. Prior to Maslow, researchers generally focused separately on such factors as biology, achievement, or power to explain what energises, directs, and sustains human behaviour. Maslow posited a hierarchy of human needs based on two groupings: deficiency needs and growth needs. Within the deficiency needs, each lower need must be met before moving to the next higher level. Once each of these needs has been satisfied, if at some future time a deficiency is detected, the individual will act to remove the deficiency. The first four levels are:

1) *Physiological*: hunger, thirst, bodily comforts, etc.;
2) *Safety/security*: out of danger;
3) *Belongingness and Love*: affiliate with others, be accepted; and
4) *Esteem*: to achieve, be competent, gain approval and recognition.

According to Maslow, an individual is ready to act upon the growth needs if and only if the deficiency needs are met. Maslow's initial conceptualisation included only one growth need—self-actualisation. Self-actualised people are characterised by: (1) being problem-focused; (2) incorporating an ongoing freshness of appreciation of life; (3) a concern about personal growth; and (4) the ability to have peak experiences. Maslow later differentiated the growth need of self-actualisation, specifically naming two lower-level growth needs prior to general level of self-actualisation and one beyond that level. They are:

5) *Cognitive:* to know, to understand, and explore;
6) *Aesthetic:* symmetry, order, and beauty;
7) *Self-actualisation:* to find self-fulfilment and realise one's potential; and
8) *Self-transcendence:* to connect to something beyond the ego or to help others find self-fulfilment and realise their potential.

Maslow's basic position is that as one becomes more self-actualised and self-transcendent, one becomes more wise and automatically knows what to do in a wide variety of situations.

Maslow's hierarchy can be used to describe the kinds of information that individual's seek at different levels. For example, individuals at the lowest level seek coping information in order to meet their basic needs. Information that is not directly connected to helping a person meet his or her needs in a very short time span is simply left unattended. Individuals at the safety level need helping information. They seek to be assisted in seeing how they can be safe and secure.

Enlightening information is sought by individuals seeking to meet their belongingness needs. Quite often this can be found in books or other materials on relationship development. Empowering information is sought by people at the esteem level. They are looking for information on how their ego can be developed. Finally, people in the growth levels of cogntive, aesthetic, and self-actualisation seek edifying information.

Maslow recognised that not all personalities followed his proposed hierarchy. While a variety of personality dimensions might be considered as related to motivational needs, one of the most often cited is that of introversion and extroversion. Reorganising Maslow's hierarchy and considering the introversion/extraversion dimension of personality results in three levels, each with an introverted and extroverted component. This organisation suggests there may be two aspects of each level that differentiate how people relate to each set of needs. Different personalities might relate more to one dimension than the other. For example, an introvert at the level of Other/Relatedness might be more concerned with his or her own perceptions of being included in a group, whereas an extrovert at that same level would pay more attention to how others value that membership.

At this point there is little agreement about the identification of basic human needs and how they are ordered.

Notice that bonding and relatedness are a component of every theory. However, there do not seem to be any others that are mentioned by all theorists. This lack of accord may be a result of different philosophies of researchers rather than differences among human beings. A person's explanatory or attributional style will modify the list of basic needs. Therefore, it seems appropriate to ask people what they want and how their needs could be met rather than relying on an unsupported theory.

Maslow's work lead to additional attempts to develop a grand theory of motivation, a theory that would put all of the factors influencing motivation into one model. An example proposes five factors as the sources of motivation: (1) Instrumental Motivation, (2) Intrinsic Process Motivation, (3) Goal Internalisation, (4) Internal Self Concept-based Motivation, (5) External Self Concept-based Motivation. Individuals are influenced by all five factors, though in varying degrees that can change in specific situations.

Factors one and five are both externally-oriented. The main difference is that individuals who are instrumentally motivated are influenced more by immediate actions in the environment whereas individuals who are self-concept motivated are influenced more by their constructions of external demands and ideals.

Factors two, three, and four are more internally-oriented. In the case of intrinsic process, the specific task is interesting and provides immediate internal reinforcement. The individual with a goal-internalisation orientation is more task-oriented whereas the person with an internal self-concept orientation is more influenced by individual constructions of the ideal self.

Social Learning

Social learning theory suggests that modeling and vicarious learning are important motivators of behaviour.

Social Cognition

Social cognition theory proposes reciprocal determination as a primary factor in both learning and motivation. In this view, the environment, an individual's behaviour, and the individual's characteristics both influence and are influenced by each other two components. Bandura highlights self-efficacy and self-regulation the establishment of goals, the development of a plan to attain those goals, the commitment to implement that plan, the actual implementation of the plan, and subsequent actions of reflection and modification or redirection.

Achievement of Motivation

One classification of motivation differentiates among achievement, power, and social factors. In the area of achievement motivation, the work on goal-theory has differentiated three separate types of goals: mastery goals which focus on gaining competence or mastering a new set of knowledge or skills; performance goals which focus on achieving normative-based standards, doing better than others, or doing well without a lot of effort; and social goals which focus on relationships among people. In the context of school learning, which involves operating in a relatively structured environment, students with mastery goals outperform students with either performance or social goals. However, in life success, it seems critical that individuals have all three types of goals in order to be very successful.

One aspect of this theory is that individuals are motivated to either avoid failure or achieve success. In the former situation, the individual is more likely to select easy or difficult tasks, thereby either achieving success or having a good excuse for why failure occurred. In the latter situation, the individual is more likely to select moderately difficult tasks which will provide an interesting challenge, but still keep the high expectations for success.

Impacting Motivation in the Classroom

There are a variety of reasons why individuals may be lacking in motivation and provides a list of specific behaviours associated with high academic achievement. This is an excellent checklist to help students develop the conative component of their lives. In addition, as stated previously in these materials, teacher efficacy is a powerful input variable related to student achievement. There are a variety of specific actions that teachers can take to increase motivation on classroom tasks. In general, these fall into the two categories discussed above: intrinsic motivation and extrinsic motivation.

Intrinsic

a) Explain or show why learning a particular content or skill is important.

b) Create and/or maintain curiosity.

c) Provide a variety of activities and sensory stimulations.

d) Provide games and simulations.

e) Set goals for learning.

f) Relate learning to student needs.

g) Help student develop plan of action.

Extrinsic

a) Provide clear expectations.

b) Give corrective feedback.

c) Provide valuable rewards.

d) Make rewards available.

As a general rule, teachers need to use as much of the intrinsic suggestions as possible while recognising that not all students will be appropriately motivated by them. The extrinsic suggestions will work, but it must be remembered that they do so only as long as the student is under the control of the teacher. When outside of that control, unless the desired goals and behaviours have been internalised, the learner will cease the desired behaviour and operate according to his or her internal standards or to other external factors.

Operant Conditioning and Social Learning Theory

After demonstrating that organisms tend to repeat actions that are reinforced and that behaviour can be shaped by reinforcement, Skinner developed the technique of programmed instruction to make it possible for students to be reinforced for every correct response. According to him, supplying the correct answer—and being informed by the programme that it is the correct answer—motivates the student to go on to the next frame; and as the student works through the programme, the desired terminal behaviour is progressively shaped.

Following Skinner's lead, many behavioural learning theorists devised techniques of behaviour modification on the assumption that students are motivated to complete a task by being promised a reward of some kind. Many times the reward takes the form of praise or a grade. Sometimes it is a token that can be traded in for some desired object; and at other times the reward may be the privilege of engaging in a self-selected activity.

Operant conditioning interpretations of learning may help reveal why some students react favourably to particular subjects and dislike others. For instance, some students may enter a required math class with a feeling of delight, while others may feel that they have been sentenced to prison.

Skinner suggests that such differences can be traced to past experiences. He would argue that the student who loves math has been shaped to respond that way by a series of positive experiences with maths. The maths hater, in contrast, may have suffered a series of negative experiences.

The Power of Persuasive Models Social learning theorists, such as Albert Bandura, call attention to the importance of observation, imitation, and vicarious reinforcement. A student who identifies with and admires a teacher of a particular subject may work hard partly to please the admired individual and partly to try becoming like that individual. A student who observes an older brother or sister reaping benefits from earning high grades may strive to do the same with the expectation of experiencing the same or similar benefits. A student who notices that a classmate receives praise from the teacher after acting in a certain way may decide to imitate such behaviour to win similar rewards.

Cognitive Views of Motivation

Cognitive views stress that human behaviour is influenced by the way people think about themselves and their environment. The direction that behaviour takes can be explained by four influences: the inherent need to construct an organised and logically consistent knowledge base, one's expectations for successfully completing a task, the factors that one believes account for success and failure, and one's beliefs about the nature of cognitive ability.

Impact of Cognitive Development

This view is based on Jean Piaget's principles of equilibration, assimilation, accommodation, and schema formation. Piaget proposes that children possess an inherent desire to maintain a sense of organisation and balance in their conception of the world. A sense of equilibration may be experienced if a child assimilates a new experience by relating it to an existing scheme, or the child may accommodate by modifying an existing scheme if the new experience is too different.

In addition, individuals will repeatedly use new schemes because of an inherent desire to master their environment. This explains why young children can, with no loss of enthusiasm, sing the same song, tell the same story, and play the same game over and over and why they repeatedly open and shut doors to rooms and cupboards with no seeming purpose. It also explains why older children take great delight in collecting and organising almost everything they can get their hands on and why adolescents who have begun to attain formal operational thinking will argue incessantly about all the unfairness in the world and how it can be eliminated.

Need for Achievement

Have you ever decided to take on a moderately difficult task and then found that you had somewhat conflicting feelings about it? On the one hand, you felt eager to start the course, confident that you would be pleased with your performance. But on the other hand, you also felt a bit of anxiety because of the small possibility of failure. Now try to imagine the opposite situation. In reaction to a suggestion to take a course outside your major, you flatly refuse because the probability of failure seems great, while the probability of success seems quite small.

Individuals with a high need for achievement have a stronger expectation of success than they do a fear of failure for most tasks and therefore anticipate a feeling of pride in accomplishment. When given a choice, high-need achievers seek out moderately challenging tasks because they offer an optimal balance between challenge and expected success. By contrast, individuals with a low need for achievement avoid such tasks because their fear of failure greatly outweighs their expectation of success, and they therefore anticipate feelings of shame. When faced with a choice, they typically opt either for relatively easy tasks because the probability of success is high or rather difficult tasks because there is no shame in failing to achieve a lofty goal.

For people to succeed at life in general, they must first experience success in one important aspect of their lives. For most children, that one important part should be school. But the traditional approach to evaluating learning, which emphasizes comparative grading, allows only a minority of students to achieve A's and B's and feel successful. The self-worth of the remaining students suffers, which depresses their motivation to achieve on subsequent classroom tasks.

Maslow's Theory of Growth Motivation

Maslow describes 17 propositions, that he believes would have to be incorporated into any sound theory of growth motivation to meet them. Referring to need gratification as the most important single principle underlying all development, he adds that "the single, holistic principle that binds together the multiplicity of human motives is the tendency for a new and higher need to emerge as the lower need fulfills itself by being sufficiently gratified". He elaborates on this basic principle by proposing a five-level hierarchy of needs. Physiological needs are at the bottom of the hierarchy, followed in ascending order by safety, belongingness and love, esteem, and self-actualisation needs. This order reflects differences in the relative strength of each need. The lower a need is in the hierarchy, the greater is its strength because when a lower-level need is activated, people will stop trying to satisfy a higher-level need and focus on satisfying the currently active lower-level need.

The first four needs are often referred to as deficiency needs because they motivate people to act only when they are unmet to some degree. Self-actualisation, by contrast, is often called a growth need because people constantly strive to satisfy it. Basically, self-actualisation refers to the need for self-fulfilment — the need to develop all of one's potential talents and capabilities. For example, an individual who felt she had the capability to write novels, teach, practise medicine, and raise children would not feel self-actualised until all of these goals had been accomplished to some minimal degree. Because it is at the top of the hierarchy and addresses the potential of the whole person, self-actualisation is discussed more frequently than the other needs.

In addition to the five basic needs that compose the hierarchy, Maslow describes cognitive needs and aesthetic needs. While not part of the basic hierarchy, these two classes of needs play a critical role in the satisfaction of basic needs. Maslow maintains that such conditions as the freedom to investigate and learn, fairness, honesty, and orderliness in interpersonal relationships are critical because their absence makes satisfaction of the five basic needs impossible.

Cooperative Learning and Motivation

Classroom tasks can be structured so that students are forced to compete with one another, work individually, or cooperate with one another to obtain the rewards that teachers make available for successfully completing these tasks. Traditionally, competitive arrangements have been assumed to be superior to the other two in increasing motivation and learning. But reviews of the research literature found cooperative arrangements to be far superior in producing these benefits.

Classroom Reward Structures

Competitive goal structures are typically norm referenced. This traditional practice of grading on the curve predetermines the percentage of A, B, C, D, and F grades regardless of the actual distribution of test scores. Because only a small percentage of students in any group can achieve the highest rewards and because this accomplishment must come at some other students' expense, competitive goal structures are characterised by negative interdependence. Students try to outdo one another, view classmates' failures as an advantage, and come to believe that the winners deserve their rewards because they are inherently better.

Some researchers have argued that competitive reward structures lead students to focus on ability as the primary basis for motivation. This orientation is reflected in the question, "Am I smart enough to accomplish this task?" When ability is the basis for motivation, competing successfully in the classroom may be seen as relevant to self-esteem, difficult to accomplish, and uncertain. These perceptions may cause some students to avoid challenging subjects or tasks, to give up in the face of difficulty, to reward themselves only if they win a competition, and to believe that their own successes are due to ability, whereas the successes of others are due to luck.

Individualistic goal structures are characterised by students working alone and earning rewards solely on the quality of their own efforts. The success or failure of other students is irrelevant. All that matters is whether the student meets the standards for a particular task. Thirty students working by themselves at computer terminals are functioning in an individual reward structure. Individual structures lead students to focus on task effort as the primary basis for motivation. Whether a student perceives a task as difficult depends on how successful she has been with that type of task in the past.

Cooperative goal structures are characterised by students working together to accomplish shared goals. What is beneficial for the other students in the group is beneficial for the individual and vice versa. Because students in cooperative groups can obtain a desired reward only if the other students in the group also obtain the same reward, cooperative goal structures are characterised by positive interdependence. Also, all groups may receive the same rewards, provided they meet the teacher's criteria for mastery. For example, a teacher might present a lesson on map reading, then give each group its own map and a question-answering exercise. Students then work with each other to ensure that all know how to interpret maps. Each student then takes a quiz on map reading. All teams whose average quiz scores meet a preset standard receive special recognition.

Cooperative structures lead students to focus on effort and cooperation as the primary basis of motivation. This orientation is reflected in the statement "We can do this if we try hard and work together." In a cooperative atmosphere, students are motivated out of a sense of obligation: one ought to try, contribute, and help satisfy group norms.

Educational Applications of Motivation

Motivation is of particular interest to educational psychologists because of the crucial role it plays in student learning. However, the specific kind of motivation that is studied in the specialized setting of education differs qualitatively from the more general forms of motivation studied by psychologists in other fields.

Motivation in education can have several effects on how students learn and how they behave towards subject matter. It can:

- Direct behavior toward particular goals
- Lead to increased effort and energy
- Increase initiation of, and persistence in, activities
- Enhance cognitive processing
- Determine what consequences are reinforcing
- Lead to improved performance.

Because students are not always internally motivated, they sometimes need situated motivation, which is found in environmental conditions that the teacher creates.

If teachers decided to extrinsically reward productive student behaviors, they may find it difficult to extricate themselves from that path. Consequently student dependency on extrinsic rewards represents one of the greatest detractors from their use in the classroom.

The majority of new student orientation leaders at colleges and universities recognize that distinctive needs of students should be considered in regard to orientation information provided at the beginning of the higher education experience. Research done by Whyte in 1986 raised the awareness of counselors and educators in this regard. In 2007, the National Orientation Directors Association reprinted Cassandra B. Whyte's research report allowing readers to ascertain improvements made in addressing specific needs of students over a quarter of a century later to help with academic success.

Generally, motivation is conceptualized as either intrinsic or extrinsic. Classically, these categories are regarded as distinct. Today, these concepts are less likely to be used as distinct categories, but instead as two ideal types that define a continuum:

— Intrinsic motivation occurs when people are internally motivated to do something because it either brings them pleasure, they think it is important, or they feel that what they are learning is significant. It has been shown that intrinsic motivation for education drops from grades 3-9 though the exact cause cannot be ascertained. Also, in younger students it has been shown that contextualizing material that would otherwise be presented in an abstract manner increases the intrinsic motivation of these students.

— Extrinsic motivation comes into play when a student is compelled to do something or act a certain way because of factors external to him or her (like money or good grades).

Cassandra B. Whyte researched and reported about the importance of locus of control and academic achievement. Students tending toward a more internal locus of control are more academically successful, thus encouraging curriculum and activity development with consideration of motivation theories.

Academic motivation orientation may also be tied with one's ability to detect and process errors. Fisher, Nanayakkara, and Marshall conducted neuroscience research on children's motivation orientation, neurological indicators of error monitoring (the process of detecting an error), and academic achievement. Their research suggests that students with high intrinsic motivation attribute performance to personal control and that their error-monitoring system is more strongly engaged by performance errors. They also found that motivation orientation and academic achievement were related to the strength in which their error-monitoring system was engaged.

Motivation has been found to be an important element in the concept of Andragogy (what motivates the adult learner), and in treating Autism

Spectrum Disorders, as in Pivotal Response Therapy.Doyle and Moeyn have noted that traditional methods tended to use anxiety as negative motivation (e.g. use of bad grades by teachers) as a method of getting students to work. However, they have found that progressive approaches with focus on positive motivation over punishment has produced greater effectiveness with learning, since anxiety interferes with performance of complex tasks.

Sudbury Model Schools' Approach

Sudbury Model schools adduce that the cure to the problem of procrastination, of learning in general, and particularly of scientific illiteracy is to remove once and for all what they call the underlying disease: compulsion in schools. They contend that human nature in a free society recoils from every attempt to force it into a mold; that the more requirements we pile onto children at school, the surer we are to drive them away from the material we are trying to force down their throats; that after all the drive and motivation of infants to master the world around them is legendary. They assert that schools must keep that drive alive by doing what some of them do: nurturing it on the freedom it needs to thrive.

Sudbury Model schools do not perform and do not offer evaluations, assessments, transcripts, or recommendations, asserting that they do not rate people, and that school is not a judge; comparing students to each other, or to some standard that has been set is for them a violation of the student's right to privacy and to self-determination. Students decide for themselves how to measure their progress as self-starting learners as a process of self-evaluation: real lifelong learning and the proper educational evaluation for the 21st century, they adduce. According to Sudbury Model schools, this policy does not cause harm to their students as they move on to life outside the school. However, they admit it makes the process more difficult, but that such hardship is part of the students learning to make their own way, set their own standards and meet their own goals. The no-grading and no-rating policy helps to create an atmosphere free of competition among students or battles for adult approval, and encourages a positive cooperative environment amongst the student body.

References

Cameron, J., Pierce, W. D., Banko, K. M., & Gear, A., (2005). "Achievement-based rewards and intrinsic motivation: A test of cognitive mediators", *Journal of Educational Psychology*.

Kohlberg, Lawrence, (1981). *Essays on Moral Development, Vol. I: The Philosophy of Moral Development*, Harper & Row.

Kuhn, D., (1999). *A developmental model of critical thinking*, Educational Researcher.

Maehr, Martin L., and Carol Midgley, (1991). "Enhancing Student Motivation: A Schoolwide Approach", *Educational Psychologist*.

Weiner, B., (2000). "Interpersonal and intrapersonal theories of motivation from an attributional perspective", *Educational Psychology Review.*

Wertsch, J.V. (ed), (1985). *Culture, communication and cognition*, Cambridge: Cambridge University Press.

11

Promoting Moral Development in Schools

Moral development is the process throught which children develop proper attitudes and behaviors toward other people in society, based on social and cultural norms, rules, and laws.

Moral development is a concern for every parent. Teaching a child to distinguish right from wrong and to behave accordingly is a goal of parenting. Moral development is a complex issue that—since the beginning of human civilization—has been a topic of discussion among some of the world's most distinguished psychologists, theologians, and culture theorists. It was not studied scientifically until the late 1950s.

Early childhood education should address the moral development of the child, especially the caring and compassionate aspects of morality. What could be more important than teaching our children a sense of caring and social responsibility? We might teach them reading, writing, math, and computer skills. We might teach them about business, history, and geography. But if we neglect to teach them to be caring and compassionate, have we really given them all they need for fulfilling their potential and achieving a sense of joy and satisfaction in their lives?

Some people argue that moral development and a sense of caring are values to be fostered at home rather than at school. However, the teaching of these values doesn't seem to be happening, as evidenced by the behaviors and attitudes of many adults in our society. A recent book by David Callahan presents a volume of research data on the selfish nature of our culture today and people's willingness to "do wrong" to get ahead. As Callahan's work indicates, our current culture reflects a serious lack of social responsibility and an unhealthy compulsion to succeed at any cost. Addressing this moral crisis will take more than the assumption – or wish – that children will just naturally evolve into caring adults who choose to make socially responsible decisions.

As positive moral characteristics do not appear spontaneously, addressing our cultural moral crisis will take the commitment and involvement of many elements of society, including early childhood education. Community involvement is especially important in light of the fact that "many children are not taught much about ethics and honesty at home…Worse, many parents may be caught up in the cheating culture themselves and set a negative example for their children". Many educators are aware of the cultural moral crisis and feel a need to promote ethical development in the classroom. Determining the best way to do this, however, isn't always understood.

Morality and moral development are sometimes defined in terms of objective norms and established standards of behaviors. This view of morality often provides the basic structure for character education programs, where a set of virtues (such as honesty, kindness, courage, determination, etc.) are identified and promoted. Lawrence Kohlberg, an internationally recognized researcher and expert in the field of moral development, used the term "a bag of virtues" in discussing the limitations of this traditional framework.

Kohlberg and others who view moral development in a more developmental and constructivist perspective believe that "goodness" is developed from the inside of an individual rather than being imposed from the outside (as the traditional character education model suggests). They recognize, as Halverson says, that, "the simplistic strategy of directly teaching ethics does not work". Robert Coles, in The Moral Life of Children, speaks to this same misunderstanding: "It is a mistake to think of morality as a set of external standards that adults somehow foist upon an unknowing or unwilling child…most of our current moral education efforts fail precisely because of this mistaken yet pervasive assumption". Alfie Kohn offers a similar critical assessment of character education in schools. He feels that character education in most schools is a form of indoctrination in which absolutes of a moral action are instilled or transmitted. An alternative proposed by Kohn is to involve children in actively assessing certain behaviors against real situations and allowing them to make moral judgments accordingly.

Developmentalists, such as Kohlberg, propose that the process of attaining moral maturity occurs over time if conditions are favorable for such growth. They also believe that a child's moral maturity is directly related to the way she thinks about concepts such as justice, rights, equality, and human welfare. Over time and through a variety of social interactions, children come to develop their own understandings of these concepts. Thus, their sense of "goodness" is constructed through their own thinking about their experiences and through dialogue with others about what these experiences mean. Children's sense of goodness is also fostered through encouragement offered by significant adults in their lives. One principal of an elementary school in Florida offers such encouragement at the end of his daily announcements by saying something like, "Remember, children, be kind to one another".

Kohlberg's theory of moral development builds on Jean Piaget's work, which focused primarily on cognitive development. According to Piaget, children construct and reconstruct their knowledge of the world through interactions with the environment. Such knowledge includes children's understandings about what is right and what is wrong. Moral development and cognitive development are thus closely intertwined. Moral reasoning is, in fact, considered to be one of the central aspects (or "building blocks") of moral functioning Being a "good" person, however, involves more than having the cognitive understanding of what is right and what is wrong. Other central aspects of moral functioning include empathy, conscience, and altruism.According to the constructivist theory of development, these central aspects of moral functioning cannot be given to children – but they can be fostered. We know that we can't give young children an understanding of such concepts as cause and effect or object permanence, yet we purposefully provide experiences that promote such understandings. In a similar way, if we want to foster goodness in children, we would do well to provide the kinds of experiences that promote moral functioning – and we would do so starting at a young age.

Moral Psychology

Moral psychology is a field of study in both philosophy and psychology. Some use the term "moral psychology" relatively narrowly to refer to the study of moral development. However, others tend to use the term more broadly to include any topics at the intersection of ethics and psychology. Such topics are ones that involve the mind and are relevant to moral issues. Some of the main topics of the field are moral responsibility, moral development, moral character, altruism, psychological egoism, moral luck, and moral disagreement.

Historically, early philosophers such as Aristotle and Plato engaged in both empirical research and *a priori* conceptual analysis about the ways in which people make decisions about issues that raise moral concerns. Moral psychological issues have been central theoretical issues explored by philosophers from the early days of the profession right up until the present. With the development of psychology as a discipline separate from philosophy, it was natural for psychologists to continue pursuing work in moral psychology, and much of the empirical research of the 20th century in this area was completed by academics working in psychology departments.

Nowadays, moral psychology is a thriving area of research in both philosophy and psychology, even at an interdisciplinary level. For example, the psychologist Lawrence Kohlberg questioned boys and young men about their thought processes when they were faced with a moral dilemma, producing one of many very useful empirical studies in the area of moral psychology. As another example, the philosopher, Joshua Knobe, recently completed an empirical study on how the way in which an ethical problem is phrased dramatically affects an individual's intuitions about the proper moral response to said problem. More conceptually focused research has recently been completed by researchers such as John Doris. He discusses the way in which social psychological experiments—such as the Stanford Prison Experiments involving the idea of situationism—call into question a key component in virtue ethics: the idea that individuals have a single, environment-independent moral character.

Kohlberg's Stages of Moral Development

Lawrence Kohlberg's stages of moral development constitute an adaptation of a psychological theory originally conceived of by the Swiss psychologist Jean Piaget. The theory holds that moral reasoning, the basis for ethical behaviour, has six identifiable developmental stages, each more adequate at responding to moral dilemmas than its predecessor. Kohlberg followed the development of moral judgement far beyond the ages studied earlier by Piaget, who also claimed that logic and morality develop through constructive stages. Expanding on Piaget's work, Kohlberg determined that the process of moral development was principally concerned with justice, and that it continued throughout the individual's lifetime, a notion that spawned dialogue on the philosophical implications of such research.

There have been critiques of the theory from several perspectives. Some argue that it emphasizes justice to the exclusion of other moral values, such as caring; or that there is such an overlap between stages that they should more properly be regarded as separate domains; or that evaluations of the reasons for moral choices are mostly post hoc rationalisations of essentially intuitive decisions.

Nevertheless, an entirely new field within psychology was created as a result of Kohlberg's theory.

Six Stages

Kohlberg's six stages can be more generally grouped into three levels of two stages each: pre-conventional, conventional and post-conventional. Following Piaget's constructivist requirements for a stage model, as described in his theory of cognitive development, it is extremely rare to regress backward in stages. Stages cannot be skipped; each provides a new and necessary perspective, more comprehensive and differentiated than its predecessors but integrated with them.

Level 1 (Pre-Conventional)

1. Obedience and punishment orientation
   (How can I avoid punishment?)
2. Self-interest orientation
   (What's in it for me?)

Level 2 (Conventional)

3. Interpersonal accord and conformity
   (Social norms)
   (The good boy/good girl attitude)
4. Authority and social-order maintaining orientation
   (Law and order morality)

Level 3 (Post-conventional)

5. Social contract orientation
6. Universal ethical principles
   (Principled conscience)

Pre-conventional

The pre-conventional level of moral reasoning is especially common in children, although adults can also exhibit this level of reasoning. Reasoners at this level judge the morality of an action by its direct consequences. The pre-conventional level consists of the first and second stages of moral development, and is solely concerned with the self in an egocentric manner.

In stage one, individuals focus on the direct consequences of their actions on themselves. For example, an action is perceived as morally wrong if the perpetrator is punished. "The last time I did that I got spanked so I will not do it again." The worse the punishment for the act is, the more "bad" the act is perceived to be. This can give rise to an inference that even innocent victims are guilty in proportion to their suffering. It is "egocentric", lacking recognition that others' points of view are different from one's own. There is "deference to superior power or prestige".

Stage two espouses the "what's in it for me" position, in which right behaviour is defined by whatever is in the individual's best interest. Stage two reasoning shows a limited interest in the needs of others, but only to a point where it might further the individual's own interests. As a result, concern for others is not based on loyalty or intrinsic respect, but rather a "you scratch my back, and I'll scratch yours" mentality. The lack of a societal perspective in the pre-conventional level is quite different from the social contract, as all actions have the purpose of serving the individual's own needs or interests. For the stage two theorist, the world's perspective is often seen as morally relative.

Conventional

The conventional level of moral reasoning is typical of adolescents and adults. Those who reason in a conventional way judge the morality of actions by comparing them to society's views and expectations. The conventional level consists of the third and fourth stages of moral development.

In stage three, the self enters society by filling social roles. Individuals are receptive to approval or disapproval from others as it reflects society's accordance with the perceived role. They try to be a "good boy" or "good girl" to live up to these expectations, having learned that there is inherent value in doing so. Stage three reasoning may judge the morality of an action by evaluating its consequences in terms of a person's relationships, which now begin to include things like respect, gratitude and the "golden rule". "I want to be liked and thought well of; apparently, not being naughty makes people like me." Desire to maintain rules and authority exists only to further support these social roles. The intentions of actions play a more significant role in reasoning at this stage; "they mean well ...".

In stage four, it is important to obey laws, dictums and social conventions because of their importance in maintaining a functioning society. Moral reasoning in stage four is thus beyond the need for individual approval exhibited in stage three; society must learn to transcend individual needs. A central ideal or ideals often prescribe what is right and wrong, such as in the case of fundamentalism. If one person violates a law, perhaps everyone would-thus there is an obligation and a duty to uphold laws and rules. When someone does violate a law, it is morally wrong; culpability is thus a significant factor in this stage as it separates the bad domains from the good ones. Most active members of society remain at stage four, where morality is still predominantly dictated by an outside force.

Post-conventional

The post-conventional level, also known as the principled level, consists of stages five and six of moral development. There is a growing realisation that individuals are separate entities from society, and that the individual's own perspective should have precedence over society's view. Because of this level's "nature of self before others", the behaviour of post-conventional individuals, especially those at stage six, can be confused with that of those at the pre-conventional level.

In stage five, individuals are viewed as holding different opinions and values. Similarly, laws are regarded as social contracts rather than rigid dictums. Those which do not promote the general welfare should be changed when necessary to meet "the greatest good for the greatest number of people". This is achieved through majority decision and inevitable compromise. Thus democratic government is ostensibly based on stage five reasoning.

In stage six, moral reasoning is based on abstract reasoning using universal ethical principles. Laws are valid only insofar as they are grounded in justice, and a commitment to justice carries with it an obligation to disobey unjust laws. Rights are unnecessary, as social contracts are not essential for deontic moral action. Decisions are not reached hypothetically in a conditional way but rather categorically in an absolute way, as in the philosophy of Immanuel Kant. This involves an individual imagining what they would do in another's shoes, if they believed what that other person imagines to be true. The resulting consensus is the action taken. In this way action is never a means but always an end in itself; the individual acts because it is right, and not because it is instrumental, expected, legal, or previously agreed upon. Although Kohlberg insisted that stage six exists, he found it difficult to identify individuals who consistently operated at that level.

Theoretical Assumptions

The picture of human nature which Kohlberg begins with is that humans are inherently communicative and capable of reason; they also possess a desire to understand others and the world around them. The stages of Kohlberg's model relate to the qualitative moral reasonings adopted by individuals, and so do not translate directly into praise or blame of any individual's actions or character. In order to argue that his theory measures moral reasoning and not particular moral conclusions, Kohlberg insists that the form and structure of moral arguments is independent of the content of those arguments, a position he calls "formalism".

Kohlberg's theory centres on the notion that justice is the essential characteristic of moral reasoning. Justice itself relies heavily upon the notion of sound reasoning based on principles. Despite being a justice-centred theory of morality, Kohlberg considered it to be compatible with plausible formulations of deontology and eudaimonia.

Kohlberg's theory understands values as a critical component of the right. Whatever the right is, for him, it must be universally valid across societies: there can be no relativism. Moreover, morals are not natural features of the world; they are prescriptive. Nevertheless, moral judgements can be evaluated in logical terms of truth and falsity.

According to Kohlberg, someone progressing to a higher stage of moral reasoning cannot skip stages. For example, an individual cannot jump from being concerned mostly with peer judgements to being a proponent of social contracts. On encountering a moral dilemma and finding their current level of moral reasoning unsatisfactory, however, an individual will look to the next level. Realising the limitations of the current stage of thinking is the driving force behind moral development, as each progressive stage is more adequate than the last. The process is therefore considered to be constructive, as it is initiated by the conscious construction of the individual, and is not in any meaningful sense a component of the individual's innate dispositions, or a result of past inductions.

Formal Elements

Progress through Kohlberg's stages happens as a result of the individual's increasing competence, both psychologically and in balancing conflicting social-value claims. The process of resolving conflicting claims to reach an equilibrium is called "justice operation". Kohlberg identifies two of these justice operations: "equality" which involves an impartial regard for persons; and "reciprocity", which means a regard for the role of personal merit. For Kohlberg, the most adequate result of both operations is "reversibility", in which a moral or dutiful act within a particular situation is evaluated in terms of whether or not the act would be satisfactory even if particular persons were to switch roles within that situation.

Knowledge and learning contribute to moral development. Specifically important are the individual's "view of persons" and their "social perspective level", each of which becomes more complex and mature with each advancing stage. The "view of persons" can be understood as the individual's grasp of the psychology of other persons; it may be pictured as a spectrum, with stage one having no view of other persons at all, and stage six being entirely sociocentric. Similarly, the social perspective level involves the understanding of the social universe, differing from the view of persons in that it involves an appreciation of social norms.

Examples of Applied Moral Dilemmas

Kohlberg established the Moral Judgement Interview in his original 1958 dissertation. During the roughly 45-minute tape recorded semi-structured interview, the interviewer uses moral dilemmas to determine which stage of moral reasoning a person uses. The dilemmas are fictional short stories that describe situations in which a person has to make a moral decision.

The participant is asked a systemic series of open-ended questions, like what they think the right course of action is, as well as justifications as to why certain actions are right or wrong. The form and structure of these replies are scored and not the content; over a set of multiple moral dilemmas an overall score is derived.

A dilemma that Kohlberg used in his original research was the druggist's dilemma: Heinz Steals the Drug In Europe.

Kohlberg's theory holds that the justification the participant offers is what is significant, the form of their response. Below are some of many examples of possible arguments that belong to the six stages:

Stage one (obedience): Heinz should not steal the medicine because he will consequently be put in prison which will mean he is a bad person. Or: Heinz should steal the medicine because it is only worth $200 and not how much the druggist wanted for it; Heinz had even offered to pay for it and was not stealing anything else.

Stage two (self-interest): Heinz should steal the medicine because he will be much happier if he saves his wife, even if he will have to serve a prison sentence. Or: Heinz should not steal the medicine because prison is an awful place, and he would probably languish over a jail cell more than his wife's death.

Stage three (conformity): Heinz should steal the medicine because his wife expects it; he wants to be a good husband. Or: Heinz should not steal the drug because stealing is bad and he is not a criminal; he tried to do everything he could without breaking the law, you cannot blame him.

Stage four (law-and-order): Heinz should not steal the medicine because the law prohibits stealing, making it illegal. Or: Heinz should steal the drug for his wife but also take the prescribed punishment for the crime as well as paying the druggist what he is owed. Criminals cannot just run around without regard for the law; actions have consequences.

Stage five (human rights): Heinz should steal the medicine because everyone has a right to choose life, regardless of the law. Or: Heinz should not steal the medicine because the scientist has a right to fair compensation. Even if his wife is sick, it does not make his actions right.

Stage six (universal human ethics): Heinz should steal the medicine, because saving a human life is a more fundamental value than the property rights of another person. Or: Heinz should not steal the medicine, because others may need the medicine just as badly, and their lives are equally significant.

Moral Development

Morals are systems of social rules that shape our interactions and guide our behaviour. Our sense or right and wrong can influence our feelings of altruism or prejudice, can affect in our daily lives and relationships with friends or at work, and can even (although perhaps not often enough) have a bearing on social policy. One important social question is how we come to behave in moral (or immoral) ways. Obviously, part of this question depends on how attitudes or reasoning connect with moral behaviour and action. But another part, which is at least as important, concerns how we come to understand or reason about these rules themselves.

The child's moral development involves a gradual immersion into the world of adults' rules and principles. Social learning theorists argue that it is, and that it is the mechanics of that learning which need to be understood by theorists.

Social Learning Theories

Aronfeed suggested that children gain an understanding of morality through a form of social conditioning. When a child behaves in a particular way they may receive feedback on their actions from others. Parents or caregivers occupy a very important role for the child's development since support or encouragement for any particular form of behaviour will increase the chances of a child repeating that behaviour later. Conversely criticism or punishment will decrease the chances of that behaviour being repeated since it entails negative consequences for the child. According to this social conditioning model it is through adults' reinforcement of certain forms of behaviour that the child comes to behave in a way which is deemed morally appropriate or inappropriate. For Aronfeed moral thought is therefore the consequence of a process of association: the child associates its behaviour and the feedback to that behaviour with the thoughts that preceded it.

A further social learning approach has been suggested by Bandura who argued that children's moral development comes about through the more indirect process of observational learning or vicarious conditioning. Bandura and McDonald found that children who observed an adult 'model' making moral judgments tended to give more mature responses themselves in a subsequent post-test. On the other hand children who had seen no adult model, but whose own responses had been reinforced whenever they reflected more mature forms of reasoning, showed no such improvement. Bandura concluded that an important mechanism for the child's moral development is the mimicking or imitation of adult behaviour.

According to Bandura the child observes, internalises and then replicates the moral judgment and behaviour of adults. As these observations increase in both depth and scope the child comes to grasp some of the complexities (and perhaps vagueries) of more mature moral thought. Both Aronfeed's and Bandura's theories share a sense in which the child absorbs a sense of morality from those around them. Yet whilst Aronfeed sees the adult as the direct conditioning agent in the child's moral development, Bandura views development of the child's judgment as rather more detached from immediate features of the relationship between adult and child.

Although social learning accounts appear empirically robust, the theoretical simplicity of the approach is not without its difficulties. For a start there is an abiding concern that social learning theories tend to relegate children's lived experiences to a behaviouristic plane, where the personal significance of social relationships is of little importance. There is also an ethical worry for Aronfeed's social conditioning model. If punishment is a key to preventing immoral behaviour and thought then it would seem that the greater the degree of punishment the more effective the moral 'education'. This, in turn, leads to a rather odd conception of morality since the rightness or wrongness of an action is determined by the strength, perhaps physical, of reactions to it.

A further difficulty for Aronfeed's theory is that children may learn to exhibit 'moral' behaviour only in the presence of those who are able to enforce punishments. Away from the watchful gaze of an adult the child might feel no constraints to producing behaviour that would not be sanctioned if an adult were present. Indeed, children can be well aware of the differences between interaction with peers and with adults and can act differently in each separate context.

Aspects of Bandura's approach also need clarification. If moral development is a product of the child's modelling of others' judgments it needs to be established whether all 'models' are equally effective in promoting development. For example, is one parent more influential than the other as a model for the child's behaviour and judgment?

Lastly, it is certainly debatable whether all children grow up simply reproducing the moral rules and norms of adults. In this sense, it would appear that the notion of the 'socialising agent' requires rather more elaboration than either Aronfeed or Bandura give it.

Parents and Moral Development

Perhaps the most prominent influence a child receives is that of the parents or caregivers. Parents not only provide the child with protection, support and basic material needs. In most cases parents also act as the principal figures who enforce moral and other rules.

Freud proposed that our sense of moral duty arises from our relationships with our parents. The importance of this relationship is a result of the parents' role as principal caregivers and as sources of comfort, support and security – or, as Freud puts it, as love objects. However, when a child does something that his or her parents disapprove of, the child is punished. This punishment leads to feelings of frustration and anger in the child and parents become objects of hate.

In the early years punishment acts as an external form of control exercised by parents. Over time this external form of control becomes internalised. However, the child does not usually enforce this internal form of control by means of self-punishment. Rather, when a child does something wrong he or she feels guilt which acts as the principal mechanism for internalised self-control. To avoid guilt, or self-punishment, the child is motivated to act morally and in accordance with the mother's or father's moral standards. Identification with the punitive parent therefore leads the child to adopt the moral standards and principles of that parent - the parent's superego. Thus moral rules move from external to internal forms of control, and a child adopts the moral standards of his or her parents.

The psychoanalytic approach, like social learning theories, places an emphasis on punishment as the principal motivator of moral development. Freud, however, presents us with a more sophisticated account of the means by which external processes of control become translated into internal processes of self-regulation. Also, by introducing the notion of identification Freud's theory allows us to conceptualise how different individuals may have a qualitatively different influence upon the child's development.

However, Freud's theory has, generally, been criticised not only for the lack of empirical evidence but also because many aspects of the theory are difficult to test. For example, Freud claims that external control leads to feelings of guilt which, in turn, motivate the child to act morally. Yet it would seem difficult to distinguish a child who refrains from certain behaviour because of guilt or, to adopt a social conditioning theory explanation, through fear. Thus whilst evidence has generally supported the proposition that children reflect the moral values of their parents it is difficult to determine whether Freud's account, or other socialisation accounts, are the best for explaining this process.

Hoffman has described how different forms of parenting might influence a child's moral reasoning. Hoffman & Saltzstein identified three different styles of parenting through interviews with parents, and then observed how others rated the behaviour of these parents' children in real life situations. The first parenting style, love-oriented discipline, involves the parent withholding affection or approval when a child behaves badly. According to Freudian theory this would be an effective form of moral education. However, the children of parents who used predominantly love-oriented forms of discipline did not show benefits (over and above other children) in their rate of moral development.

Parents who employed predominently power-assertive discipliniary techniques used a variety of punitive measures to enforce their rules, or simply gave their position of power or authority over the child as a justification for preventing the child from acting in a certain way. Results indicated that a consequence of this parenting technique is that children tended to respond only to the threat of sanction. Thus, away from adult supervision children showed little sense of how to behave appropriately. With the third parenting style, inductive discipline, parents explained to their children the reasons behind a particular moral prohibition. Pointing out the consequences of certain forms of behaviour and the reasons for not acting in a particular way was the most effective in ensuring a child developed a moral sense for themselves.

Hoffman's work suggests that moral development is promoted when children are given rationales for their moral behaviour and judgments. Similar work by Baumrind has also indicated that combining parental authority with justifications for the rules that parents enforce is the most effective form of helping children to attain social competence and avoid deviance up to adolescence.

There are however problems establishing a link between parenting styles and development. The relationship between a child and his or her parent is something that researchers can only ever hope to capture briefly, or second-hand from either self-reports or reports from others involved with the child and parents. Such reports may be subject to some inaccuracies if not all participants in the research judge by the same criteria when reporting behaviour, or fail to present themselves to researchers in an entirely candid fashion. Moreover, the work of Baumrind and Hoffman provides evidence of only a correlation between parenting styles and children's reasoning or behaviour. For example, it may be that authoritative or inductive disciplinary techniques are more prevalent amongst parents from middle class backgrounds and so there is at least a possibility that different, over-arching social factors might also have a causal role in the positive outcomes associated with inductive or authoritative parenting styles.

Society and Morality

A child's parents have an important influence upon a their moral development. Yet an emphasis upon parents and other adults as the principal socialisers of a child runs the risk of neglecting the role of the wider social context in a child's development. Durkheim suggested that a sense of moral duty arises from a feeling of connectedness to society; "we are moral beings only to the extent that we are social beings". What binds individuals together is the recognition that "society" is something more than the sum of the individual's who make it up. It is the source of all moral knowledge and the authority by which morality can be held to be legitimate.

For Durkheim morals possess power because they regulate behaviour between people as a sort of social bond or contract. Mature moral reasoning therefore reflects an awareness of the importance of maintaining our social relationships. In spite of the sociological basis of Durkheim's theory, the consequences of his theory for moral education are rather similar to traditional social learning accounts. In order to understand morality, Durkheim argued, the child must come to understand the rules which preserve social relations. Moral development can therefore only come about through the imposition of these rules by the adult upon the child.

Moral education, according to Durkheim, requires that the child forms a 'spirit of discipline' in respect to his or her moral thought and conduct. The spirit of discipline is principally instilled when the child goes to school.

At home family feelings of altruism and solidarity can obscure the need for hard and fast rules. At school, on the other hand, the child has his or her first experience of a more formal, social institution which, in turn, demands a more rigorous adherence to collective rules. The teacher possesses social authority and acts as an intermediary between society and the child.

A strength of Durkheim's theory is that it allows a conceptualisation of morality as a social process: moral judgments possess a power because they locate an individual in a society or social group which shares certain practices and rules. However, an (at least tacit) implication of Durkheim's theory is that to act morally is nothing more than to conform to the rules of society. Thus there is little room for any meaningful development in social morality beyond the status quo.

A second difficulty lies in Durkheim's claim that all morality is imposed upon the child by the group or (in the case of the teacher) a representative of society. It is important to remember that this imposition of morality does not function in quite the same way as it does for social learning theories. Durkheim's conception of 'society' allows us to invoke an idea of morality as something more than, in its strictest sense, self-interest.

Student's Character Formation

There are three major issues in the education of young people today. The first is the development of a vision for one's life that includes the discovery and/or defining of one's life mission and desired lifestyle. The second is the development of one's character, dealing with concerns of direction and quality of life. The third deals with the development of competence that deals with concerns of how well one is able to do something.

In general, character, good or bad, is considered to be observable in one's conduct. Thus, character is different from values in that values are orientations or dispositions whereas character involves action or activation of knowledge and values. From this perspective, values are seen as one of the foundations for character. In the context of the model of human behaviour presented at this site, values includes both cognitive and affective components, but not necessarily conative or behavioural components. Character includes all four components.

Scholarly debate on moral development and character formation extends at least as far back as Aristotle's Nichomacean Ethics and Socrates's

Meno and continues through to modern times. In the last several hundred years, character education has been seen as a primary function of educational institutions. For example, John Locke, 17th century English philosopher, advocated education as education for character development. This theme was continued in the 19th century by English philosophers John Stuart Mill and Herbert Spencer. The American philosopher, John Dewey, an influential philosopher and educator of the early 20th century, saw moral education as central to the school's mission.

Spears's survey of members of Phi Delta Kappa on goals of education showed the following ranking of the goals of public schools:

1. develop skills in reading, writing, speaking, and listening;
2. develop pride in work and feeling of self-worth; and
3. develop good character and self-respect.

In terms of defining good character, educators stated that this should include developing:

1. moral responsibility and sound ethical and moral behaviour;
2. capacity for discipline;
3. a moral and ethical sense of the values, goals, and processes of a free society;
4. standards of personal character and ideas.

In two more recent Gallup surveys of public attitudes toward public schools, 79 percent of respondents indicated they favour "instruction in schools that would deal with morals and moral behaviour."

Character Education

Whether at work, at home, or at play, there are basic values that define ethical behaviour. These values are not political, religious or culturally biased. Josephson Institute calls them the Six Pillars of Character, and they form the basis of all programmes and materials.

Trustworthiness

This pillar encompasses a variety of qualities: honesty, integrity, reliability, and loyalty. Being trustworthy means keeping promises and doing one's best not to deceive, even with white lies or statements that one might defend as "technically true."

Respect

The Golden Rule is the most useful guide here: Treat others as you wish to be treated. That means being courteous, listening to others, and accepting individual differences.

Responsibility

This pillar includes accountability, self-control, and the pursuit of excellence. Being responsible also requires that we carefully consider the consequences of our choices before we make them.

Fairness

Being fair means playing by the rules and not taking advantage of others. A fair person makes informed judgements without favoritism or prejudice and does not blame others carelessly.

Caring

Kindness, compassion, altruism - these are the heart of ethics. Of course, some ethical decisions inevitably cause pain, but the caring person acts to minimise hardship and to help others whenever possible.

Citizenship

Good citizens work to make their community better. They are committed to protecting our environment and to making our democratic institutions work. They know the law, and they often do more than it requires and less than it allows.

Trends in Character Education

Since the 1960's teacher education has downplayed the teacher's role as a transmitter of social and personal values and emphasized other areas such teaching techniques, strategies, models and skills. Educational psychology, rather than philosophy and religion, has become the basis of teacher training. In most cases, educational psychology focuses on the individual, separated from the social context. Additionally, modern education has been heavily influenced by the behavioural approach, which has proved adept at developing instructional methods that impact achievement as measured by standardised tests. In the opinion of most researchers in the area of character and moral development, additional emphasis must be placed on the philosophical "why" of education in addition to the technical "how."

The two educational goals most desired by both the public and educators—academic competence and character development—are not mutually exclusive, but complementary. Competence allows character to be manifested in highest forms and vice versa.

There are four major questions to be addressed when focusing on character development:

1. What is good character?
2. What causes or prevents it?
3. How can it be measured so that efforts at improvement can have corrective feedback? and
4. How can it best be developed?

As previously discussed, good character is defined in terms of one's actions. Character development traditionally has focused on those traits or values appropriate for the industrial age such as obedience to authority, work ethic, working in group under supervision, etc. Modern education must promote character based on values appropriate for the information age: truthfulness, honesty, integrity, individual responsibility, humility, wisdom, justice, steadfastness, dependability, etc.

In terms of what influences character development, the following are major factors in the moral development and behaviour of youth:

1. heredity
2. early childhood experience
3. modeling by important adults and older youth
4. peer influence
5. the general physical and social environment
6. the communications media
7. what is taught in the schools and other institutions
8. specific situations and roles that elicit corresponding behaviour.

These sources of influence are listed in approximate order of least tractable to most tractable in order to suggest why we often seek solutions to social problems through schools. It is important to realise that while schools do and should play a role in the development of character, families, communities, and society in general also have an important influence.

The measurement of character has proven difficult since character, by definition, involves behaviour, but character is often defined in terms of traits (i.e., honesty, integrity, etc.). Some possible measures that are suggested are:

1. student discipline;
2. student suicide rates;
3. crimes: assault, burglary, homicides;
4. pregnancy rates of teenage girls; and
5. prosocial activities.

Even a cursory glance would indicate that our society is changing in ways that produce discomfort for most of us. While Gross Domestic Product has risen dramatically relative to the growth in population, with a corresponding increase in spending on social programmes, data on indicators that might be used as a measure of the nation's character show movement in the opposite direction. This type of analysis is quite beneficial because it is at a level that includes the influence of all of the major social institutions that influence character development in our young people, not just schools. However, schools do have an important influence and we should use that influence judiciously.

There are a variety of alternatives to dealing with moral and character education in the schools. First, we can ignore it completely which assumes the issue is outside the bounds of proper curriculum. The interest by professional organisations and the public suggests that this view is inappropriate. Second, we can take a "values neutral" stance and provide opportunities for students to clarify and defend their own values without making recommendations or advocating a particular viewpoint. This is the position taken by the advocates of the values clarification movement and assumes that in important ways no values or character traits are more valid than others. However, to the extent that certain values or character traits are more likely to lead to socially desired outcomes, it would seem inappropriate to not identify these as "better" values. This is not to say that the techniques used in values clarification have no merit, but that when educators and the public have developed a consensus about the worth of certain values, it seems entirely appropriate to teach those to students.

A third approach is to teach students a specific process to follow when making decisions and putting these into action. This is the approach of the analysis view used in values education and assumes moral and character decisions are made rationally.

Another cognitively-oriented approach is to engage students in discussions of relevant moral issues with the expectation that students who hear their peers discuss the issue from a higher level will gravitate to that position. This position is expounded in the moral development approach of Lawrence Kohlberg whose theory was based on the cognitive development theory of Jean Piaget. While the techniques used in both of these approaches have been shown to be effective in changing thinking, there is scant evidence to support the belief that changing thinking will automatically lead to a change in behaviour. And it is impact on behaviour that distinguishes values education from character education.

A fifth approach is to teach students a given set of values and accompanying appropriate actions. This is the position taken by the inculcation approach to values clarification. This approach assumes a set of absolute values agreed upon by society that are unchanging and that be applied equally appropriately in all situations.

A final approach is to use the inculcation, values education, analysis, and moral development approaches described above when and where appropriate and then to have students put their thoughts and feelings into action in a variety of social actions as suggested in the action learning or service learning approaches. This combination of approaches is much more likely to impact the two important aspects of character not included in values education—volition and action.

From the perspective of a systems view, which is most compatible with the action learning and service learning approaches to character education, we need to define character development in terms of the three components of mind: and the component of behaviour as depicted in the systems model of human behaviour. The cognitive component of character consists of both a knowledge base of right and wrong as well as the rational and creative processes necessary to work with that knowledge base to make sound moral decisions. There is a related value system that defines what the individual holds in high esteem or to which he or she is attached. These are the criteria that students use to make moral or ethical judgements. Students learn to value what is in their knowledge base; they will also more deeply esteem what they critically and creatively think about. These two components influence what students are willing to commit to, what they are willing to set goals for, what they are willing to plan for and put energy towards accomplishing. As students make these commitments and plans, it adds to their knowledge base and strengthens their thinking skills and values. These three components then influence the final component, overt behaviour. This behaviour has two aspects: personal virtues such as being courageous and self-disciplined and social virtues such as being compassionate, courteous, and trustworthy. As students reflect on their behaviour, it adds to the knowledge base, strengthens their thinking skills, and impacts their values. Of course, behaviour can also be directly influenced through the application of consequences as described by operant conditioning theory and through observation and modelling as described by social learning theory.

The basic principle of this model is that much of the knowledge and values that students hold are implicit and have been obtained though observation, modelling, and the application of consequences. As important as it is to impact overt moral behaviour, it is equally important to help students make explicit one's own knowledge base, value system, and the process of committing and planning so as to make that behaviour more intentional. This multifaceted view of character development is more similar to Bandura's social cognition theory with its emphasis on reciprocal determinism than it is to a behavioural, cognitive, or humanistic view, each of which is more likely to focus on one component to the detriment of the others.

In assisting students to develop their morals and character, we should acknowledge that these components come into play within a rapidly changing context and therefore, we cannot teach our students all the specific knowledge, values, or behaviours that will lead to success in all aspects of their lives. We must therefore acknowledge that some values are relative and teach students to develop their own views accordingly. At the same time, we must acknowledge that there are some absolutes with respect to morality and character as accepted by commonalties among members of specific communities, major world religions, and moral philosophers. We, therefore, have an obligation to teach these in the family, in our religious organisations, and to support this effort in our communities.

Moral and character development is integral to the development of self, and is as much the responsibility of early caregivers as it is of later educators.

In sum, as parents, educators, affiliates of religious organisations, and community members, we have an obligation to provide young people with training appropriate to their age level that would assist them in holding to the absolutes that are common across philosophies and the scriptures of the major religious traditions, while at the same time helping them clarify and defend their own acquired values.

Any framework for impacting moral and character development is arbitrary unless it is based on some philosophical foundation. Since no current approach to moral education is consistent with all philosophies and meta-ethical theories, educators must first decide these and then develop curriculum. An atmosphere of adult harmony is vitally important. Schools effectively assisting pupil character development are:

1. directed by adults who exercise their authority toward faculty and students in a firm, sensitive, and imaginative manner, and who are committed to both academics and pupil character development;
2. staffed by dedicated faculty who make vigourous demands on pupils and each other;
3. structured so that pupils are surrounded by a variety of opportunities for them to practise helping conduct;
4. managed to provide pupils—both individually and collectively—with many forms of recognition for good conduct;
5. oriented toward maintaining systems of symbols, slogans, ceremonies, and songs that heighten pupils' collective identities;
6. dedicated to maintaining pupil discipline, via clear, widely disseminated discipline codes that are vigourously enforced and backed up with vital consequences;
7. committed to academic instruction and assigned pupils significant homework and otherwise stressed appropriate academic rigour;
8. sensitive to the need to develop collective pupil loyalties to particular classes, clubs, athletic groups, and other subentities in the school;
9. sympathetic to the values of the external adult society, and perceive it as largely supportive and concerned with the problems of the young;
10. always able to use more money to improve their programs, but rarely regard lack of money as an excuse for serious programme deficiencies;
11. open to enlisting the help, counsel, and support of parents and other external adults, but willing to propose important constructive changes in the face of (sometimes) ill-informed parent resistance;

12. disposed to define "good character" in relatively immediate and traditional terms.

Approaches to Values Education

One of the most significant advances made during the past 15 years of research and theory on social development has been the discovery that children's conceptions of morality and social convention are not aspects of single developmental system of morality, but constitute distinct conceptual and developmental domains. More recently we have begun to make progress in applying these findings from developmental psychology to what we call "domain appropriate" values education.

The domain approach to values education emerges from the discovery that children's social concepts do not form a single conceptual system, but are structured within discrete areas of social knowledge that account for qualitatively differing aspects of societal and interpersonal regulation. Within this framework, morality pertains to the set of interpersonal actions such as hitting and hurting that have non arbitrary consequences for the rights or welfare of persons. Moral issues, then, are treated as categorical, and universalisable; specific moral concepts (i.e., it is wrong to hit and hurt another) are structured by underlying conceptions of justice, rights, and welfare (beneficence).

Whereas morality deals with issues inherent in interpersonal relations, social conventions such as modes of dress, forms of address, sex roles, manners, and aspects of mores regarding sexuality are the arbitrary and agreed-upon uniformities in social behaviour determined by the social system in which they are formed. Thus, conventions are seen as alterable, and context dependent. Through accepted usage, however, these standards serve to coordinate the interactions of individuals within systems by providing them with a set of expectations regarding appropriate behaviour. In turn, the matrix of social conventions and customs serves as one element in the structuring and maintenance of the general social order. Judgements about social convention are structured by underlying conceptions of social organisation.

Three forms of evidence are offered in support of the moral-conventional distinction. First, interview studies with children as young as 2 1/2 years-of-age have reported that subjects distinguish between matters of morality and social convention. In these studies it has been found that subjects view moral transgressions as wrong irrespective of the presence of governing rules, while conventional acts are viewed as wrong only if they are in violation of an existing standard. Interview studies have also found that individuals view conventional standards as alterable, while moral prescriptions are viewed as universal and unchangeable.

The second form of evidence comes from observational studies of children's and adolescents' social interactions in family, school, and playground contexts. These studies have reported that the forms of social interactions in the context of moral events differ qualitatively from interactions in the context of conventions. It was found that children's and adults' responses to events in the moral domain focus on features intrinsic to the acts, while responses in the context of conventions focus on aspects of social order. The general pattern of results reported in the interview and observational studies have been replicated with subjects in other cultures indicating that the distinction between morality and convention is not confined to subjects reared in Western societies.

The third piece of evidence comes from developmental studies examining age-related changes in children's moral and conventional judgements. These studies have reported that concepts in the moral and conventional domains follow distinct developmental patterns. The sequence of changes observed in the moral domain indicates that as children develop, they form increased understandings of benevolence, equality, and reciprocity. In the conventional domain development entails transformation in the child's underlying conceptions of social organisation and moves toward an understanding of convention as constitutive of social systems and as important for the coordination of social interactions.

Morality and Convention in Interaction

Often social situations will contain elements from both domains. For example, conventions sometimes result in injustices, as in the case of sex conventions that discriminate against women. In other cases, conventions, such as waiting in line to purchase theatre tickets, act in the service of fairness. When people reason about such issues they tend to do one of three things:

1. Emphasize on one domain and subordinate the other: For example, people worried about, or committed to maintaining the existing social order may not even recognise the potential injustice in existing sex role

conventions that give greater privileges to men than women. Others, on the other hand, focusing on such injustices may not take into account the impact on social organisation in such contexts as family structure, that might result from a single-minded focus on rights and equality.

2. Experience conflict between the two, and engage in inconsistencies and vacillation with an absence of resolution or reconciliation of the components
3. Coordination of the two components, so that the two are taken into account in consideration of the issue. For example, concerns for fairness and equality are coupled with changes in the conventions regarding household tasks, child care, etc., that allow for family life to go forward in an organised and functional way.

This view of social reasoning is consistent with a reinterpretation of earlier, global theories of social development, such as Kohlberg's stages of moral development, as an approximation of the age-related changes in domain coordinations. From the distinct domains perspective, however, one would not interpret such interdomain coordinations as representing a stable context-independent cognitive structure. From this perspective one would predict a great deal more intraindividual, and cross-cultural variation in social reasoning than is permitted by Kohlbergian stages of moral judgement, since morality is but one element to be interrelated in the process of generating actions in multifaceted social contexts.

Basic Principles of Domain Appropriate Education

One educational implication of these psychological findings is that values instruction be coordinated with domain of the issues addressed in a given lesson. The first step in such an approach, would entail the teacher's analysis and identification of the moral or conventional nature of social issues employed in values lessons. Such an analysis would be necessary to ensure that the issues discussed are concordant with the domain of the values dimension they are intended to affect. A related function of the teacher would be to focus student activity on the underlying features concordant with the domain of the issue. Thus, students dealing with a moral issue would be directed to focus on the underlying justice or human welfare considerations of the episode.

With respect to conventions, the focus of the student activity would be on the role of social expectations and the social organisational function of such social norms. As we noted earlier, not all issues of social right and wrong fall simply into one domain or the other. Cases of domain overlap would involve both the domain concordant practices just outlined as well as activities that would involve students in reasoning that necessitates the coordination of knowledge from more than one social dimension.

The second general principle is that the activities and questions posed to students be appropriate for their developmental level. Students in the 8th grade and 9th grades are approximately 13 to 15 years-old. In terms of their conceptions of convention, the majority of such young adolescents are either at Level 4 negation, in which conventions are viewed as the arbitrary and unimportant dictates of authority, or are in the process of shifting toward Level 5 affirmation, in which conventions are understood to be constitutive of social systems. At Level 4, students' lack of understanding of the role conventions play in organising and structuring social systems, coupled with their knowledge that the specific conventions of society are arbitrary leads them to either downplay or discount the importance of convention, "What's the difference if I eat my peas with a fork or a butter knife?", or conform to convention out of fear of peer or adult sanctions, "Sure, I refer to my teachers by Mr. and Mrs. instead of first names. I have enough trouble being in school; who needs more?"

Sometimes, as in the case of teacher names, Level 4 adolescents will go along with conventions in order not to cause moral harm in the form of perceived hurt feelings or disrespect that may come from violating someone else's strongly held convention. These Level 4 adolescents, however, do not understand why anyone's feelings should be hurt, and simply conform in order not to be gratuitously hurtful.

It is at Level 5 that the person's conceptions of convention can first be described as reflecting an understanding of society as a system. For the first time, students clearly perceive that while individual conventions are arbitrary, they form the set of norms that structures society in particular ways.

People who are members of a society are obligated to adhere to conventions in order for society to function. History teachers are probably familiar with the kinds of difficulties that arise when students are not at a point where they have achieved this Level 5 understanding of social systems and their relations to conventions and customs. Many school districts respond to this developmental transition by delaying the teaching of world history until the sophomore year of high school when most students are 15 to 16 years of age and generally at Level 5 in their conventional understandings. In doing so, schools wait for development, rather than contributing to it. The materials and practices described below are based on a different premise, namely that the transition point from Level 4 and 5 presents a great opportunity to link the teaching of particular school subject matter with the dynamics of development. Done well, such a link carries with it payoffs in the form of student motivation, and interest in the subject matter as well as increased sophistication in their understanding of the academic content.

In the moral domain adolescents are generally beyond childhood conceptions of fairness as "raw justice", and are beginning to apply their moral understandings to issues that require an integration of concerns for equal treatment with concerns for equity. Fairness is understood as requiring more than a simple tit-for-tat approach to social interactions. At this age, adolescents are also beginning to couple their moral understandings with a broadening sense of their moral community. By engaging students at this age in coordinating their concerns for morality with their emerging conceptions of society, teachers can begin to contribute to the ability of students to take a moral perspective in relation to society as a whole.

Emotional Development

According to Erik Erikson, the socialisation process consists of eight phases - the "eight stages of man." His eight stages of man were formulated, not through experimental work, but through wide - ranging experience in psychotherapy, including extensive experience with children and adolescents from low - as well as upper - and middle - social classes. Each stage is regarded by Erikson as a "psychosocial crisis," which arises and demands resolution before the next stage can be satisfactorily negotiated. These stages are conceived in an almost architectural sense: satisfactory learning and resolution of each crisis is necessary if the child is to manage the next and subsequent ones satisfactorily, just as the foundation of a house is essential to the first floor, which in turn must be structurally sound to support and the second story, and so on.

Learning Basic Trust Versus Basic Mistrust (Hope)

Chronologically, this is the period of infancy through the first one or two years of life. The child, well - handled, nurtured, and loved, develops trust and security and a basic optimism. Badly handled, he becomes insecure and mistrustful.

Learning Autonomy Versus Shame (Will)

The second psychosocial crisis, Erikson believes, occurs during early childhood, probably between about 18 months or 2 years and 3½ to 4 years of age. The "well - parented" child emerges from this stage sure of himself, elated with his new found control, and proud rather than ashamed. Autonomy is not, however, entirely synonymous with assured self - possession, initiative, and independence but, at least for children in the early part of this psychosocial crisis, includes stormy self - will, tantrums, stubbornness, and negativism. For example, one sees may 2 year olds resolutely folding their arms to prevent their mothers from holding their hands as they cross the street. Also, the sound of "NO" rings through the house or the grocery store.

Learning Initiative Versus Guilt (Purpose)

Erikson believes that this third psychosocial crisis occurs during what he calls the "play age," or the later preschool years (from about 3½ to, in the United States culture, entry into formal school). During it, the healthily developing child learns: (1) to imagine, to broaden his skills through active play of all sorts, including fantasy (2) to cooperate with others (3) to lead as well as to follow. Immobilised by guilt, he is: (1) fearful (2) hangs on the fringes of groups (3) continues to depend unduly on adults and (4) is restricted both in the development of play skills and in imagination.

Industry Versus Inferiority (Competence)

Erikson believes that the fourth psychosocial crisis is handled, for better or worse, during what he calls the "school age," presumably up to and possibly including some of junior high school. Here the child learns to master the more formal skills of life: (1) relating with peers according to rules (2) progressing from free play to play that may be elaborately structured by rules and may demand formal teamwork, such as baseball and (3) mastering social studies, reading, arithmetic. Homework is a necessity, and the need for self-discipline increases yearly. The child who, because of his successive and successful resolutions of earlier psychosocial crisis, is trusting, autonomous, and full of initiative will learn easily enough to be industrious. However, the mistrusting child will doubt the future. The shame - and guilt-filled child will experience defeat and inferiority.

Learning Identity Versus Identity Diffusion (Fidelity)

During the fifth psychosocial crisis (adolescence, from about 13 or 14 to about 20) the child, now an adolescent, learns how to answer satisfactorily and happily the question of "Who am I?" But even the best - adjusted of adolescents experiences some role identity diffusion: most boys and probably most girls experiment with minor delinquency; rebellion flourishes; self - doubts flood the youngster, and so on.

Erikson believes that during successful early adolescence, mature time perspective is developed; the young person acquires self-certainty as opposed to self-consciousness and self-doubt. He comes to experiment with different - usually constructive - roles rather than adopting a "negative identity" (such as delinquency). He actually anticipates achievement, and achieves, rather than being "paralysed" by feelings of inferiority or by an inadequate time perspective.

In later adolescence, clear sexual identity - manhood or womanhood - is established. The adolescent seeks leadership (someone to inspire him), and gradually develops a set of ideals (socially congruent and desirable, in the case of the successful adolescent). Erikson believes that, in our culture, adolescence affords a "psychosocial moratorium," particularly for middle - and upper-class American children. They do not yet have to "play for keeps," but can experiment, trying various roles, and thus hopefully find the one most suitable for them.

Learning Intimacy Versus Isolation (Love)

The successful young adult, for the first time, can experience true intimacy - the sort of intimacy that makes possible good marriage or a genuine and enduring friendship.

Learning Generativity Versus Self-Absorption (Care)

In adulthood, the psychosocial crisis demands generativity, both in the sense of marriage and parenthood, and in the sense of working productively and creatively.

Integrity Versus Despair (Wisdom)

If the other seven psychosocial crisis have been successfully resolved, the mature adult develops the peak of adjustment; integrity. He trusts, he is independent and dares the new. He works hard, has found a well - defined role in life, and has developed a selfconcept with which he is happy. He can be intimate without strain, guilt, regret, or lack of realism; and he is proud of what he creates - his children, his work, or his hobbies. If one or more of the earlier psychosocial crises have not been resolved, he may view himself and his life with disgust and despair.

These eight stages of man, or the psychosocial crises, are plausible and insightful descriptions of how personality develops but at present they are descriptions only. The best rudimentary and tentative knowledge of just what sort of environment will result, for example, in traits of trust versus distrust, or clear personal identity versus diffusion. Helping the child through the various stages and the positive learning that should accompany them is a complex and difficult task, as any worried parent or teacher knows. Search for the best ways of accomplishing this task accounts for much of the research in the field of child development.

Socialisation, then is a learning - teaching process that, when successful, results in the human organism's moving from its infant state of helpless but total egocentricity to its ideal adult state of sensible conformity coupled with independent creativity.

Factors Affecting Emotional Development

Temperament

Temperament is a set of in-born traits that organize the child's approach to the world. They are instrumental in the development of the child's distinct personality. These traits also determine how the child goes about learning about the world around him. These traits appear to be relatively stable from birth. They are enduring characteristics that are actually never "good" or "bad." How they are received determines whether they are perceived by the child as being a bad or good thing.

When parents understand the temperament of their children, they can avoid blaming themselves for issues that are normal for their child's temperament. Some children are noisier than other. Some are more cuddly than others. Some have more regular sleep patterns that others. When parents understand how their child responds to certain situations, they an learn to anticipate issues that might present difficulties for their child. They can prepare the child for the situation or in other cases they may avoid a potentially difficult situation all together.

Parents can tailor their parenting strategies to the particular temperamental characteristics of the child. They can also avoid thinking that a behaviour that reflects a temperament trait represents a pathological condition that requires treatment. Parents feel more effective as they more fully understand and appreciate their child's unique personality.

When the demands and expectations of people and the environment are compatible with the child's temperament there is said to be a "goodness-of-fit." When incompatibility exists, you have what is known as a "personality conflict." Early on parents can work with the child's temperamental traits rather than in opposition to them. Later as the child matures the parents can help the child to adapt to their world by accommodating to their temperamental traits.

The 9 temperamental traits are;

1. *Activity Level*: This is the child's "idle speed or how active the child is generally. Does the infant always wiggle, more squirm? Is the infant difficult to diaper because of this? Is the infant content to sit and quietly watch? Does the child have difficulty sitting still? Is the child always on the go? Or, does the child prefer sedentary quiet activities? Highly active children may channel such extra energy into success in sports; may perform well in high-energy careers and may be able to keep up with many different responsibilities.
2. *Distractibility*: The degree of concentration and paying attention displayed when a child is not particularly interested in an activity. This trait refers to the ease with which external stimuli interfere with ongoing behaviour. Is the infant easily distracted by sounds or sights while drinking a bottle? Is the infant easily soothed when upset by being offered alternate activity? Does the child become sidetracked easily when attempting to follow routine or working on some activity? High distractibility is seen as positive when it is easy to divert a child from an undesirable behaviour but seen as negative when it prevents the child from finishing school work.
3. *Intensity*: The energy level of a response whether positive or negative. Does the infant react strongly and loudly to everything, even relatively minor events? Does the child show pleasure or upset strongly and dramatically? Or does the child just get quiet when upset? Intense children are more likely to have their needs met and may have depth

and delight of emotion rarely experienced by others. These children may be gifted in dramatic arts. Intense children tend to be exhausting to live with.

4. *Regularity*: The trait refers to the predictability of biological functions like appetite and sleep. Does the child get hungry or tired at predictable times? Or, is the child unpredictable in terms of hunger and tiredness? As grown-ups irregular individuals may do better than others with traveling as well as be likely to adapt to careers with unusual working hours.
5. *Sensory Threshold*: Related to how sensitive this child is to physical stimuli. It is the amount of stimulation (sounds, tastes, touch, temperature changes) needed to produce a response in the child. Does the child react positively or negatively to particular sounds? Does the child startle easily to sounds? Is the child a picky eater or will he eat almost anything? Does the child respond positively or negatively to the feel of clothing? Highly sensitive individuals are morc likely to be artistic and creative.
6. *Approach/Withdrawal*: Refers to the child's characteristic response to a new situation or strangers. Does the child eagerly approach new situations or people? Or does the child seem hesitant and resistant when faced with new situations, people or things? Slow-to-warm up children tend to think before they act. They are less likely to act impulsively during adolescence.
7. *Adaptability*: Related to how easily the child adapts to transitions and changes, like switching to a new activity. Does the child have difficulty with changes in routines, or with transitions from one activity to another? Does the child take a long time to become comfortable to new situations? A slow-to-adapt child is less likely to rush into dangerous situations, and may be less influenced by peer pressure.
8. *Persistence*: This is the length of time a child continues in activities in the face of obstacles. Does the child continue to work on a puzzle when he has difficulty with it or does he just move on to another activity? Is the child able to wait to have his needs met? Does the child react strongly when interrupted in an activity? When a child persists in an activity he is asked to stop, he is labeled as stubborn. When a child stays with a tough puzzle he is seen a being patient. The highly

persistent child is more likely to succeed in reaching goals. A child with low persistence may develop strong social skills because he realizes other people can help.

9. *Mood*: This is the tendency to react to the world primarily in a positive or negative way. Does the child see the glass as half full? Does he focus on the positive aspects of life? Is the child generally in a happy mood? Or, does the child see the gall as half empty and tend to focus on the negative aspects of life? Is the child generally serious? Serious children tend to be analytical and evaluate situations carefully.

Temperament is the innate behaviour style of an individual that seems to be biologically determined. Although some experts feel that labeling a child too quickly as "difficult" may create a self-fulfilling prophecy of problematic parent-child interaction, knowing what kind of temperament your child has may make the difference between a happy and a troubled child - and between an accepting and frustrated parent.

Adolescent Stages of Development

Children must pass through several stages, or take specific steps, on their road to becoming adults. For most people, there are four or five such stages of growth where they learn certain things: infancy (birth to age two), early childhood (ages 3 to 8 years), later childhood (ages 9 to 12) and adolescence (ages 13 to 18). Persons 18 and over are considered adults in our society. Of course, there are some who will try to act older than their years. But, for the most part, most everybody grows in this same pattern. Parents learn much about taking care of their babies and young children. At the hospital or with the doctor, you might pick up information about what to feed them or how long they should sleep.

Later, school staff may remind you about the importance of talking and reading to your young children. You can also see how your friends or relatives treat their kids. You cannot say the same thing about learning to talk with teenagers (adolescents). It seems like everyone, even teachers and neighbors, have problems understanding them. Giving up, you might turn to doing and saying the same things your parents did with you. But those were other times! You can begin to understand this age group if you look at its place on the growth sequence. Notice how it's right next to the adult stage, the last step before being an adult. This is a time for adolescents to decide about their future line of work and think about starting their own families in a few years.

One of the first things they must do is to start making their own decisions. For example adolescents can begin to decide what to buy with their own money or who will be their friend. To do this they must put a little distance between themselves and their parents. This does not mean that you can't continue to "look after them" or help them when needed. You should, as much as possible, let them learn from the results of their actions. Adolescents also need to be around other adults, both male and female. These can be relatives, neighbors, or teachers. Of course, they should be positive role models. Your teenagers can learn from them about things like how to fix the car, getting along with others, or ideas for future jobs. Finally, don't worry if they want to spend time alone. Adolescents can "spend hours" day dreaming about their future life. They might be planning the things they can do or will buy "when they grow up." Remember, to travel far, one begins with the first few steps!

Chronic Health Conditions

Children with chronic health conditions and disabilities should not be excluded from fitness activities; they receive the same positive benefits from exercise. Some activities may need to be modified or adapted to your child's disability. Certain activities are dangerous for some health conditions. Consult your child's doctor about the safety of fitness activities for your child with a disability.

As children develop, so do their physical skills. Children ages 4 and 5 play in an increasingly coordinated manner and can participate in organized games. Four- and 5-year-olds can roll large balls, play catch and may be able to navigate a bike with training wheels. However, children this age cannot safely maneuver a bicycle in areas where there is traffic because they lack judgment and safety awareness as well as coordination skills. Swimming is an excellent fitness activity and teaches a valuable skill. Other fitness activities they may enjoy include dance, skiing or skating.

No matter what the sport or activity, parents should remember that events should always be fun. If your child isn't having fun, ask why and try to resolve what is bothering your child or find some other fitness activity. This is particularly true of organized sports. Kids who are pressured to compete may develop a negative attitude toward fitness or injure themselves while trying to please others with their performance. Make sure your child's time is not overscheduled; this may cause stress. Unstructured time allows your child to learn important skills and time to wind down. If your child refuses to participate in any fitness activity, it can be an indication of a physical or psychological problem. Children who complain of pain when they play or consistently refuse to join other children in outdoor play may need to be seen by a doctor. Even a shy child needs to play with other kids.

Physical Fitness

As a parent, you need to encourage healthy habits - including exercise - in your youngsters. Physical activity should become as routine a part of their lives as eating and sleeping. Reassure them that sports such as cycling (always with a helmet), swimming, basketball, jogging, walking briskly, cross-country skiing, dancing, aerobics and soccer, played regularly, are not only fun but can promote health. Some sports, like baseball, that require only sporadic activity are beneficial in a number of ways, but they do not promote fitness. Physical activity can be healthful in the following ways:

— Increase cardiovascular endurance
— Improve large muscle strength and endurance
— Increase flexibility
— Maintain proper weight
— Reduce stress
— Increase Cardiovascular Endurance

More Americans die from heart disease than any other ailment; regular physical activity can help protect against heart problems. Exercise can improve your child's fitness, make him feel better and strengthen his cardiovascular system. Aerobic activity can make the heart pump more efficiently, thus reducing the incidence of high blood pressure. It can also raise blood levels of HDL (high-density lipoprotein) cholesterol, the "good" form of cholesterol that removes excess fats from the bloodstream. Even though most cardiovascular diseases are thought to be illnesses of adulthood, fatty deposits have been detected in the arteries of children as young as age 3, and high blood pressure exists in about 5 percent of youngsters.

At least three times a week, your middle-years child needs to exercise continuously for 20 minutes to 30 minutes at a heart rate above his resting level. As a guideline, the effort involved in continuous brisk walking is adequate to maintain fitness. Each exercise session should be preceded and followed by a gradual warm-up and cool-down period, allowing muscles, joints and the cardiovascular system to ease into and out of vigorous activity, thus helping to guarantee a safe workout. This can be accomplished by stretching for a few minutes before and after exercise.

Improve large muscle strength and endurance

As your child's muscles become stronger, he will be able to exercise for longer periods of time, as well as protect himself from injuries - strong muscles provide better support for the joints. Modified sit-ups (knees bent, feet on the ground) can build up abdominal muscles, increase lung capacity and protect against back injuries. For upper body strength, he can perform modified pull-ups (keeping the arms flexed while hanging from a horizontal bar) and modified push-ups (positioning the knees on the ground while extending the arms at the elbow).

Increase flexibility

For complete physical fitness, children need to be able to twist and bend their bodies through the full range of normal motions without overexerting themselves or causing injury. When children are flexible like this, they are more agile. Although most people lose flexibility as they age, this process can be retarded by stretching to maintain suppleness throughout life, beginning in childhood. Stretching exercises are the best way to maintain or improve flexibility, and they can be incorporated into your child's warm-up and cool-down routines. In most stretching exercises, your child should stretch to a position where he begins to feel tightness but not pain, then hold steady for 20 seconds to 30 seconds before relaxing. He should not bounce as he stretches, since this can cause injury to the muscles or tendons.

Maintain proper weight

Twelve percent of children in the prepuberty years are overweight, but few of these youngsters are physically active. Exercise can effectively burn calories and fat and reduce appetite. Ask your pediatrician to help you determine whether your youngster has a healthy percentage of body fat for his or her age and sex.

Reduce stress

Unmanaged stress can cause muscle tightness, which can contribute to headaches, stomachaches and other types of discomfort. Your child needs to learn not only to recognize stress in his body but also to diffuse it effectively. Exercise is one of the best ways to control stress. A physically active child is less likely to experience stress-related symptoms than his more sedentary peers.

Perhaps the best way to get children to enjoy exercise is to make it a family affair, with parents setting a good example and encouraging the youngsters to join the fun. The entire family can participate together in many physical activities, from swimming to cycling to hiking. Not only will everyone's fitness improve, but the unity of the family can be strengthened too. If you can get your child interested in fitness at a young age, you will improve the chances that physical activity will become a lifetime habit.

Personality Development

To study successful personality development one must first have a way of thinking about the course of lives and a way of assessing how adaptational processes are patterned over time. There are three general approaches to this conceptual problem: growth models, lifespan models, and life-course models. Each of these social-developmental approaches provides a framework for understanding adaptational processes and the coherence of personality development by focusing on the distinctive ways individuals organise their behaviour to meet new environmental demands and developmental challenges.

Growth Models of Personality Development

Growth models of personality development are not homogeneous in their orientation, but are based on different traditions and conceptual backgrounds. For example, humanistic theories of personality development are best known for emphasising the potential for positive development. People can take charge of their lives and direct them toward creativity and self-actualisation which involves self-fulfilment and the realisation of one's potential. In contrast, psychoanalytically oriented models tend to emphasise the growth of ego through age stages.

Integrity is the goal of successful development in Erikson's theory, as well as in Loevinger's model of ego development and in the model of Labouvie-Vief which integrates Piaget's theory of cognitive development with emotions and social relations. Erikson's theory covers eight stages across the lifespan. Each stage involves a crisis or an age-specific challenge that should be satisfactorily resolved for optimal development.

The theory states that a successful resolution of each crisis results in the refinement of a predominantly positive quality, such as trust in infancy. The psychosocial crises to be solved in adulthood concern intimacy versus isolation, generativity versus stagnation, and integrity versus despair. Common virtues or ego skills such as hope, will, purpose, and skill in childhood, fidelity in adolescence, and love, care, and wisdom in adulthood emerge as successful outcomes of the crises. Development is based on successful resolution of psychological crises leading finally to integrity in old age.

The passage from one developmental stage to another is also central to Levinson's work, who has studied what he calls "life structures": things that a person finds important in work and love, as well as the values and emotions that make these important. Life structures are subjected to change during transitional periods when people reappraise and restructure important things in their lives. According to Levinson, people spend about half their adult lives in transitional periods.

Sanford, another psychodynamically influenced theorist, described a fully developed person as one characterised by high degrees of both differentiation and integration. Specifically, the fully developed person has a rich and varied impulse life, a broad and refined conscience, a strong sense of individuality, and a balance of control and expression of needs. As for when people reach this stage, Sanford placed the development of impulse control in adolescence and the development of ego, or the controlling function of personality, in adulthood. In both cases, Sanford did not presuppose that personality ever stopped changing: "The highly developed person is always open to new experience, and capable of further learning."

Lifespan Models

Research on lifespan personality development is concerned with three major influence systems:

— agegraded influences (e.g., education) which shape individual development in relatively normative ways;

— history-graded influences (e.g., wars) which make development different across historical periods; and

— nonnormative influences (e.g., accidents) which may have powerful effects on an individual's development.

Lifespan development theories hold that psychological functioning is not fixed at a certain age. Rather, "during development, and at all stages of the life span, both continuous (cumulative) and discontinuous (innovative) processes are at work". Development is defined as "selective age-related change in adaptive capacity" and special attention is given to the developing person's contribution to the creation of his or her own development. Individuals steer their physical, cognitive, social, and personality development by constructing strategies for coping with various developmental challenges, by setting goals, and by making choices.

According to Brandtst¨ adter, such intentional self development over the life span is geared to the realisation and maintenance of normative representations that individuals construct of themselves and their future. Pulkkinen, Nurmi, and Kokko discuss how individuals steer their development by setting goals and making choices as responses to developmental challenges. On the one hand, personal goals reflect major agegraded transitions and normative demands. On the other hand, individual differences in personal goals reflect motivational orientations, such as security seeking or aiming at personal growth, which result in intraindividual coherence in goal patterns.

An agentic conception of human nature is also central in Heckhausen's work on control. Heckhausen proposes that humans strive to maximise primary control of their environment throughout life. However, control capacities undergo radical changes and losses and individuals have to disengage from unattainable goals and manage their own emotional responses to such loss experiences. This type of control that is directed at the internal world of the individual is referred to as secondary control.

Heckhausen shows how the age-normative structure of life-course transitions allows individuals to anticipate decremental changes in the opportunities to attain developmental goals. For example, an individual can increase primary control striving when approaching "developmental deadlines" (e.g., union formation, health-maintenance in old age) and use secondary control to compensate for potential negative affect and self-evaluation associated with failure to meet or resolve developmental deadlines successfully.

Brandtst adter's work on intentional self-development is also striking in its appreciation of the tension between gains and losses in lifespan development. Although lifespan models do not articulate what is success, some commentators have noted that developmental models that emphasise freedom of individual decision and action are plagued by a Western bias associated with an individualistic cultural base. There is a clear need for cultural psychologists to engage lifespan researchers in testing the limits of the developmental models that have been advanced. Still, the models that have been put forth are exciting because they articulate hypotheses about how individuals at different junctures in their lives struggle to derive meaning from and make sense of life events, and of their part in these events.

Life-course Models

Especially beyond childhood the study of successful adaptation becomes more complicated, and it may be that a purely psychological approach is insufficient for the study of personality development as the individual increasingly negotiates social roles defined by the culture. Whereas lifespan theories specify the temporal order of life stages, such as childhood, adolescence, and adulthood, life-course researchers tend to emphasise social-role demands at different ages. Social trajectories are influenced by four factors. First, they are influenced by human agency, the choices that persons make about their own lives.

Second, they are influenced by the timing of life-course events in relation to other events in an individual's life. Third, they are influenced by linked lives, because social changes are expressed in an individual's life through the experiences of related others. Finally, they are influenced by historical changes. Lifespan and life-course models are complementary. Biological changes across the life span and social demands across the life course define typical life events and social roles in people's lives. Indeed, some psychological researchers have found it useful to adopt a sociocultural perspective and to conceive of the life course as a sequence of culturally-defined, agegraded roles that the individual enacts over time.

Helson introduced the concept of a "social clock project" as a framework for studying lifespan development. The concept of a social clock focuses attention on the age-related life schedules of individuals in particular cultures and cohorts, and organises the study of lives in terms of patterned movements into, along, and out of multiple role-paths such as education, work, marriage, and parenthood. In this fashion, the life course can be charted as a sequence of social roles that are enacted over time, and adaptational processes can be explored by investigating the ways different persons select and perform different social-cultural roles. In her 30-year longitudinal study of female college seniors, who were first studied in 1958-60, Helson examined the personality antecedents and consequences of adherence to a Feminine Social Clock (FSC) and a Masculine Occupational Clock (MOC). For example, women who adhered to the FSC were earlier in life characterised by a desire to do well and by a need for structure; women in this birth cohort who adhered to a MOC were earlier in life more rebellious and less sensitive to social norms. Helson et al. were thus able to identify "culturally salient need-press configurations through time" and to show predictable and meaningful relations between personality and behaviour in different social settings at different ages.

Laursen and Williams explore the role of ethnic identity, a personally and politically-charged topic that is also a profound source of strength. The authors conceive of ethnic identity as a personality variable that shapes the nature and course of successful adolescent adjustment, and describe how ethnic identity offers an important mechanism through which minority adolescents cope with the tension between the inner self and the psychological environment of the majority culture. Silbereisen and his colleagues have capitalised on a "natural experiment" - the unification of Germany during the 1990s - to examine how historical changes shape the nature of adolescent transitions.

Bouchard correctly argued that a purely sociocultural perspective on the life course "ignores the fact that lifehistories themselves are complex evolved adaptations," and suggests that an evolutionary perspective may complement the sociocultural perspective by exploring how personality variation is related to those adaptively-important problems with which human beings have had to repeatedly contend. Evolutionary psychology thus focuses attention on the coherence of behavioural strategies that people use in, for example, mate selection, mate retention, reproduction, parental care, kin investment, status attainment, and coalition building.

It focuses research on the genetically-influenced strategies and tactics that individuals use for survival and reproduction. An evolutionary perspective on successful life-course development could thus offer a fusion of concerns in evolutionary theory, behaviour genetics, and demography. For example, using the evolutionary perspective, Draper and Belsky and Gangestad and Simpson have offered intriguing hypotheses about personality characteristics and reproductive strategies that facilitate adaptations in different environments at different ages Ormel tackles this problem from a somewhat different perspective and introduces social production function (SPF) theory as a heuristic for studying successful development. The theory attempts to integrate the various strengths of psychological theories and economic consumer/household production theories. It identifies two ultimate goals that all humans seek to optimise (physical well-being and social wellbeing) and five instrumental goals by which they are achieved (stimulation, comfort, status, behavioural confirmation, affection). The core notion of SPF theory is that people choose and substitute instrumental goals so as to optimise the production of their well-being, subject to constraints in available means of production.

Personality Differences

The starting point for such work should be a system for describing individual differences in personality dispositions and temperamental traits. This is not to suggest that these psychological constructs are the only way to study the contribution of personality differences to successful development. Indeed, motivational concepts in personality are better represented in much of the research on adult development. Over the past 15 years, the intensity and productivity of psychological research on the dimensionality of adult personality has been phenomenal, and has influenced research in diverse fields such as organisational behaviour, psychiatry, and genetics. An emerging consensus points to the existence of five important factors: Extraversion (active, assertive, enthusiastic, outgoing), Agreeableness (generous, kind, sympathetic, trusting), Conscientiousness (organised, planful, reliable, responsible), Neuroticism (anxious, self-pitying, tense, worrying), and Openness to Experience (artistic, curious, imaginative, having wide interests). Each superfactor covers a broad domain of individual differences and includes a number of more specific personality dimensions or facets.

Some developmental researchers have noted that this Five-Factor Model of personality does not provide a theory of personality, which is correct to the extent that most personality taxonomies are focused on describing regularities in behaviour rather than examining dynamic and developmental processes. Other critics have noted that researchers interested in the Five Factor Model have not paid attention to issues of personality development. Indeed, whereas the study of personality structure in adulthood has influenced research on adult development and aging, the study of personality structure in childhood has been all but neglected. But these are criticisms of what has been done, not of what can be accomplished.

An especially important area of integration involves efforts to connect existing models of infant and child temperament with studies of adult personality structure. What are normally understood as personality traits may be aspects of temperament differentiated in the course of life experience. But, surprisingly, there has been virtually no contact between child psychologists who study temperament and personality psychologists who are concerned with personality differences. Halverson and colleagues have made a strong case that research on lifespan personality development will remain unintegrated unless child psychologists begin to study the structure of personality. Research linking temperament to the development of personality will be facilitated by two parallel achievements: the development of a consensual system for describing the structure of personality differences in adulthood, as noted earlier, and the development of such a system for temperamental traits.In the domain of temperament, conceptual reviews and factor-analytic studies have identified several "consensus" dimensions of infant and childhood temperament that might show influences on later developmental outcomes. For example, some researchers cling to the notion that temperament can only be assessed in the young infant and that temperament cannot be shaped by experience.

Rothbart and Putnam define temperament as "constitutionally based individual differences in reactivity and self-regulation, influenced over time by heredity and experience." Reactivity refers to the excitability, responsivity, or arousability of the behavioural and physiological systems of the individual, and self-regulation refers to the behavioural processes that modulate this reactivity. Importantly, Rothbart and Putnam note that such temperament differences develop and they are not immune to experience. Recent research shows that infants' temperament is shaped by experience even before birth.

Moreover, behavioural genetic studies have established that individual differences in temperament, measured even during the first year of life, are only partially heritable and are influenced significantly by unique environmental events, suggesting that younger age of measurement does not guarantee that temperament is purely "constitutional."

Promoting Moral Functioning in Young Children

The constructivist model of moral development suggests that we should avoid giving children a list of do's and don'ts (or virtues and vices) to guide their behavior. Yet we all know that children must learn to act in certain socially acceptable ways to get along well in society and to maintain a healthy sense of self. They must learn, for example, to follow certain rules of etiquette while eating, to use the bathroom appropriately, and to express their feelings of anger and frustration without hurting others. While it is important for children to learn and abide by these "rules," teaching such rules isn't what moral education is all about. Just as morality involves more than thinking, so does it involve more than a set of behaviors. We may be able to get children to do certain things or "to behave themselves" as we want them to, but that doesn't mean they've developed a sense of goodness or morality. Morality runs much deeper than behaving according to the rules set down by others. Morality includes a sense of justice, compassion, and caring about the welfare of others. It also includes perspective-taking ability – that is, the ability to discern how someone might be thinking or feeling.

While some people may think that preschool children aren't cognitively or emotionally ready to be concerned about anyone but themselves, research indicates otherwise. Caring behavior becomes evident during the first year of life. Many infants show signs of distress when another baby cries, and toddlers become uneasy when another child gets hurt or is punished. Some two-year-olds even display the same emotion as the child being punished. Such behaviors indicate a sense of caring and the ability to take the perspective of someone other than self. Helping children grow in this perspective-taking ability should be a major goal of moral education at the early childhood level. Following are six guidelines and suggestions on how to promote moral functioning with young children, especially in relation to caring for others.

1. Help children understand the reason behind rules, especially rules relating to such moral concerns as justice, fairness, and other aspects of human welfare. Discuss the reasons why one behavior is preferable to another (e.g, sharing a box of crayons is preferable to pushing another child away from the art area). In discussing these contrasting behaviors with a young child, the focus should be on how what the child does affects someone else (e.g., sharing crayons makes a play partner happy while pushing the child away makes the other child sad). Such

discussions foster empathy, higher levels of moral reasoning, and altruism. These types of discussions also help children develop perspective-taking abilities in that it focuses on how someone else might think or feel in a given situation.

Discussions with children should take the form of "true dialogue" as described by Noddings. True dialogue occurs, Noddings says, when participants engage "in mutual exploration, a search for meaning, or the solution of some problem". In true dialogue, teachers refrain from giving all the right answers. They solicit, listen to, and seriously consider the child's point of view. Such interactions never become just a "telling session" on the part of the adult. In fact, some of the most effective discussions for promoting moral development occur between child and child versus child and adult. The adult, however, will often serve as a facilitator in child-to-child discussions, especially on issues of morality.

2. Match your response to conflict situations to the children's level of cognitive and social development. It's important to remember that cognitively young children have differing understandings of the social and physical world than do older children and adults. Young children are egocentric and will thus judge events and behaviors on how such happenings directly affect them. They will find it difficult to simultaneously take into account their own view of things with the perspective of someone else.

   If four-year-old Alex is playing with toys in the sandbox and doesn't want to stop playing, it's not likely that he will automatically be sympathetic to the fact that Lisa, another, has been waiting for ten minutes to have her turn. We, as adults, need to understand Alex's position. This doesn't mean that we allow Alex to play as long as he pleases. It does suggest that we establish rules or procedures to protect the interests and rights of all the children and that the reasons behind these rules are shared with the children. In fact, in many cases, it's best to develop the rules with the children. The involvement of children in making rules promotes their moral development and fosters their self esteem. Developing a rule about time limits for using the sand box, for example, would include a discussion with the children about how most children enjoy the sand toys in the sand box and about how they feel sad when they don't get a turn. While having and enforcing the time limit rule may not result in Alex suddenly empathizing with the other child's feelings, he should be reminded that there is a rule and that the rule was developed to protect the rights and feelings of all the children.

According to Kohlberg, "following the rules" represents the first level of moral reasoning – a level characterized by judgments being based on concrete, individual perspectives and typical of how young children think. Children at this level are motivated to follow the rules to avoid punishment and/or to get rewards. Thus, they follow the rules when they can see that it is to their benefit to do so – that is, they get a reward or avoid negative consequences. Alex should thus be praised for following the rule when he gives up the sand toys, as this praise may motivate him to follow rules in the future. Yet, praise for following the rule should be paired with a comment about how his behavior affected his classmate. To promote Alex's moral development, a teacher might say "Thank you, Alex, for giving Lisa her turn. Do you see how happy that made her feel?"

By talking about how someone else feels in relation to a specific action, we encourage children to understand and care about the feelings of others. Such caring represents an added dimension to Kohlberg's model of moral development. Kohlberg emphasized the concepts of fairness and justice as critical aspects of moral functioning. More recent work on moral development calls attention to the morality of care, as well. In Kohlberg's model, we have the injunction not to treat others unfairly (that is, to do what is just); in this newer model, we have the added injunction not to turn away from someone in need (that is, to show that we care when someone else is hurting or needs something).

3. Attend to the victim first when one child hurts another. It's always important to focus on the feelings of others when dealing with hurtful interpersonal conflicts or transgressions of established classroom rules. Instead of focusing on the concern that "the rules have been broken," we should focus on the outcome of how "someone has been hurt" (or was put in danger of being hurt). This response not only attends to the victim's needs but also helps the offending child develop a sense of morality, as caring about the welfare of others is critical to moral functioning.

4. Use children's literature to share examples of caring. Early childhood educators should be aware that using children's literature to foster caring in children is both supported and criticized in the professional literature. The well-established practice of bibliotherapy – where carefully chosen literature is used to help people solve problems – certainly supports the idea. Yet, there are others who criticize the practice of using "moral stories" to build character. They suggest that labeling a complex set of behaviors with one word like "respect" or "loyalty" does not help children understand its meaning. They also suggest that the use of children's literature in this way is not consistent with constructivist theory – in that it represents an effort to give children a sense of morality rather than providing them with experiences to develop their own understandings about what it means to do the right thing.

   While it's important to keep these criticisms in mind, it's also wise to refer back to the idea of interactive discussion as an effective strategy in helping children construct their views of morality. Children's literature often serves as an excellent stimulus for such discussion. Rather than just reading a book from cover to cover with children, teachers should help children "uncover" the meaning and personal implications of the story through thoughtful discussion. Such discussion should be based on the understanding that books can't give children morality but that they can serve as stimuli for meaningful social interaction. Readers should be reminded that morality arises out of social interactions and social relationships.

5. Include animals in the classroom and involve children in the care of the animals. Tending to the needs of animals requires children to give thought and attention to something outside of themselves and supports the practice of caring. The professional literature suggests that as children care for animals, they become more caring towards people as well. Related research also indicates that as children learn to treat animals with care and respect, they become less likely to treat humans in a violent, disrespectful way. Thus, while bringing animals into the classroom requires careful thought, planning and commitment, the benefits to children suggest that the effort is indeed worthwhile.

6. Model, encourage, and reward acts of caring. Children need to seeothers engaged in acts of kindness and expressions of caring. There

are many opportunities for teachers to put this in practice throughout the day. For example, if one child has been absent for several days because of illness, you might suggest making a get-well card for her. It's also important to observe children's behavior closely and note any acts of kindness and caring. Children should then be praised when they show empathy for others. Teachers should also suggest ways in which children can practice acts of kindness in their daily routines – for example, holding the door for each other, sharing desired materials, helping when someone has a "mess" to clean up, etc.

Helping children achieve success has long been recognized as one of the goals of early childhood education. Defining the meaning of success, however, isn't always easy. Some see success as getting good grades in school and getting a good job after graduation. Good grades and good jobs, however, don't always lead to the practice of "goodness" and a sense of fulfillment.

References

Crain, William C., *Theories of Development,* 2Rev Ed, Prentice-Hall, 1985.

Hedl, John J.; Glazer, H. and Chan, F. "Improving the Moral Reasoning of Allied Health Students". *Journal of Allied Health* 34 (2): 121–1. 2005.

Kohlberg, Lawrence, *Essays on Moral Development, Vol. I: The Philosophy of Moral Development*, Harper & Row, 1981.

McShane, John, *Cognitive development: An information-processing approach*, Cambridge, MA: Basil Blackwell. 1991.

Rest, James. *Development in Judging Moral Issues.* University of Minnesota Press. 1979.

Woolfolk, A. E., Winne, P. H., & Perry, N. E., *Educational Psychology,* Toronto, Canada: Pearson, 2006.

Bibliography

Alessi, G. K., & Kaye, J. H. (1983). *Behavior assessment for school psychologists.* Washington, DC: National Association of School Psychologists

American Psychological Association (1998). *Archival description of school psychology.* Washington, DC: Author

Calhoun, E. F. (1994). *How to use action research in the self-renewing school.* Alexandria, VA: Association for Supervision and Curriculum Development.

Cameron, J., Pierce, W. D., Banko, K. M., & Gear, A., (2005). "Achievement-based rewards and intrinsic motivation: A test of cognitive mediators", *Journal of Educational Psychology.*

Cerbin, W., (1992), *A learning centered course portfolio for educational psychology,* Unpublished manuscript.

Cole, M, et al., (2005). *The Development of Children,* New York: Worth Publishers.

Connecticut State Board of Education Regulation (2002). School psychology endorsement, p. 33-34. Hartford, CT: Author.

Crain, William C. (1985).*Theories of Development* (2Rev ed.). Prentice-Hall.

Eggen, P., & Kauchak, D., "The teaching of educational psychology: A research agenda", *Paper presented at annual meeting of the American Educational Research Association,* San Francisco.

Good, T. & Brophy, J. (2002). *Looking in classrooms, 9th edition.* Boston: Allyn & Bacon.

Harvey,V.S., and Struzziero, J.A. (2000). *Effective supervision in school psychology.* Bethesda, MD:Author

Hedl, John J.; Glazer, H. and Chan, F. "Improving the Moral Reasoning of Allied Health Students". *Journal of Allied Health* 34 (2): 121–1. 2005.

Huitt, W. (Compiler), (1992), *Philosophy and education,* Valdosta, GA: Valdosta State University.

Jacob, S. and Hartshorne,T.S. (2003). *Ethics and law for school psychologists (4th ed.).* Hoboken, NJ: John Wiley & Sons, Inc.

Jones, V. & Jones, L. (2006). *Comprehensive classroom management: Creating communities of support and solving problems, 6th edition.* Boston: Allyn & Bacon.

Kauchak, D., and Eggen, P. (2008). *Introduction to teaching: Becoming a professional* (3rd ed.). Upper Saddle River, NJ: Pearson Education, Inc.

Kazdin, A. E. (Ed.) (2002). *Encyclopedia of psychology*. New York: Oxford University.

Kohlberg, Lawrence, *Essays on Moral Development, Vol. I: The Philosophy of Moral Development*, Harper & Row, 1981.

Kuhn, D., (1999). *A developmental model of critical thinking*, Educational Researcher.

Lave, J. and Wenger, E. (1991). *Situated Learning, Legitimate peripheral participation*, Cambridge: University of Cambridge Press.

Maccoby, Eleanor, (1974), *The psychology of sex differences*, Stanford, CA: Stanford University Press.

Maehr, Martin L., and Carol Midgley, (1991). "Enhancing Student Motivation: A Schoolwide Approach", *Educational Psychologist*.

Marshall, H., (1998), *Teaching educational psychology: Learner-centered constructivist perspectives*. In N.M. Lambert & B.L. McCombs (Eds.) How students learn: Reforming schools through learner-centered education, Washington, DC: American Psychological Association.

McShane, John, (1991), *Cognitive development: An information-processing approach*, Cambridge, MA: Basil Blackwell.

National Association of School Psychologists. (2000). *Guidelines for the provision of school psychological services*. Bethesda, MD: Author

New Brunswick Department of Education (2001). *Guidelines for professional practice for school psychologists*. Fredericton, NB: Author.

Ortiz, S.O. (2002). Best practices in nondiscriminatory assessment. In A.Thomas and J. Grimes (Eds.), *Best practices in school psychology IV*. Bethesda, MD: National Association of School Psychologists.

Raimy, V. C. (Ed.). (1950). *Training in clinical psychology*. Englewood Cliffs, NJ: Prentice Hall.

Repp, A. C., & Horner, R. H. (Eds.). (1999). *Functional analysis of problem behavior*. Belmont, CA: Wadsworth.

Reschly, D. J., & Ysseldyke, J. E. (1995). School psychology paradigm shift. In A. Thomas & J. Grimes (Eds.), *Best practices in school psychology III* (pp. 17–31). Washington, DC: National Association of School Psychologists.

Rest, James. *Development in Judging Moral Issues*. University of Minnesota Press. 1979.

Reynolds, C.R. and Gutkin,T.B. (1998). *The Handbook of School Psychology (3rd ed.)*. New York: John Wiley & Sons, Inc.

Sherman, L., (1995), "A post modern, constructivist pedagogy for teaching Educational Psychology, assisted by computer mediated communications", *Paper presentation to the CSCL95 Conference*, Bloomington Indiana.

Shinn, M. R. (Ed.). (1989). *Curriculum-based measurement: Assessing special children*. New York: Guilford Press.

Thomas & J. Grimes (Eds.), *Best practices in school psychology IV* (pp. 483–501). Bethesda, MD: National Association of School Psychologists.

Vygotskii, L. S, (1997). *Educational psychology*, Trans. Robert Silverman. Boca Raton, FL: St. Lucie Press.

Weiner, B., (2000). "Interpersonal and intrapersonal theories of motivation from an attributional perspective", *Educational Psychology Review.*

Wertsch, J.V. (ed), (1985). *Culture, communication and cognition*, Cambridge: Cambridge University Press.

Woolfolk, A. E., Winne, P. H., & Perry, N. E., (2006). *Educational Psychology,* Toronto, Canada: Pearson.

Ysseldyke, J., Burns, M., Dawson, P., Kelley, B., Morrison, D., Ortiz, S., et al. (2006). *School psychology: A blueprint for training and practice II*I. Bethesda, MD: National Association of School Psychologists.